Complicit Sisters

Oxford Studies in Gender and International Relations

Series editors: J. Ann Tickner, University of Southern California, and Laura Sjoberg, University of Florida

*Windows of Opportunity:
How Women Seize Peace
Negotiations for Political Change*
Miriam J. Anderson

*Women as Foreign Policy Leaders: National
Security and Gender Politics in Superpower
America*
Sylvia Bashevkin

*Enlisting Masculinity: The Construction
of Gender in U.S. Military Recruiting
Advertising during the All-Volunteer Force*
Melissa T. Brown

*The Politics of Gender Justice at the
International Criminal Court: Legacies and
Legitimacy*
Louise Chappell

*Cosmopolitan Sex Workers: Women and
Migration in a Global City*
Christine B. N. Chin

*Intelligent Compassion: Feminist Critical
Methodology in the Women's International
League for Peace and Freedom*
Catia Cecilia Confortini

*Gender and Private Security
in Global Politics*
Maya Eichler

*This American Moment: A Feminist
Christian Realist Intervention*
Caron E. Gentry

*Scandalous Economics: Gender and the
Politics of Financial Crises*
Aida A. Hozić and Jacqui True

*Rewriting the Victim: Dramatization as
Research in Thailand's Anti-Trafficking
Movement*
Erin M. Kamler

*Equal Opportunity Peacekeeping: Women,
Peace, and Security in Post-Conflict States*
Sabrina Karim and Kyle Beardsley

*Gender, Sex, and the Postnational
Defense: Militarism and Peacekeeping*
Annica Kronsell

*The Beauty Trade: Youth, Gender,
and Fashion Globalization*
Angela B. V. McCracken

*Rape Loot Pillage: The Political Economy of
Sexual Violence
in Armed Conflict*
Sara Meger

*From Global to Grassroots:
The European Union, Transnational
Advocacy, and Combating Violence
against Women*
Celeste Montoya

*Who Is Worthy of Protection? Gender-
Based Asylum and US Immigration Politics*
Meghana Nayak

*Revisiting Gendered States: Feminist
Imaginings of the State in International
Relations*
Swati Parashar, J. Ann Tickner, and
Jacqui True

*Gender, UN Peacebuilding, and the Politics
of Space: Locating Legitimacy*
Laura J. Shepherd

*A Feminist Voyage through International
Relations*
J. Ann Tickner

*The Political Economy of Violence
against Women*
Jacqui True

*Queer International Relations: Sovereignty,
Sexuality and the Will to Knowledge*
Cynthia Weber

*Bodies of Violence:
Theorizing Embodied Subjects
in International Relations*
Lauren B. Wilcox

COMPLICIT SISTERS

Gender and Women's Issues across North–South Divides

Sara de Jong

Oxford University Press is a department of the University of Oxford. It furthers
the University's objective of excellence in research, scholarship, and education
by publishing worldwide. Oxford is a registered trademark of Oxford University
Press in the UK and certain other countries.

Published in the United States of America by Oxford University Press
198 Madison Avenue, New York, NY 10016, United States of America.

© Oxford University Press 2017

First issued as an Oxford University Press paperback, 2019

All rights reserved. No part of this publication may be reproduced, stored in
a retrieval system, or transmitted, in any form or by any means, without the
prior permission in writing of Oxford University Press, or as expressly permitted
by law, by license, or under terms agreed with the appropriate reproduction
rights organization. Inquiries concerning reproduction outside the scope of the
above should be sent to the Rights Department, Oxford University Press, at the
address above.

You must not circulate this work in any other form
and you must impose this same condition on any acquirer.

Library of Congress Cataloging-in-Publication Data
Names: Jong, Sara de, author.
Title: Complicit sisters : gender and women's issues across North–South
divides / Sara de Jong.
Description: New York : Oxford University Press, [2017] | Series: Oxford
studies in gender and international relations | Includes bibliographical
references and index.
Identifiers: LCCN 2016027845 (print) | LCCN 2016040898 (ebook) |
ISBN 9780190626563 (hardcover) | ISBN 9780190055882 (paperback) | ISBN
9780190626570 (Updf) | ISBN 9780190648688 (Epub)
Subjects: LCSH: Women in development—Developing countries. | Women
volunteers in social service—Developing countries. | Non-governmental
organizations. | Women—Developing countries—Social conditions. |
Feminism—Developing countries.
Classification: LCC HQ1240.5.D44 J66 2017 (print) | LCC HQ1240.5.D44 (ebook) |
DDC 305.42094—dc23
LC record available at https://lccn.loc.gov/2016027845

CONTENTS

Acknowledgments   *vii*

1. Introduction   *1*
2. Feminist Trajectories   *15*
3. Global Responsibilities   *46*
4. Bridging Distance   *88*
5. Interlocking Connections   *131*
6. Postcolonial Configurations   *160*
7. Conclusion: Complicit Sisters   *191*

Notes   199
Bibliography   201
Index   219

ACKNOWLEDGMENTS

I could not have written this book without the support of a number of people. First of all, I would like to thank the women that I interviewed for their willingness to share their thoughts with me, for their openness, their time, and their hospitality when I traveled to meet them. As they are in the book, I could not have written it without them; I learned much and sometimes recognized much about myself speaking to them. I am also grateful to those who suggested potential research participants to me.

I want to thank all my friends and former colleagues from the Centre for the Study of Social and Global Justice, School of Politics and International Relations and the School of Sociology and Social Policy at the University of Nottingham for inspiring conversations and for sharing a social life beyond academia with me at the time of the research for this book. Bernhard Weicht, the only one who read an early version of the manuscript in its entirety without professional obligation, has played an important role in the book's and my own development. I want to thank Simon Tormey for encouraging me to become a researcher and Vanessa Pupavac for her enthusiastic sharing of her expertise in critical development studies. Lucy Sargisson has given me both intellectual and emotional support, and her faith in and her commitment to my project extended far beyond her duty. I am very grateful for Saskia Wieringa's and Petra Dannecker's continued insistence that I should finish my book manuscript, and for providing an intellectual home at respectively Atria, Institute on Gender Equality and Women's History, and the Department of Development Studies, University of Vienna. With their critical and supportive reading, Silke Roth and Wendy Harcourt have made this a much better book than it would have been without their extensive feedback. I thank Laura Sjoberg, editor of the Gender and International Relations series at Oxford University Press, for encouraging me to submit my book proposal to her book series, when overhearing a conversation about my manuscript during a conference dinner; with her help I found the perfect publisher. I am also grateful to her and her series coeditor,

J. Ann Tickner, for their editorial guidance. Angela Chnapko has been an immensely patient, persistent, and always helpful commissioning editor; in the last stages of finalizing this book I have much benefited from the support of her assistant, Princess Ikatekit. I want to thank Wangechi Mutu for giving her permission to reproduce her evocative art work *Madame Repeateat* (2010) on the cover of this book. The Fund for Women Graduates, the Dr. Catharine van Tussenbroek Fonds, the OeAD Ernst Mach Grant, and the Marie Skłodowska-Curie Fellowship (EU FP7; grant agreement no 624577) have generously funded various research periods during the last years.

To close with those who are closest to me: I want to thank Clemens Pfeffer for inspiring new ways of thinking and living. I am very grateful to my parents who were the first to teach me to read and think critically, for always letting me go and welcoming me back, together with my brothers, with whom I never need to be an academic. I hope my father will give this book a place on the shelves in his bookshop. This book is dedicated to my mother, the first feminist I met.

Complicit Sisters

CHAPTER 1
Introduction

INTRODUCTION

This book takes up questions about power and positionality in relation to women in the global North who want to "do good" by supporting women in or from the global South. They do this, either by engaging in international work, for instance in the field of development, conflict, and governance, or by working for national and local projects in European states targeting female migrants. As the title of this book suggests, drawing on black and postcolonial feminism, I understand these women as "complicit sisters," whose normative engagement with other women across North–South divides is itself embedded in the inequalities and power relations they seek to address. For example, women from the global North whose work is to support women in the global South displaced by war have benefited in their careers from the global dominance of English, which is rooted in the same colonialism that also lies at the source of much ethnic conflict. And the global unequal distribution of resources that prompts some women to migrate to the global North in search of better opportunities has enabled other women to travel and develop a cosmopolitanism that inspired them to set up support services for these underprivileged migrant women.

The aim of this study is to understand the perspectives of women situated at the nexus of feminist, postcolonial, and development critiques. The women's work plays out at the intersection of divisions inside the women's movement around "race," class, and sexuality; contentions around the postcolonial articulation of colonial global material inequalities and ideological frames about civilization, rationality, modernization; and issues of organizational accountability, funding relations, representation, and empowerment of marginalized groups. Hence in this research I ask why the women do the work they do and how they relate to those targeted by their organizations as well as how the women work in and through the power structures in which their organizations are embedded. Do they reflect on the contentiousness of their positions, in light of the strained relationship between privileged women and their "subordinate sisters," the continuities between the colonial civilizing mission and development, and the more recently emerging disillusionment with the less-noble-than-expected nonprofit sector? And if so, how? This also implies a second goal for this study, which is an evaluation of the current relevance of a range of critiques that started to be strongly articulated in the 1980s and 1990s by activists and scholars in women's and gender studies, postcolonial and critical race studies, and critical development studies, as well as those studying the emergence of global civil society and global citizenship. Finally, drawing on these normative critiques and on the rich, impassioned interview narratives of the women that are the subjects of this study, I tease out strategies for moving beyond subjectivities that reinscribe dominance.

Feminist critical race scholar Sherene Razack addresses the relational positions women have taken when making sense of global relations of inequality: as "the saviour," "progressive," "subordinate," or "innocent."

> We need to examine how we explain to ourselves the social hierarchies that surround us. We need to ask: Where am I in this picture? Am I positioning myself as the saviour of less fortunate peoples? as the progressive one? as more subordinated? as innocent? These are moves of superiority and we need to reach beyond them.[1] (Razack 2001, 170)

Razack's statement reflects the critique articulated by the black women's movement in the 1980s, which asserted that their experiences were not taken into account by the mainstream white, middle-class feminist movement (hooks 1981, 1986; Lorde 1984; Carby 1992; Hill Collins 2000; Lazreg 2000). As they pointed out, the foregrounding of gender oppression through an emphasis on "sisterhood" came at the expense of recognizing the ways in which patriarchy is "interlocking" with other forms of oppression, such as racism, homophobia, and classism (Hill Collins 1993). Holding on to "innocence" by denying complicity in the oppression of others or engaging in a "competition" of subordinations are both effects of a one-dimensional understanding of gender inequality and, as Razack claims, amount to gestures of superiority. The reference to the positions of "saviour" and "progressive," moreover, conjures up the ambivalent history of women's transnational activism. Postcolonial feminists have traced this history from imperial feminism to second-wave feminism's depictions of the "average third world woman," to Laura Bush–inspired interventions to "save" the women in Afghanistan (Mohanty 1984; Von der Lippe and Väyrynen 2011).

The latter inspires us to read Razack's quote in the light of critiques that have emerged in relation to international development work. While this is most obviously captured in her reference to the "saviour" position, her call to interrogate the claim to be "progressive" or "innocent" resonates with accusations that international development is a neoimperial and postcolonial project that draws on the imperial history of the civilizing mission (Shiva 1989; Escobar 1995; Stirrat and Henkel 1997; Kothari 2005; Nederveen Pieterse 2006). Within the field of development, but also beyond it, in the wider field of normative civil society politics, nongovernmental organizations (NGOs) were initially hailed for their progressiveness and inclusion of marginalized voices, such as those of women, in comparison with state institutions. More recently, however, the role of NGOs, and hence of NGO workers, came to be "viewed with less naivety and more discrimination concerning the institutional, discursive, economic and political constraints under which they operate" (Nederveen Pieterse 2006, 85). Razack's demand for a critical reflexivity concerning relational subjectivities, the way we understand ourselves in global social hierarchies, can therefore also be interpreted as addressed to the growing class of "global citizens," the transnational elite who practice their responsibility globally (Anheier et al. 2001; Taylor 2002; Desforges 2004; Baker and Chandler 2005; Grewal 2005).

The idea for this study emerged in the context of personal experiences and reflections during volunteer work for a UK-based NGO that supports refugees. The fact that Sherene Razack uses the personal pronoun "I" in the quote above indicates that she does not exempt herself from critical introspection and reflection. I also see this as a duty, being positioned as neither more "innocent" nor more "progressive" than the women I interviewed (cf. Tickner 2006). Volunteering for different projects of this NGO, I was confronted with my complicity in perpetuating different structures of inequality, not merely outside the volunteering, but inside this space of "doing good." For instance, in one project we would go out in teams consisting of one refugee or asylum seeker and one "native" British person to raise awareness about refugees among, for instance, police officers and firefighters. My whiteness and Dutch nationality not only meant that I could pass as "British-native-volunteer," erasing my migrant status, but also that I would be ascribed and could revel in the role of middle-class, university-educated expert on the asylum process, reinforcing hierarchies of knowledge. The volunteer refugee colleague accompanying me would be placed in the role of adding the "oral history" or "local knowledge" by speaking about his or her experiences, which black feminist Patricia Hill Collins (1993, 42) has described as the "voyeurism" common to relationships across power differences. In another program for female asylum seekers I failed to critically interrogate my colleagues or change the structure of the project when we addressed the women mainly as mothers and facilitated cooking and handicraft activities, even though this drew on and perpetuated gender and racial stereotypes. Neither theoretical reflections nor my knowledge of the feminist movement and its struggles presented immediate strategies for productively disrupting the apparent contentment of both the female asylum seekers attending the sessions and my volunteer colleagues. This made me interested in hearing the perspectives and approaches of other women who occupied privileged locations, who were positioned on the "helping" side and negotiated North–South relationships, in a field that has a tradition of struggle, but also of reflection: women's and gender politics. While the next chapter will present this history of struggle and reflection that forms the backdrop of this study, I will begin by situating this research with reference to three key components: subjectivities and reflections; feminism and gender; organizations and locations.

SITUATING THIS STUDY

Subjectivities and Reflections

This book's focus on the reflections of women supporting women along a North–South axis is situated within a genre of critical development literature, which addresses the subjectivities, experiences, and identity constructions of NGO and development workers (Goetz 2001; Goudge 2003; Eriksson Baaz 2005; Charlés 2007; Cook 2007; Heron 2007). This genre was given significant impetus from "insiders" of the development and aid industry, who, inspired by their accumulated unease with certain practices and by macrocritiques of development and NGOs, drew on their embodied experiences as the impulse for further critical research (Vaux 2001; Goudge 2003; Charlés 2007; Heron 2007; Mosse 2011; Eyben 2012; Hacker 2012). These scholarly and popular scientific publications, as well as others that have focused on the perspectives and experiences of development and humanitarian workers, have introduced a new language of reflection and demonstrated the gaps between official visions and day-to-day dilemmas. Previously, critiques concerning development institutions and NGOs focused mainly on organizational dimensions and policy effects (Petras 1997; Stirrat and Henkel 1997), as also noted by Fechter (2012). Through attention to subjectivity and identity, these studies managed to capture the relations between microlevel experiences, meso phenomena such as organizational structures, and macrolevel structures of global inequality (Goetz 2001; Eriksson Baaz 2005; Cook 2007; Hödl 2010; Fechter and Hindman 2011; Roth 2015).

This book should be read as part of this set of studies, as it employs reflections on individual experiences as material to explore wider structural issues of inequality and power. I align myself with other research on Northern NGO and development workers that takes a postcolonial approach and situates their experiences in the context of continuities between colonialism and the current "postcolonial" era (Eriksson Baaz 2005; Cook 2007; Heron 2007). This book contributes to this field by combining postcolonial perspectives with those of black feminism, critical development literature, and theories of global citizenship and civil society.

The following chapters present a close reading of interview extracts from the empirical material consisting of twenty-one semistructured interviews, conducted in 2007–2008, to demonstrate how these macrocritiques are reflected in the ways these women make meaning of their work. While I bring the dilemmas and reflections of the women in those positions to life by making extensive use of interview material, this study is not intended to "name and shame" individuals. Rather, the analysis should offer what Spivak calls a "constructive reading," which is "unaccusing, unexcusing, attentive, situationally productive through dismantling" (Spivak 1999, 81).

Feminism and Gender

By focusing on the experiences of women who specifically work on women and gender issues within their organizations, this book adds an additional layer to those studies among the aforementioned works, which have highlighted the experiences of female development workers or offered reflections on gender dynamics at work (Goetz 2001; Cook 2007; Heron 2007; Verma 2011; Eyben 2012). It takes feminist history and gender theory as central points of departure and engages with the role of sisterhood, generations of feminism, the public/private divide, and understandings of "the political." In order to highlight the interconnected dynamics of gender, "race," class, and age in the positions of the women in this study, many of whom, though not all, are white and middle class, I use an intersectional perspective.

I work with Avtar Brah's assumption that "members of dominant groups occupy 'privileged' positions within political and material practices that attend these social divisions although the precise interplay of this power in specific institutions or in interpersonal relations cannot be stipulated in advance, may be contradictory, and can be challenged" (Brah 1996, 112). Hence, throughout this book I will be attentive to how different categories, such as gender, "race," class, and nationality, intersect in the lived experience of the women. I discuss how different meanings are attributed to positions and categories, and I look into the relational aspect of identity with reference to how the women understand themselves vis-à-vis their target group. In this way I employ an intersectional approach to combine the macrostructures of social divisions with the microlevel of subjective experiences and to explore how structures of domination interact.

Black feminists' observation that the experiences of black women could not be theorized when analyses of "race" and gender were separated demonstrated the need for an approach that is attentive to the interaction between different categories of subordination. In this context, Kimberlé Crenshaw (2000) coined the concept "intersectionality" in 1989 in her article "Demarginalizing the Intersection of Race and Sex." Here she introduced her famous image of a black woman on a traffic intersection with discrimination flowing to and from the different lanes. If an accident happens to the woman standing on the crossroads, it could have been caused by one car from any of the directions, or by several cars at the same time. This is similar to the situation of harm through discrimination where the source of the specific discrimination (e.g., racism, sexism, or classism) can often not easily be identified and separated (Crenshaw 2000). Brah and Phoenix provide a useful definition of "intersectionality," which captures its multidimensionality, as denoting "the complex, irreducible, varied, and variable effects which ensue when multiple axes of differentiation—economic, political, cultural, psychic, subjective and experiential—intersect in historically specific contexts" (Brah and Phoenix 2004, 76). In this book I draw on their careful use of the term "differentiation" rather than "discrimination," which signals that an intersectional approach is also productive for analyzing "mixed" or privileged positions in addition to its original and significant impetus to analyze the experiences of black women facing multiple oppressions (AWID 2004; Yuval-Davis 2006; Verloo 2009). This is also in line with postcolonial interventions, such as articulated by Jenny Sharpe, who suggests that "the problematic needs to be reversed so that we can explain not how European women transformed colonialism but how colonialism left its indelible mark on European women" (Sharpe 1993, 94; cf. Stoler and Cooper 1997; McEwan 2009).

To position myself as a researcher in this study, I borrow a statement by Bridget Byrne from her book *White Lives: The Interplay of "Race," Class and Gender in Everyday Life*: "I have not chosen to research myself, but have chosen to research those who are quite like myself" (Byrne 2006, 40). In line with an intersectional perspective that understands identity as relational, this has a few implications. In each interview different parts of my own identity and position were foregrounded when establishing commonalities with my interview partners. As suggested by Ruth Frankenberg in her study about white women and "race," her "ability to conduct interviews successfully involved a complex set of adjustments in self-presentation, but never a presentation of [her]self as neutral" (Frankenberg 1993, 32). Depending on whom I was interviewing, the women perceived me as "mainly" someone who had also lived in different countries, with a similar academic background, primarily Dutch, particularly young, or, foremost, a white woman.

Since one of my interview questions specifically addressed how identity played out in the women's work, and the majority of the research participants can be categorized as white, Western, and middle class, it is likely that they were more comfortable sharing with me how their identity affected their work, since I am also white, Western, middle class, and a woman. This observation does not imply that this openness was necessarily better; rather it underlines the fact that the data are produced in the interaction of the specific interview setting (Letherby 2003). I will make this explicit at certain points in this book when I make my questions visible and present the interview material in the form of a dialogue between the women I interviewed and myself. Sometimes I was perceived as a "white ally": moments where my silence in the interviews was taken as agreement produced problematic tensions between research ethics and normative political convictions. They also reinforced my complicity in structures of racism such as the perpetuation of colonial racial stereotypes, when I left these unchallenged (Armbruster 2012, 45). Many of the women I interviewed had university degrees in a social science subject, making us share "a common intellectual language" (Puwar 1997, 10.2), since members of transnational feminist networks are often "highly educated social scientists" (Moghadam 2005, 102). At the same time, some of my (perceived) identity markers posed barriers between the research participants and me. I was surprised that age or seniority became topics that surfaced in almost every interview despite the fact that none of my questions directly addressed these. Moreover, I had the impression that this was mirrored in how the interviewed women related to me, especially in how frank they chose to be about their own reflections on their work practice. Generally speaking, the younger women in their twenties and thirties appeared to more closely identify with me as a young woman, which fostered openness in relation to their doubts and dilemmas. At the same time, many older and, in some cases, more "established" women tended to explain to me how their work functioned, undoubtedly also inspired by the fact that I have not worked in development or international NGOs myself. This unsettled the way power relations between (feminist) researcher and research participant are commonly conceived (Letherby 2003, 115; Sprague 2005, 59). Feminist writings from the 1980s emphasized that in contrast to mainstream research where the power differential between researcher and research participant was significant, feminist research with female researchers interviewing female participants narrowed this power gap. Later interventions acknowledged that it is too simplistic to attribute the "coziness" between researcher and participants to shared gender and that such experiences were the result of a combination of other common positions, such as class and "race" (Phoenix 1994; Puwar 1997). The expectation that female interviewers and research participants immediately establish rapport also problematically assumes that both have the same agendas, and that the interview participant would agree with the analysis of the interviewer, which cannot be guaranteed in much critical research (Byrne 2006), such as presented in this book.

Organizations and Locations

The organizations[2] the women worked for comprised a range of organizational forms: (headquarters of) membership organizations with branches in different countries, independent associations, networks, platforms, umbrella organizations, and intergovernmental institutions, which varied in size and institutional history, with the oldest dating back a century and the youngest being founded only a few years ago. As will become clear in the next chapter, which provides an overview of women's engagement across North–South divides and describes some of the organizations that the women interviewed for this study worked for, this is reflective of the broad variety of ways in which women have organized themselves to make their voices heard and work toward achieving justice and equality (Goetz 1997; Fraser and Tinker 2004). The thematic span of the women's work ranged from reproductive issues, health, development, peace, and trade, to political leadership and participation, sex work, and migration. The interviewed women occupied different hierarchical positions and had various roles, at the time of interview as well as in their previous jobs, including secretary general, interim director, policy director, advocacy officer, technical officer, network officer, and project worker, exemplifying Fechter's (2011) and Roth's (2015) observations about the diversity of "Aidland." A few women were the original founders of their organizations.

Importantly for the purpose of this study, which was to gain insight into the perspectives and reflections of women who support women across North–South divides, the interviewed women—though selected on the basis of their work for certain organizations—spoke in their personal capacity and not as representatives of their institutions. Since confidentiality was a precondition for the women's openness, I provide context with regard to their biographies, organizations, and thematic work remit but use pseudonyms and do not name their organizations. I have chosen to highlight the contextual information that I consider relevant to the thematic emphasis of each chapter, while leaving out other details that would more likely make the women identifiable.[3] Where I foreground organizational over biographical details, there is no expectation that the reader recalls the latter information from previous chapters.

All of the interviewed women were located in Europe at the time of the interview, more specifically, the UK, the Netherlands, Denmark, Sweden, Austria, Belgium (Brussels), and Switzerland (Geneva). The seemingly simple criterion of women's work across a North–South axis included a range of different institutions and locations. First, my sample includes women who work for international organizations with offices in Geneva and Brussels, as centers for international politics. Either they work for women's organizations or for organizations with a wider thematic remit, such as development and humanitarian aid in dedicated gender units or as gender officers. Second, there were women based in other European capital cities who engage in international work; as with those based in Brussels or Geneva, some work for women's organizations and others work on gender issues within larger organizations. Finally, my sample includes a third group of women in European cities who support women who have migrated to the global North, for example, as sex workers or asylum seekers.

I describe these three groups to provide a picture of the various arenas of work, not to introduce them as types that will structure a comparative tripartite analysis. As I will discuss in more detail later, the analysis in the subsequent chapters focuses on what the women as a group have in common. Nevertheless, in order to give further biographical context to the women in this study, I want to note that they do differ in their degree of "geographical promiscuity" (Nowicka 2005, 138), the extent to which they have experience with moving between different countries and continents, use several foreign languages in their work, and have multilingual families.

Since none of the women from the first category of organizations (those based in Brussels and Geneva) were born in Belgium or Switzerland and most have relocated several times, this label suits them; it also describes to a lesser extent the second group, who were based in other European cities working internationally. However, the label of "geographical promiscuity" is hardly applicable to the third group, who worked with migrant women. Where these biographical and organizational differences become meaningful, I highlight this in the analysis, for instance when discussing location and distance in chapter 3.

This book introduces distinct issues related to space, distance, and transnationality by centering on women in the global North, unlike the majority of studies in the field that this book contributes to, which have predominantly researched those working "on the ground" in the global South. The more limited research on international work from the global North, such as Frantz (2005) on careers of German NGO workers, Hopgood (2006) on employees at Amnesty International's headquarters in London, and Krause (2014) on desk officers in Western relief NGOs, still maintains a distinction between international humanitarianism or development and national work with migrants. Combining organizations who work internationally and nationally, that is, combining my groups 1 and 2 with group 3, is indeed uncommon. For example, Kathleen Staudt, who started working at the US–Mexican border with immigration NGOs after a career in development, anticipates in her short memoir the following question from her readers: "Have I lost my ways, diverting from research and action on women internationally?" before she argues that she considers her local community also international (Staudt 2004, 323).

As David Lewis has argued in relation to the strong separation between the UK domestic third (non-profit) sector and its international development sector, this division is "artificial and ahistorical" and relies on a refusal to recognize the linkages between global trade, migration, poverty, and development, as well as on a postcolonial insistence on distinguishing the "developing" from the "developed" world (2011, 188). The latter arguably mirrors a colonial separation between the colony and the metropole, which critical scholarship has sought to address by explicitly linking the two together (McClintock 1995). According to Lewis, this compartmentalization in both scholarship and practice ignores the parallel concerns with issues such as "accountability, challenges of resource mobilisation, tensions between advocacy and service delivery roles, and the nature of relations with the state" (Lewis 2014, 1137). In proposing that there are meaningful similarities and convergences between the issues that emerge in the work of women who support women in the global South (group 1 and 2), and those who work with migrant women nationally (group 3), I align myself with Lewis's argument. Moreover, I agree with Wendy Harcourt (2009), who posits that the tendency of gender and development analysis to separate phenomena occurring in the global North and global South, despite their obvious interrelatedness, is mistaken (cf. Jain 2004). I foreground the relation between migration, colonialism, and the aid industry, in particular in the light of the feminization of migration, against the commonly held idea that "the lives of female migrants are not ... part of the gender, trade and development nexus" (Harcourt 2009, 84). The next chapter will connect the scholarly debates on gender and development with issues emerging in the field of gender and migration.

As this book demonstrates, encounters between the global North and the global South in the context of "aid" broadly conceived take place in multiple arenas as a result of various mobilities. Appadurai (1990, 297) uses the term "ethnoscape" as "the landscape of persons who constitute the shifting world in which we live." These ethnoscapes are "inhabited" with and framed by encounters between asylum seekers, economic migrants, sex workers, NGO workers, and development workers, whose mobilities are differently valued (Grewal 2005; Kreutzer and Roth 2006). These "landscapes" are not just physical but also imagined worlds, as Appadurai stresses, which underlines the significance of relations that are mediated through images, memories of previous field visits, and stories, in addition to the "real" physical encounters, as chapter 4 will discuss. This book thus locates global relations inside, as well as between, nation-states and underlines parallels in the dynamics between North–South relations that play out inside the global North, and North–South relations between Northern and Southern regions. While "global North" and "global South" have become established terms within the context of postcolonial perspectives to denote a relational power dynamic that is rooted in colonialism and that goes beyond geographical correspondence, it is important to extend this with attention to the East–West axis, equally marked by imperialist politics and Othering processes. Following a range of studies on Eastern Europe and the Balkans that have successfully applied postcolonial theory to analyze how this region functions as Western Europe's "Other" (Bakic-Hayden and Hayden 1992; Buchowski 2006), in this book I generally include Eastern Europe under the umbrella term "global South." In some instances, however, I will pay particular attention to the specific dynamics of the East–West axis that exceed the global North–global South frame (Harcourt 2009, 29; Ghodsee 2014; Roth 2015, 10–11).

OVERVIEW OF THE BOOK

This book draws on and synthesizes four distinct yet interrelated sources of critique and tools for analysis of "doing good" across North–South divides: feminist theories, global citizenship/civil society theories, postcolonial theories, and critical development literature. Chapters 2 and 3 place the emphasis on the women's *self-understanding* with respect to the work they engage in, whereas chapters 4 and 5 focus on the ways in which they understand their *relations* with the women they support, and chapter 6 concentrates on *conceptions of the Other*. Together the chapters capture the continuum of subjectivities and relations that underpin the women's engagement.

In the next chapter, "Feminist Trajectories," I provide an overview of the history of transnational feminism, women's organizations' engagement, Gender and Development as well as the political struggles and dilemmas that have emerged in this context, for the purpose of contextualizing the work by the women studied here, as well as their feminist biographies. I argue that the different generations of women in this study reflect distinct feminist and work trajectories and that their positioning demonstrates the continued relevance of key debates within feminism concerning institutionalization, backlashes, essentialism, and inclusion/separatism.

Chapter 3, "Global Responsibilities," discusses the women's sense of responsibility and their self-understanding as professionals who make choices about their private time as well as about the location from which they work. Drawing on global citizenship theory, I suggest that many women articulate their sense of responsibility with reference to the opportunities they have enjoyed, disregarding the relationality between privilege and marginalization. The narratives of the women show their awareness of and their implication in the persistent discourse critical of professionalization of (feminist) NGO work, in which careerism is seen as incompatible with "moral work." I argue that the process of drawing the boundaries of the public and the private, the professional and the personal, is vital for the women; while the notion of the public serves to maintain their idea(l) of professionalism, the notion of the private is central to underlining their passionate commitment. The final section of this chapter focuses on those women who work from European cities to support women internationally in the global South and argues that these women respond to and justify their location in response to a dominant discourse in which distance is negatively evaluated.

Chapter 4, "Bridging Distance," further elaborates the theme of spatial location by analyzing the women's strategies for reaching across distance.

I first discuss field visits and storytelling as strategies to "stay in touch." Subsequently, I argue that the main strategy for bridging distance is contact with partner organizations in the South, in which partner organizations play a bridging role and, in some cases, eventually "replace" the intended beneficiaries. I situate the interview narratives about these strategies and their function to address distance in the context of critical development literature, which has problematized field visits and myths as inaccurate and has highlighted the ways in which partnerships are marked by power imbalances. I argue that the interview narratives are evidence of the mutual dependency between partner organizations, but that this mutuality is masked and fails to radically interrogate power imbalances. Finally, this chapter engages with representation, which has raised critical issues that include but are not limited to concerns with distance. I argue that representation, as well as alternative models, inevitably implies dynamics of construction.

In chapter 5, "Interlocking Connections," I discuss relationality, focusing on the women's understanding of the relation between themselves and the women in or from the global South whom they support. I observe that the contested notion of "sisterhood" still has currency and connect this to a "race to innocence" in which women foreground their own subordinate position when reflecting on the implications of their own identity for their work practices. In the final section of this chapter I draw on the interview narratives to trace alternative conceptualizations of connections between women globally that move beyond sisterhood. I derive from this analysis four building blocks that can provide a foundation for building solidarities, and subsequently discuss each: resisting divisions; establishing connections through experience; recognizing the instability of one's own position; and solidarity as a process rather than a given.

In chapter 6, entitled "Postcolonial Configurations," I shift my attention to the understanding of the Other, in a way approaching relationality from the other side. Drawing on postcolonial theories—and on similar yet distinct contributions of decolonial thought—that have highlighted how colonialism continues to inform a postcolonial era, I observe how the women's unprompted references to the colonial era, which tend to situate colonialism firmly in the past, reconfirm its persisting presence. Subsequently, I trace how the predominance of (racial) cultural lenses to interpret Otherness obscures socioeconomic structures as well as power dynamics. I argue that this focus on (not) understanding cultures introduces a language of knowledge that legitimizes, on the one hand, a distancing based on cultural relativism and, on the other hand, facilitates quick-fix solutions that bring the ambivalent Other under control. Finally, I contrast the interview narratives that employ a strong racialized cultural language with those that eschew such language or exceed cultural explanations to demonstrate important differences, but also perhaps unexpected similarities.

The concluding chapter of this book offers a synthesis by linking together the self-understandings of women in the global North who try to "do good" with their perceptions of (their relations with) women in or from the global South, addressing their positionality as "complicit sisters." The chapter outlines the contributions this book makes in its specific engagement with the continuities between migration and development and its focus on women's and gender issues. It presents further implications of this study's findings and offers suggestions for future research. It finally highlights the productive synergies between the different fields of critique that inform this book: feminist and postcolonial perspectives, global citizenship/civil society theory, and critical development approaches.

CHAPTER 2
Feminist Trajectories

TRANSNATIONAL FEMINISM, WOMEN'S NGOS, AND GENDER AND DEVELOPMENT
Women for Women and the Transnational

There is a rich, but also ambivalent tradition of women working to improve the circumstances of other women. This chapter will present this history in order to contextualize the work of the women in this study across North–South divides. It will introduce some important organizations and policy milestones in the field of gender and development and the transnational women's movement, while paying particular attention to the dilemmas and strategies that have emerged in the context of women's global engagement. Subsequently, against this backdrop, I will analyze the feminist biographies of the women in this study and look at the ways their feminist vision was facilitated, hampered, or questioned in the organizational settings in which they operated.

The NGO and voluntary sectors have historically strong associations with women. Bourgeois white women sought to find a place in the public sphere of colonial empires through philanthropy and missionary work (Heron 2007; Dimock 2010). Deborah Mindry (2001) points to the continuities between the Victorian colonial discourse of feminine virtue and current discourses of benevolence in relations between women NGOs from the global North and women from the global South. The shift from colonialism to the aid industry has been described as a "move away from the masculinity of colonialism to the more feminine subjectivity of aid" (Duffield 2007, 61). Also, women have historically been associated with peace movements (and femininity with peace), with more recent examples including women's involvement in the postwar NGO sector in Bosnia-Herzegovina and the dominant donor (essentialist) representations of these women as apolitical and nonnationalist peacemakers, mothers, and nurturers (York 1998; Helms 2003; Eyben 2007a; Pupavac 2010).

The women's movement itself has had an international orientation from the beginning, though globalization has changed the nature of this orientation (Naples 2002a; Ferree and McClurg Mueller 2004). First-wave feminists already organized internationally around issues such as abolitionism and women's suffrage (Burton 1994) and engaged with the United Nations (UN) through organizations such as the Women's International League for Peace and Freedom (WILPF) and the Young Women's Christian Association (YWCA), an organization building women's leadership. The NGO WILPF, formally founded in 1919, was in 1948 one of the first NGOs to obtain consultative status with the UN Economic and Social Council (ECOSOC). WILPF, a Western organization with a majority of white middle- and upper-class members, has an international reach, with national sections in each continent (Confortini 2012). The YWCA had its first world conference in 1898, its internationality linked to the British Empire, and has since grown into a global network of autonomous national YWCA quarters in 120 countries, coordinated by the World YWCA office in Geneva (Walker 2000; Desai 2002; Moghadam 2005; Higgs 2016).

The transnational impetus of this early feminism got renewed impulse from second-wave feminism (Fraser and Tinker 2004). In 1975 the UN declared International Women's Year and organized the first international women's world conference in Mexico City. This was followed by the declaration of the UN's International Women's Decade, in which the Copenhagen conference (1980) and the Nairobi conference (1985) were organized, prepared by the Commission on the Status of Women (CSW) (Desai 2002; Fraser and Tinker 2004; Moghadam 2005). The United Nations Decade for Women and the parallel NGO forums have been pivotal in making gender issues visible and providing opportunities to establish international networks between women (Razavi 1998). In the memoirs of those who played a seminal part in these developments, excitement about the momentum women's movements managed to generate and pride concerning their multiple achievements are still palpable (Fraser and Tinker 2004). At the same time, these memoirs, as well as other sources, speak of the tensions between women from the global South and the global North, which had emerged in the years leading up to the Nairobi conference through a divergence of interests and understandings of women's issues. Whereas Southern women focused on women's position in relation to the consequences of colonization, poverty, and other non-gender-specific issues, women from the North generally concentrated on body politics and male-female relations (Snyder 2004; Moghadam 2005). The dominance of the Northern women's movement only exacerbated those tensions.

The Nairobi conference is generally regarded as an important breakthrough moment in cooperation and communication between women from the global South and those from the global North and as the moment when "a collective sense of injustice" (Moghadam 2005, 1) and a "reflexive solidarity" (Desai 2002, 27) was formulated. This was facilitated by the fact that many women from Africa were present at the conference. Northern women could meet with Kenyan rural women's groups, and by that time economic issues, such as the erosion of the welfare state, had become more pressing concerns in the global North as well. Devaki Jain, feminist economist and activist, recalls how in the preparation for Nairobi, she "suggested panels and platforms from which women from the developing countries could present their own act, a presentation of views from the South, recalling those moments of distance and discomfort that we from the Third World had felt in the North" (2004, 135). Women from the global South started incorporating issues that had previously mainly been the focus of Northern-based feminism, such as violence against women. Another important impetus for Nairobi was the emergence of Development Alternatives with Women for a New Era (DAWN), an initiative by women from the global South. DAWN situated women's experiences in the (neo) colonial context and developed more inclusive understandings of feminism for those who had previously distanced themselves from feminism as a Western, antimale, and antifamily import (Goetz 1998; Antrobus 2004; Snyder 2004; Timothy 2004). Right after Nairobi, another important network was established, Women in Development Europe (WIDE), which took much inspiration from DAWN's vision on development. From 1993, the WIDE network had its main office in Brussels to facilitate its advocacy and lobbying work, coordinating national platforms of different women's organizations in a large number of European states (Moghadam 2001). In 2011 WIDE was dissolved and replaced by the informal cooperation structure of WIDE+ (WIDE+ newsletter, no. 1, 2012).

Global Civil Society and NGOs

Ten years after Nairobi, in 1995, the Fourth World Conference on Women took place in Beijing. This is generally regarded as one of the marking points of the emergence of "global civil society" (Munck 2002). The term "civil society" became *en vogue* again with the Latin American revolutions and the breakdown of the Soviet regime, and in Western societies the term "civil society" was taken up as an attempt to revitalize democracy (Van Rooy 1998; Anheier et al. 2001). While most agree that some significant shift took place in the early 1990s, there is also the accusation of "presentism," the exaggerated focus on global civil society as a new phenomenon and the lack of recognition of historical continuities with regard to earlier internationalist movements (such as the women's suffragist movement) often ignored by the traditionally statist discipline of International Relations (IR) (Munck 2002). In the Platform for Action agreed on in Beijing, NGOs are presented as important players in achieving change and maintaining links with marginalized constituencies, creating a platform for different voices. Compared to state or private sector institutions, they became positively celebrated as innovative, participatory, and efficient. In the years leading up to the Beijing conference, there was an increase in the number of women's NGOs and a growing involvement of women in them, and larger international NGOs moved to incorporate gender policies or independent gender subunits (Mayoux 1998). The "deceptively short acronym" NGO refers to a diverse sector, as it comprises highly professionalized organizations and small-scale volunteer organizations, with a broad range of political views (Naples 2002b, 274; cf. Silliman 1999; Smillie 2000). NGOs were conventionally defined as nongovernmental, nonprofit, and nonviolent and derived part of their moral status from these features (Willetts 2002). The astonishing growth in the number of (international) NGOs in the last decades, and their increasing interconnectedness and embedding in institutions of global governance like the UN and the World Bank, meant that they became a political force to be reckoned with (Anheier et al. 2001; Taylor 2002; Desforges 2004; Baker and Chandler 2005; Duffield 2007).

Since the 1990s, the engagement of national and international NGOs, whether operating in the field of development, women's rights, health, or migration, has increasingly been under critical scrutiny (Shiva 1989; Escobar 1995; Sogge 1996; Miller and Razavi 1998; Kothari 2005; Nederveen Pieterse 2006; Kane 2013). The three dimensions that importantly defined NGOs (independence from the state, nonprofit status, and their nonviolent nature) started to be questioned because of, respectively, NGOs' increased reliance on state donor funding and involvement in global governance, the aid sector's transformation into an industry where aid workers act as moral entrepreneurs, and finally, NGOs' support for Western military (humanitarian) interventions. Nowadays NGOs are often contrasted with social movements, with the former being characterized as more bureaucratic, depoliticized, hierarchical, and dependent on external funding than the latter (Petras 1997; Tully 2005). Many critics of NGOs in general, and women's NGOs in particular, tend to favor autonomous social movements as a locus of politics "from below," over the more top-down NGOs.

Critics have also pointed out that NGOs, rather than being answerable to those they seek to represent and provide services for, are in fact only accountable to their donors. Donors generally encourage a concentration on service delivery over political advocacy (Miller and Razavi 1998; Eyben 2006). Though one of the results of the "NGOization" of the women's movement has been relative job security for some former activists, it is also feared that this has led to a reduction of radical feminist political spaces, to an increasing dependence on the state, to a legitimization of the state's pullback in welfare provision, and to project-based work that negates long-term political goals (Lang 1997; Alvarez 1998; Mayoux 1998; Menon 2004; de Alwis 2009). Postcolonial feminist Chandra Mohanty speaks of a "mainstreaming of the feminist movement" in which feminism has been replaced by (women's) rights discourses (Mohanty 2003, 249). Furthermore, because only a few organizations have the material and economic capacity to transform themselves into NGOs with high-status networks, it is feared that the divide between professional NGOs and informal organizations mirrors other inequalities along the global North–global South axis (Moghadam 2005).

Deliberations, Dilemmas, and Divisions

The efforts by the women's movement to influence institutional change in development and beyond led to a number of strategic deliberations, dilemmas, and divisions inside the movement and among feminists (Harcourt 2016). As will be sketched below, these range from addressing institutional strategies to discursive framing, programmatic choices, and the heterogeneity of, as well as power dynamics between, women. The celebration of the successes of the women's movement has gone hand in hand with recognition of struggles and the need for critical reflection. One of the points of contention has centered on whether to remain outside dominant institutions and act from independent and autonomous positions, or whether to enter bulwarks of male power, such as state institutions, to try to achieve change from within. Carol Miller and Shahra Razavi (1998) describe the latter strategy in terms of "entryism," requiring a double move of being both "missionary" in terms of working to convert others to a (feminist) ideology and "mandarin" in adapting to organizational and bureaucratic logics. Another common term to describe women working in established contexts is "femocrat," a word that emerged in the Australian context of the 1970s when women's policy machinery was created by the state (Sawer 1998). Femocrats who operate inside mainstream bureaucratic institutions have to combine technical with political skills, and their success is additionally seen as dependent on maintaining relations with the autonomous women's movement outside their institution. This can be hindered by the fact that femocrats, especially those who have not been politicized inside the women's movement, are oftentimes observed critically by feminists who choose to remain outside established institutions (Miller and Razavi 1998). As Razavi has (1998) argued, a politics of total disengagement from mainstream institutions could, however, be considered even more risky.

Feminist engagement with institutions required further strategic reflection in relation to which discourses to employ to articulate women's needs, from aligning feminist claims with dominant discourses (e.g., on efficiency or rights) to intervening with alternative frames. This is a balancing act between, on the one hand, finding ways to be heard and having gender issues be recognized as legitimate and, on the other hand, risks of co-optation and instrumentalization (Miller and Razavi 1998). While many have recognized the successes and achievements related to the women's movement's engagement with the UN—for example, in terms of agenda setting through slogans such as "Women's rights are human rights"—it is also argued that women's NGOs have been co-opted into the UN agenda (Silliman 1999; Desai 2002; Moghadam 2005; Reeves 2012). Feminists have, however, undoubtedly made a strong imprint on the field of international development through their international activism, lobbying, and networking.

Feminist interventions in the field of development from the early 1970s led to the introduction of the policy framework of "Women in Development" (WID). WID introduced women as previously overlooked independent actors of development, rather than passive beneficiaries (Miller and Razavi 1998). WID has more critically been described as an approach that emerged in the global North, especially the United States, and which followed a liberal individualist ideology that focused on adding women without challenging the definition of development (Razavi 1998; Bhavnani and Coulson 2003). The subsequent "Women and Development" (WAD or WAND) approach was a response to this latter shortcoming, "suggest[ing] that women and development must be seen synonymously, each drawn to recast the other" (Bhavnani and Coulson 2003, 83; Antrobus 2004). More prominent than WAD, however, has been the later "Gender and Development" (GAD) approach, which emerged in the 1990s. GAD considers gender (rather than women) to be a more constructive tool in capturing gendered power relations in the context of development (Desai 2002; Bhavnani and Coulson 2003; Fraser and Tinker 2004). The intention behind GAD was also to address what had been identified as a problem with the implementation of WID policies, namely that they improved women's material conditions, but less so their social and economic status in relation to men (Goetz 1997). It therefore moved from the "integrative project" of WID to include women, to a focus on intervening at the level of gendered power relations (Goetz 1998). While the three labels, WID, WAD, and GAD, are meant to reflect different historical periods as well as ways of conceptualizing sex and gender and related political strategies, White (2006) argues that in practice it is difficult to neatly distinguish the three from one another, as they are often combined and sometimes tell us more about organizational politics than anything substantial in relation to policy content. Though each subsequent policy change was intended as an improvement over the previous policy, some now argue that the GAD approach has depoliticized the original feminist intentions (Piálek 2008). More positively the dilution and instrumentalization of the gender agenda has been considered as an inevitable side-effect of any political advocacy work (Razavi 1998).

There are a number of major milestones for the international women's movement that remain significant for current-day NGO and movement practice. At the Mexico City conference in 1975, the predecessor of what became UNIFEM and now is called UN WOMEN, the Voluntary Fund for the UN Decade for Women (VFDW), was set up (Fraser and Tinker 2004; Snyder 2004). Other achievements are the adoption of the Convention on the Elimination of All Forms of Discrimination against Women (CEDAW) in 1979, adopted and presented to governments at the 1980 Copenhagen conference, which remains a key instrument for NGOs, and the Beijing Declaration and Platform for Action (1995) (Fraser and Tinker 2004). The United Nation's Conference on Women in Beijing 1995 also marked the start of the prominence of the concept of "gender mainstreaming" (Rees 2002). A short definition is formulated by Rees: "Mainstreaming is the systematic integration of gender equality into all systems and structures, policies, programmes, processes and projects, into ways of seeing and doing, into cultures and their organisations" (2002, 1). Gender mainstreaming, a strategy associated with GAD (Squires 2007, 44), was originally hailed as a radical and all-encompassing approach, as it encourages taking gender into account across all programs and topics. Increasingly, however, some have argued that gender mainstreaming in development has become a technocratic rather than a feminist instrument (Piálek 2008, 279; cf. Verloo 2001, 13; Squires 2007, 137; de Jong 2016a). The Beijing Platform for Action also formed a starting point for the organizing and lobbying that led to the drafting and subsequent unanimous adoption of UN Security Council Resolution 1325 on Women, Peace and Security in 2000. This resolution stresses women's role in conflict resolution, the need for a gender perspective in peacekeeping, and the significance of participation of women in peace negotiations, and forms the backdrop for political mobilization by women's and feminist peace organizations (Hill, Aboitiz, and Poehlman-Doumbouya 2003).

Increasing women's participation, however, is a guarantee neither for representation of feminist agendas nor for addressing the needs of a diverse groups of women. Demands for women's participation are also hindered by other exclusionary mechanisms that women face, or constitute a burden for women in terms of resources and commitment (Mayoux 1998). More generally, one can ask how "success" of the women's movement in achieving women's empowerment is measured. For example, there have been concerns about the fact that some issues have found a more ready acceptance in mainstream institutions in the context of neoliberal capitalism, while other feminist concerns have not been taken up (Fraser 2009). On the one hand, this illustrates the compromises feminist activists have felt compelled to make, in terms of rhetoric and strategic alliances. On the other hand, it reveals something about the interests of those dominant institutions and programs (Razavi 1998). For example, the perceived success of women's microcredit programs for poverty relief, which were initiated by organizations such as the Self Employed Women's Association (SEWA), an Indian trade union founded in 1972, due to women's efficient repayment of loans, has been assessed as aligning closely to the interests of banks. Women's so-called efficiency can come at the cost of a devaluation of women's unpaid skills and labor as well as a reinforcement of decontextualized, gendered stereotypes of women as caring (grand)mothers and men as egoistic family members (Crewe and Harrison 1998; Mayoux 1998; Wilson 2011). Hence activists have witnessed the transformation of some of their key principles into popular buzzwords and have warned against the promise of quick-fix solutions. For instance, the term "women's empowerment" to denote achievement of autonomy and choice has quickly become popularized despite (or because of) the fact that there is no agreed-on definition (Kardam 1997; MacKenzie 2012). As Ackerly has mockingly put it, combining the critiques of microcredit programs and "empowerment": "'Empowered,' the borrower wisely invests money in a successful enterprise, her husband stops beating her, she sends her children to school, she improves the health and nutrition of her family, and she participates in major family decisions" (1995, 56).

The global women's movement hence brought women together in unprecedented ways around the theme of development, while also making divisions visible. When women's issues started to be recognized as important in development, women were increasingly incorporated into the NGO world, albeit in very different positions; at its most extreme, some became the professionals working for NGOs on gender projects, some the proposed beneficiaries of projects (White 2006). While these women shared experiences of gender oppression in their own countries, different "race" and class positions negated this gender unity. Gayatri Spivak conjures up a poignant image when she states in the context of the work of the UN and hegemonic women's NGOs that "one group of women of the Northern hemisphere . . . are helping to exploit another, quite as the old colonial subject used to do the dirty work of the colonisers" (2000, 123). As the above account has made clear, these different locations and positions do not just surface between "recipient" and NGO worker, but are also visible inside feminist networks that engage with global gender issues. For example, I suggest that a close reading of the volume *Developing Power: How Women Transformed International Development*," edited by Arvonne S. Fraser and Irene Tinker (2004), which collects different contributions from scholars and practitioners from the North and the South who offer their memoires, reveals celebration and tension alongside each other. This concerns not only what is discussed and celebrated as achievement, but also how the "story" of women and development is being narrated. As Devaki Jain states, addressing issues of ownership:

> Such celebration, however, has also raised difficult questions. Who really uncovered the shroud, coined a phrase, or fostered a movement? Because the written word and its dissemination are dominated by the English-speaking North, the South is often denied the credit it is due for the many discoveries made there, especially in the field of development. (2004, 136)

Jain's statement is also an important disclaimer for the retelling and retracing of transnational feminism, women's NGOs, and gender and development that this section has offered so far. This goes beyond concerns about giving credit where credit is due and extends to a more general need to be alert to what is told and what is excluded from what can be considered the canonical account of the engagement of the transnational women's movement with international development. Kristen Ghodsee (2014), for example, has written a powerful critique of the historiography of the international women's movement, by demonstrating the importance of the alliances between the "Second" and "Third World" for transnational feminism, which are commonly ignored. She describes how the Mexico City conference provided a platform for networking and collaboration between women from Eastern bloc countries and women representing African states (Ghodsee 2014).

Moreover, while the history of the transnational women's movement is testimony to the connections between the local and the global, as has become clear from the above, it is striking to see that accounts of engagement at the national level are often limited to case studies of countries in the global South or national foreign ministries in the global North providing aid to the South. There is no equivalent comprehensive history written about local-level engagement comparable to the "canonical account" on gender and development, despite both contemporary and historical parallels. For example, similar "race"- and class-mediated imperatives that inspired structurally advantaged women to do philanthropic work in the colonies can be found in the legacy of voluntary work by middle- and upper-class women in the metropole, in the nineteenth and first part of the twentieth centuries (Mahood 2008). The disconnect between, on the one hand, accounts of women's engagement and encounters inside the global North and, on the other, the gender-and-development narrative, is underlined by Harcourt's observation that marginalized women from the global South "disappear" out of the gender and development frame the moment they cross to the global North as female migrants (2009, 84). The study presented in this book considers these two locations and types of engagement under one umbrella, as I explained in the previous chapter. In the next section I will therefore draw connections between the dilemmas, deliberations, and divisions sketched above, and those that have emerged in North–South encounters in women's civil society engagement in the North.

From the Local to the Global and Back

The continuities between gender, sexuality, migration, and development and between international and national women's movement engagement can be illustrated with the example of the issue of sex work. A central topic in the context of feminist activism across North–South divides generally and a key issue for some of the women interviewed for this study, this is one of the most intensely debated topics within contemporary feminism. Feminists have been deeply divided in their assessment of sex work and about their mobilizing strategies. The organizations that are included in this study have no consensus on this topic either and operate according to different standpoints. As Augustín points out, the choice of position is not solely read in conceptual or ideological terms, but as casting people "as good feminists or caring persons" (2005, no page number). Roughly, the main division is between abolitionist feminists and sex work activists. The first, often inspired by radical feminism, regard prostitution, as they insist on calling it, a symptom of oppressive patriarchy, which is inherently demeaning for women and therefore should be criminalized. Their current reference point is the Swedish model of criminalization of (male-connoted) buyers of sex, introduced in 1998 and subsequently adopted in other countries (Bernstein 2012). Important representatives of abolitionist feminism are the US-based Coalition Against Trafficking in Women (CATW), and, in Europe, the Brussels-based European Women's Lobby (EWL), the largest umbrella organization of women's associations in the European Union. The EWL was founded in 1990 and has advisory status in both the UN ECOSOC and the Council of Europe. Feminist sex work activists, on the other hand, do not consider prostitution as oppressive per se. They prefer the term "sex work" in order to conceptualize it as (legitimate) labor, and initiate interventions geared toward improving working conditions and combating potential violence, for example, by advocating for decriminalization and building alliances with trade unions (Augustín 2005).

While these opposing positions cannot be mapped onto a North–South divide, since both "camps" include activists and scholars from different regions, the debate has revealed tensions along a North–South axis. Scholar and sex work activist Doezema (2001) accuses Western feminist activists of imposing their particular Western ideas of sexuality and victimhood on Third World sex workers/prostitutes. The North–South dimension is particularly pertinent in relation to the issue of trafficking of women for sex work, with its links to migration, border control, and security. From the mid-1990s, shifts occurred in women's mobilization around sex work and trafficking and the framing of this issue; shifts that are connected to developments in the international women's movement as described above. Feminist antitrafficking campaigners were able to construct successful transnational alliances with evangelical groups and law enforcement institutions—as well as, arguably, building professional careers as antitrafficking activists—at a time that the UN increasingly provided a platform for NGOs. The Beijing World Conference on Women is cited as a location where "trafficking as a labor issue was first transformed into a sexual violence and slavery issue" (human rights activist quoted in Bernstein 2012, 252). The aforementioned "women's rights as human rights" frame has, according to its critics, lent itself to an emphasis on sexual violence and protection against bodily harm over gender power relations as embedded in social and economic inequalities (Bernstein 2012).

Strategic and ideological decisions concerning the scope for engagement and cooperation with the state, which I have discussed earlier in relation to femocrats, have also been prominent with regard to sex work and trafficking, with feminists being divided about the opportunities and risks (Bernstein 2012). More recently the state has started "courting" migrant, especially Muslim, women's organizations, with increased funding and access to politicians and policymakers, for example in the Netherlands and the UK (Roggeband 2010; Wadia 2015). This interest in the voices of migrant women is in marked contrast to years of neglect by the state, as well as, to an extent, by the white women's movement and male-dominated ethnic community organizations (Mügge and de Jong 2013). It is also highly selective, as studies on headscarf debates in Austria, Germany, and France have demonstrated, with the voices of particular women, for example secular women with a Muslim background, receiving more attention (Freedman 2001; Hadj-Abdou 2011). In their study of what they call majority-minority relations in contemporary women's movements, Line Nyhagen Predelli and Beatrice Halsaa (2012) investigate in how far the critique voiced by racialized women against the white women's movement, which I briefly described in the introduction to this book, remains relevant for today. They draw on the account of US-based second-wave feminisms—explicitly in the plural—by Benita Roth (2004), who has traced the development of the African American, white, and Chicana feminist movements alongside one another, each making strategic choices with regard to its distinct contexts. With reference to three case studies of the women's movements in the UK, Spain, and Norway, Predelli and Halsaa observe an increased acknowledgment by majoritized women's movements that racism is relevant for feminism and that ethnic minority women have specific experiences and interests. At the same time, they found that "minoritised women's issues are still largely perceived as different from the issues of majoritised women, or as being specific to minority women's experiences" and that this framing restricts the scope for cooperation (Predelli and Halsaa 2012, 262).

In transnational feminist networks on the European level, two majority organizations, Women Against Violence Europe (WAVE) and the aforementioned EWL, follow a strategy of inclusion of minority women's issues in their agenda as well as cooperation with minority organizations, but invest less in the integration of minority women within their own organizational structures. This raises issues of representation that are similar to those experienced in transnational feminism around development, with the interests of migrant and African diaspora women "not articulated *by* them but *for* them" (Agustín and Roth 2011, 240–241), as I will discuss in more detail in chapter 4. In this context, minority organizations' strategies include integration in the mainstream as well as self-representation as a form of empowerment (Agustín and Roth 2011). While these rich empirical national and transnational studies (Merill 2001; Roth 2003), which document conflicts and divisions as well as spaces of cooperation and "bridging" between different movements, are not written into the canonical account of women's networking around issues of international development that I recounted in the previous section, there are many overlapping dynamics and concerns. Also on the level of historiography I suggest that there are powerful resonances. For example, Ghodsee's (2014) previously mentioned critique concerning the erasure of "Second World" feminism from the history of women's organizing around development is joined by Roth's (2004, 7) rectification of the "white-washing" of second-wave feminism and the silence on class (as intersecting with "race" and ethnicity).

Returning to the relation between ethnic minority women and the state, it is clear that the state's investment in migrant and racialized women has emerged both from a victim frame in which (especially Muslim) migrant and ethnic minority women are regarded as "least integrated" in Western society, and from a discourse that understands these women as gendered agents who play a key role as mothers and wives in the "civilization," that is, integration, of their male family members (Roggeband 2010; Wadia 2015). Such instrumental attention to migrant women can also be found in the recent interest of international institutions in migrant women as "sacrificing heroines" for both monetary and social remittances at the nexus of migration and development (Schwenken 2008). I suggest that the fact that these stereotypes bear close resemblance to those articulated in the context of microcredit programs, which I have discussed above, is one of many illustrations of the continuities between discourses and debates in the context of gender and development, on the one hand (cf. Grewal 2005), and those concerning migrant and racialized women in the global North, on the other hand. These parallels find their expression both in the discursive realm and in material structures. For example, African American women and women in Africa "meet" not only in being depicted as mothers of too many children and as dependent on welfare (the first being seen as "unworthy recipients of aid," the latter as "unresponsive to aid"), but also in being negatively affected by the gendered, classed, and racial policies of privatization and welfare state entrenchment (Hill Collins 2000, 241). The fact that this is designated in some global locations as a "development issue" and in others as a "social issue" cannot hide that these are "two sides of the same coin" (Hill Collins 2000, 240).

FEMINIST BIOGRAPHIES

The previous section has presented a snapshot overview of the transnational women's movement, gender and development, and women's NGOs, drawing connections between the different positions, strategies, and dilemmas in the international development context and those that have emerged in women's movements in the North. Against this backdrop, I will now introduce and situate the women of this study, in particular their diverse understandings of gender and feminism. I will do so both in relation to their personal trajectories that have informed their understandings of their work and in relation to the positions taken by their organizations. I will show that it matters that some of the women can be counted among the pioneers in gender and development as described above, while later generations entered an already crafted field of gender and development. I will argue that instead of analyzing the situated narratives of the women workers according to the classical fault lines of liberal, radical, and socialist feminism (Bulbeck 1998), their everyday negotiations can be better understood in the context of some of the major debates and contentions that have marked feminism(s). These include generational differences between feminists, (responses to) different backlashes against feminisms, the institutionalization of the women's movement in the academy, separatism versus inclusion, and intersectionality.

While working on women's and gender issues is no guarantee for a feminist perspective, the majority of the women I interviewed explicitly and spontaneously defined themselves as feminists. This was generally more pronounced among those who worked internationally than those who worked nationally with migrant women, as I will further discuss below. What they understood under "feminism" was diverse and was often linked to their biographies, as I will demonstrate. Despite their divergent understandings of feminism, a common and recurrent theme that emerged from their accounts was that "the personal is political." This reflects one of the most significant claims of feminists who insisted that women's experiences were not merely personal but reflected gendered power relations on a wider scale, including those in the public sphere (Enloe 1989). A powerful example of this is the account of Stacey, a Canadian woman in her midthirties, who studied political science and works on gender and health for an international organization. She says the following:

> [My interest in inequalities] with respect to women . . . came as I grew older and had my own experiences based on gender-based violence and abuse and seeing things around myself. There was a shooting . . . where somebody killed only

women—only women, just because they were women trying to be engineers.... And so as a woman and having gone through things that I only experienced as a woman, that definitely influenced things.

Here Stacey neatly weaves together her own gendered experiences with her observations about gender-based violence around her. For Stacey, who is one of the few non-white women among those that I interviewed, her awareness of her own gendered positioning was preceded by her awareness of her racialized and ethnic identity. She qualifies her feminism by stressing that her interest in gender inequality does not mean that she is blind to other oppressions:

So of course being a woman affects things. Does that mean that I don't feel for the discrimination and the inequality and injustices that my cousin is facing in fighting to marry his partner who is HIV positive? Of course not! Does it mean that I am not sensitive to other forms of inequalities? Of course not!

In this statement, Stacey clearly states that her convictions cannot be reduced to her personal gendered experiences. The relevance of this assertion as well as the critique concerning blindness toward other forms of subordination will be discussed more substantially in chapter 5's section titled "Racing to Innocence."

Stacey's narration can be juxtaposed with that of a young white woman in her late twenties called Sophie, who also studied political science and now works for an international member organization in a European capital city on reproductive rights. While Sophie similarly stresses in the interview the importance of class and ethnicity in line with the influence of intersectional approaches and contrasts herself with other feminists who solely focus on gender, she admits that this insight is something she had to develop: "I think I came to this work with that approach, that if you solve the gender problem, you also solve all other power relations in society."

Stacey, by contrast, describes how, growing up in a small conservative city where she attended a white school, she was made aware of her "difference" at an early age: "not a difference based on my sex, it was a difference based on my culture, it was a difference based on my skin color, based on my ethnicity." Informed by the history of her immigrant parents who had experienced poverty, she recounts that when she grew older, she became concerned with economic inequalities. Her early awareness of class, "race," ethnicity, and religion is contrasted with the later acquisition of her consciousness about gender issues.

Stacey: "I'm not sure that I can say from the beginning that I was concerned with inequalities only with women, because that was really something that evolved throughout. Probably I would say it sort of all came together when I was at university doing my undergraduate degree." Stacey's expression "it sort of all came together" describes how her university time helped her to synthesize her earlier experiences with theories about gender oppression. In Stacey's narrative it is not clear whether she experienced "gender-based violence" before she learned to put that label on it during her university studies or whether it came at a time when she was already able to recognize it as such. While Stacey's experiences differ from those of the white women because of her racialized and ethnic identity as well as her class status, through her age (and educational background) she shares with other women from her generation the encounter with women's and gender studies.

Anna, a white woman and fellow Canadian, slightly younger than Stacey, who works on engendering constitutions explains:

> During my university years, when I was engaged with academic study of gender issues, I was very, very engaged with women and that being part of my identity. It was very much the Ani DiFranco[1] stage of my life as well, and this was very much like "This is who I am." And a lot of how I responded to life was filtered through my own perceptions of whether they were responding to me as a woman.

Sylvia, a middle-class woman who works internationally on gender and peace, describes herself as a "classic thirty-year-old American white woman." She started her degree in political science in the mid-1990s and explains:

> I was very involved in women's issues when I was in university and in high school, mostly because reproductive rights was a very hot topic and it was something that, at that point as a young woman, it was an incredibly important issue for me in terms of being a politically active person in my youth.

The experiences of these three young, mobile, North American women, who work from the global cities of Brussels and Geneva, are the product of a historical development of the 1980s, when second-wave feminism "matured" and women's studies slowly became institutionalized in the academy (Scott 2008).

Sylvia continues by stressing that her experience of being a woman does not mean that a gender perspective comes naturally to her: "Because you are a woman does not mean that you are constantly thinking about how to integrate gender into your programming or your project. Just like a man working on an issue, I need to have the same kind of 'Don't forget the women!' reminder." Sylvia attributes the fact that a "gender balance is not instinctive for her" to the fact that she regards herself part of the "kind of postfeminist generation where it is not quite as important to us anymore. It is like the feeling of, well, as far as gender parity in our own countries is concerned, that we have come so far that it is not quite as passionate an issue for us. So it is not at the forefront of our mind when we are doing things."

Though her reference to "us" and "our own countries," draws me as the interviewer (correctly) into the same age group as well as into "the West"—creating a global hierarchy—she hastens to add that this speculation "might be a gross generalization not applicable to anyone else." Postfeminism, as McRobbie describes it, "positively draws on and invokes feminism as that which can be taken into account, to suggest that equality is achieved, in order to install a whole repertoire of new meanings which emphasize that it is no longer needed, it is a spent force" (2004, 28). As such, Sylvia's continued commitment to gender equality does not neatly map onto this definition of postfeminism. However, the link she draws between what she regards as feminist achievements and a waning of urgency indeed resonates with postfeminist sentiments. Here institutionalization of women's studies, and later gender studies, comes to meet depoliticization, as feared by those critically observing feminism's institutionalization (Wiegman 2005).

This depoliticization appears more pronounced in the narrative of a thirty-two-year-old white Western European woman, Gisela, who studied sociology and also attended gender courses. She is also based in one of the "global cities" and, perhaps surprisingly, works for what is recognized as a strong and well-known international feminist organization on gender and development. The apparent mismatch between the organization's vision and Gisela can be seen as sign of the way in which "career feminists" have been attracted by the professionalization of the women's movement brought about by NGOization (as will be discussed in more detail in the next chapter). I argue, however, that it serves as a reminder that in the highly fluctuating international NGO world, we should not be tempted to equate official organizational mission with the everyday actions and understandings of staff members. After she tells me that she had not heard of the organization before she came across the vacancy, I ask her whether she was specifically looking for gender-focused positions. Gisela then explains: "I saw this at a peace-and-women list, and this is really something that relates to something that I have done before, and I am interested in gender. I mean, I am also interested in peace. It is not that I only work on gender, but I am interested in it."

In light of this, it is not surprising that Gisela tells me that she "could work in another organization. For me an organization that is really big, like Oxfam, for instance, and that has maybe a more diluted political view. I can also work there." This cannot be dismissed as simple career-oriented pragmatism, but needs to be placed in Gisela's biography as a woman from a poor background with her parents living on social benefits. She became politically active as a teenager in the humanist movement. As she has embraced the ideal that every individual should think critically and that all perspectives are partial, for her a gender approach can neither have all answers, nor does working for a less radical organization preclude critical work.

In the context of her organization, which has as a matter of policy only women in key positions, Gisela tells me that she would like to include more men "because I feel like I am for inclusive groups and this is not an inclusive group." Her oscillation between paying lip service to the importance of women-only spaces in a recognition of feminist history and her own (tentative) humanist standpoint illustrates that she feels distanced from this tradition and willing to listen to other views: "Ideally I would like to see mixed groups everywhere, in every organization, and I know this is not realistic in the situation that we are in, and it is good for the women to have these spaces."

Sonia, a young woman from a Latin American country, working on peace in Geneva, identifies as a feminist in the interview. She links this to her experience of growing up in "a very macho culture." In a different register, she is also concerned with male-female relations in feminism, and she immediately hastens to add: "But I am not a sort of feminist that thinks, 'Oh I hope all men die.' No, I am not such an extremist. I believe we can improve the situation of women, which at the same time will probably improve the situation for men. And that's great, but I am not any extremist, not at all."

Backlashes against particular (stereo)types of feminism and subsequent disavowal mentioned in the interviews—or put more simply, explicit descriptions of "what they were not"—provide clues to situate the women that I interviewed in relation to feminisms. They also shed light on lived responses to some of the ambivalences and struggles within the movement as well as backlashes against feminism. Sonia's statement could reveal a classical prejudice, reminiscent of feminists as angry "bra-burners," that would not be shared by many of the women. However, she is not alone in insisting that she is not antimale. It might therefore be more productive to read Sonia's exceptionally strong expression in the context of her background as a woman from the global South, where the label "feminist" as an import from the West carries negative connotations, such as antifamily and antimen, as also discussed later in this chapter.

Sonia's exclamation can also be usefully situated in relation to research into young women's attitudes toward feminism, which has found that while many refuse to call themselves feminists, they do support feminist issues and recognize gender inequalities (Aronson 2003; Valenti 2007, 5–6; Scharff 2011). Aronson found that "young women's development of a feminist perspective and identity is tied closely with institutions that support and nurture such a perspective—particularly women's studies programs" (Aronson 2003, 919). This resonates with the "awakening" accounts above, in which many associated their "feminist awakening" with their university years. At the same time that feminism became institutionalized, other sources such as the media were communicating negative stereotypes of feminism that have been internalized by some women (Aronson 2003).

Catherine, who is in her midthirties, has worked since her early twenties for the same umbrella organization with a broad thematic remit. She observes this disavowal of the label "feminist" among young women and combines her experience with the strong backlashes against feminism, with faith in the potential nurturing function of institutions:

> We had a project about young women and it was twenty young women, and none of them, or maybe only two, would call themselves feminists on the first day. And all of them would call themselves feminists on the last day, so it is all a question of perception. It does not seem so difficult to change, but there is ongoing undermining work.... To speak the war language: the enemies of feminism are getting more powerful in the last years, I think, so that does not make the work easier: the conservative forces, the pro-life movement.

To understand the broader implication of generational shifts, it is helpful to complement McRobbie's previously quoted definition of postfeminism as one that has been pushed by popular media, with what Gillis and Munford (2004) present as late-1990s academic definitions of postfeminism. This is a feminism inspired by poststructuralism, which foregrounds issues of difference over equality. With this broader conceptualization of postfeminism, I argue that Gisela's consideration about the inclusion of men can be read together with Sylvia's claim to be part of a postfeminist generation and Anna's reflections on her own experience with feminism. Despite their differently articulated and developed understandings of and positions within feminism, they share a coming of age in a different, that is, later era than some of the other women that I interviewed. This also shows that the way in which Anna—the white Canadian woman who explains that her womanhood was "a real strong part" of her identity at college—describes the shift in her understanding of feminism is coherent with the developments of the 1990s and 2000s.

After Anna recounts her experience at university, where "a lot of how I responded to life was filtered through my own perceptions of whether they were responding to me as a woman," she adds that she thinks that

> the strength of that waned in a good way because I found that there was a lot of anger associated with that, and not necessarily positive anger.... It was more the kind of, "You are just saying this because I am a woman." So now I feel that yes, it is an important part of my identity, but no more or less so than it should be for anyone else, or for a man for that matter or for someone of both genders. For me it comes back again to choice, that who I am, I get to decide who I am.

This account is rich not only in its evocation of the well-established stereotype of angry feminists, but also in the emphasis on choice and autonomy, which is associated with postfeminism as defined by McRobbie (2004). Importantly, Anna's narrative also marks a shift from women to gender(s), which is mirrored in the shift from women's studies to gender studies. This academic trajectory has been negatively associated with "an endorsement of . . . post-structuralism [against] material accounts of womanhood," and, more positively, has been considered a political and theoretical move toward building coalitions with the discipline of transgender and queer studies (Hemming 2008, 272–274). Similarly, the move from WID to GAD has been welcomed by some and critically assessed by others. Some of the women I interviewed who witnessed the arrival of programs targeting men instead of women with the argument that women no longer need to be the focus were, for instance, critical.

The younger women I interviewed entered education and employment at a time in which women's and gender studies, as well as gender programs in development and other justice issues, were already established, though arguably still marginalized. This development made it possible for Sophie, a woman in her late twenties who works for a member organization in a European capital city on reproductive rights, to say that she "always had the idea . . . to work with gender and development in a very loose sense, gender and international work," once she obtained her politics degree. And also for Sonia, who is of a similar age, to say vaguely: "I wanted to work with something that had to do with gender." Their benefitting from these tangible achievements of the women's movement, as well as their encounters with older colleagues, put them in an inevitable relation with this herstory, even if their relation was expressed through distancing.

Gisela, for example, who has worked for a year and a half for a feminist network, says that she is still finding her feet in her job. She contrasts herself with more experienced colleagues who can rely on their long-term experiences:

> Also because I am not so long in [the network] I think it is not always easy. I mean you have women that have been working in this movement for ten, twenty years, and they have a perspective on the Beijing Platform for Action. I am not really familiar with this. I am learning now. I don't have the same experiences yet. I cannot really be totally angry and say, "Yeah, but on the ground this policy has this effect," because I read this basically from documents and hear it from the people I meet, and I try to understand and grasp it.

And Sylvia, for instance, openly describes generational interactions when she says:

> We had situations where we have older feminist peace builders and then younger women who are now working on women's issues and gender issues and peace building and you get this kind of tension almost between the people who were already feminists before I was born and [we who] now are coming with new ideas.... Or we are still facing the same situations in developing countries that existed thirty years ago, and then there is the feeling of the older generation that it is a judgment on them, that "they did not do enough." Or it [can be seen as] self-importance for us, that we are now somehow better or better feminists than they were, or something stupid like that. It is ridiculous, but at the same time it is the product of our own reality. And the good thing is for us that I think I did not grow up feeling conspicuously female; therefore I am not as aware of it in my thinking all the time.

The kind of "new ideas" of young feminists that Sylvia refers to, which are associated with more recent developments in feminism, will be discussed further in the next section of this chapter. Sylvia's narrative reveals an interesting contradiction where, on the one hand, she describes her generation in relation to a story of feminist achievement, which allowed her and others of her age to grow up without a strong consciousness of being a girl. At the same time, this story of progress gets disrupted when she refers to what she considers the static situation in developing countries.

The juxtaposition that Sylvia posits here between developed and developing nations, which also surfaced in an earlier quoted extract from the interview with her ("It is like the feeling of, well, as far as gender parity in our own countries, that we have come so far that it is not quite as passionate an issue for us") needs further unpacking. I will do so later in this chapter as well as in more detail in chapters 5 and 6.

The tensions described by Sylvia demonstrate that intergenerational feminist dialogues within organizations working on women's and gender issues are not always straightforward and smooth. They could have productive potential, though. Catherine, the woman in her midthirties, already shows some nostalgia regarding her younger self when she says that when she entered her organization in her early twenties, "It was a club of old ladies, frankly.... They saw me as a baby." She continues:

> But now of course I have gotten older, unfortunately.... It was a very different position, and in some ways more interesting when I was a young woman in this organization, because I could see that just being there was being different and was bringing something new. Now I don't have that anymore, I am bringing expertise.

Catherine contrasts the energy and freshness of youth with the experience and expertise brought in by older feminists. She struggles with the feeling that her status has changed now. In order to continue tracing the ways in which the women understood their own feminist positioning and related to other feminists, I will now discuss the interviews with those who were regarded by the young feminists as their older colleagues, or, in Catherine's words, the "old ladies."

In contrast to Sylvia, who considers herself part of the postfeminist generation, as well as other women for whom their university experience was significant in their process of identification as a feminist, the older interviewees told a different story. Casey's and Elisa's narratives, which both stress that they have been oriented toward gender struggles since they were young, are in marked contrast with the "feminist awakening" accounts of those who came into contact with feminism at secondary school or university. Casey is a woman in her fifties who has been working in the field of development for different organizations since 1985 and who has recently began working for an international membership NGO on reproductive issues. She, for example, says: "The gender orientation is something from my childhood and family upbringing." Her description of entering the field of development is in marked contrast with Sophie's and Sonia's early ambition to work in gender and development. She told me instead that there were no career structures by means of which to go into development work in the early 1980s. Because it was an untrodden career path, it was the lack of other job opportunities that made her consider her student activism in the field of international development as a basis for a career: "That sounds like a good idea, to find a job in an area you are really interested in! But at the time it was very different, very unusual." Once in a job, she, as well as some others of a similar generation, experienced her work terrain as male dominated. This played out even more strongly because her training as a sociologist held less status than the masculine-connoted technical training of the majority of her male colleagues in development.

Elisa, a slightly older woman from the same generation, also a sociologist, who works for a smaller international NGO in another European capital focusing on women as agents of change, explains: "I do think that for me my feminist identity was always out of the question, it was always something which was a part of me, in how I am and how I want a better world." She refers to her feminism as a "socialist feminism," saying that it is "not about women versus men, this is an outdated concept," and describes her socialist feminism in current terms as "gender justice." Elisa thereby draws both on classical second-wave narratives and on gender discourses that were developed later. Given that earlier in this section, young women that I interviewed were eager to point out that they were not antimen, it is interesting to juxtapose this anxiety with Elisa's firm relegation of such ideas to the past when she says that the idea of women versus men "is an outdated concept."

There is a tension, however, between Elisa denouncing simple male/female divides as outdated and her other statements in the interview. When she speaks about women's reliability in microcredit programs, she draws on essentialized images reminiscent of a radical feminism that juxtaposes women and men:

> Because women involved in, especially on the grass-roots level, microcredit, they are so incredibly reliable. They love to give it to women because the repayment is almost 100 percent. If you give the loans to men, you know what happens, alcohol, all kind of abuses involved. But women are reliable and somehow on this level are the heart of the community, and they are very concerned about their children. And even now in the credit [crunch] the issue emerged that there would have been fewer kind of [problems] if more women would have been involved.

Elisa presents a polarized picture in which men are necessarily unreliable and women are naturally reliable and "instrument[s] of development" (Dogra 2011, 340) as mothers and as the "heart of the community." As mentioned before, these images of men as selfish and competitive and of women as giving and caring have a long history. Eyben (2007a) found comparable images of women in the publication material of the British Overseas Development Assistance in the late 1980s, when the message was that the inclusion of women in development projects increased efficiency and effectiveness. These also have been reinvigorated during the credit crisis, as uncritically repeated by Elisa. Following the collapse of Icelandic banks, the *Guardian* featured an article titled "After the Crash, Icelandic Women Lead the Rescue" (Sunderland 2009). Around the same time, Christine Lagarde, then France's finance minister, later head of the IMF, responded to a journalist that "if Lehman Brothers had been 'Lehman Sisters,' today's economic crisis clearly would look quite different" (*International Herald Tribune*, May 10, 2010). She referred to her own comments as a "quip," but one that "reveals a bit about how I view things." The fact that this was echoed by many others, including Neelie Kroes (*Forbes*, August 19, 2009), then vice president of the European Commission responsible for the Digital Agenda, and UK deputy Labour leader Harriet Harman (*Independent*, August 3, 2009), and resonated with attributes classically associated with women, such as composure and a sense of responsibility, demonstrates the contemporary currency of such stereotypes.

For Elisa, as she explains, the famous second-wave women's movement slogan "The personal is political," which will be discussed in more detail in the next chapter, remains relevant. She refers to it to explain how her own feminism has changed with her biographical experience. In her case, becoming a mother made her aware of a wider range of gender issues and dilemmas as well as facilitating connections with other women across North–South divides. Here Elisa's account of the influence of motherhood on her feminism corresponds with the interview narratives of younger women who were mothers as well.

FEMINISM IN (SPITE OF) ORGANIZATIONS

This section continues the analysis of the views on gender and feminism that emerged from the interviews, but situates them in relation to the orientation of organizations that the women worked for. In the previous section, I argued that it is important not to presuppose an exact congruence between organizational mission and personal views. When I asked Sonia, the young woman from a Latin American country working in a junior position on peace in Geneva, why she focused particularly on women in her work, her hesitation and her wording makes apparent that there is a gap between her reproduction of the organization's gender analysis and her own, less clearly articulated views:

> Because women are affected, I mean everyone is affected by war, but maybe women's role or women's situation is not as recognized or discussed. That's why—I mean, I did not create the NGO—but that's why we look into helping them . . . to speak for themselves, and have them explaining what it is they are going through.

Other interviews showed that organizations can be spaces to develop a feminist identity. Hence it is possible that the current gap between the ideology of Sonia's organization and her own views might close over time. Fay, for instance, a woman in her early thirties who is working for an organization that supports migrant sex workers, states that she "basically grew up here; a very important part of my political socialization took place here."

Sarah, a woman in her early thirties, also identifies a disjuncture between the organizational discourse and her personal outlook, but can accept this discourse for strategic purposes. Because she works on peace and women, I ask her whether she and her organization align themselves with the discourse that associates women with peacefulness. She responds:

> You know, I hear it a lot, but I don't subscribe to it. You know, Roman mothers sent their sons to war and told their sons, "Come back with your shield or on it." I think it is a misperception. I think it is a perpetuation of misogyny! But it is something that initially some women are attracted to in this organization: "I am a woman, so I am more peaceful." . . . On a personal basis I think it is a load of crap, but it can be exploited for particular issues. For example, . . . in some places our members do mother's day antiwar events and are successful. It is attractive to media as it plays into an understood role and so society understands things, so people are more likely to connect. . . . So it has its advantages and again, opening a dialogue, but it also has a disadvantage in pigeonholing and not being fully accurate.

Though for Sarah, the link between women and peace is not only historically inaccurate but also misogynistic, she recognizes the power of the image both in terms of boosting membership and in attracting media attention. The connection between women and peace can be traced from Ancient times to the Old Testament and continues in current representations in international politics (Helms 2003; Sjoberg and Gentry 2008; Pupavac 2010). Feminists themselves have also promoted the notion of women as peaceful. Famously, second-wave radical feminist Robin Morgan, for example, in her much-lauded and much-criticized book *Sisterhood Is Global*, speaks about "the historical, cross-cultural opposition women express to war" (Morgan 1996, 4). More recent feminist IR scholarship addresses this problematic association of women with peace and points to the blind spots it has generated (Alison 2004; Fox 2004; Sjoberg and Gentry 2007).

Scholars and activists within one of the most contested fields within feminism, sex work/prostitution and trafficking, as already referred to above, have explicitly addressed the effects of reductive characterizations, in this case the "victim narrative" (Andrijasevic 2007; Berman 2010). Claudia Aradau, for example, traces how a "politics of pity" advocated by humanitarian actors got combined with a "politics of risk," and subsequently got co-opted into the securitization of trafficking (2004, 254). Some feminist organizations, despite their recognition of the "inaccuracy and damaging effects of the stereotype" of the term "trafficking in women," continue to use this term as a strategy to obtain funding and publicity (Doezema 1999). As Doezema claims:

> Attempts to combat the myth while using the terminology of trafficking are doomed by the limits to the discursive space imposed by the myth. Each repetition ... serves merely to reinforce the myth that campaigners are also attempting to break down, thus turning this into a futile effort. (1999, 45)

This demonstrates that such strategic framing carries risks and dilemmas much beyond the question of whether Sarah personally can reconcile herself with this strategic framing. Given that Sarah, in contrast to Sonia, is in a senior position in her organization, she has much more power to influence the strategic direction of her organization. Indeed she also more explicitly reflects on when and where this essentialism is an appropriate tactic, while at the same time admitting that there is no consensus around this issue within her organization.

At other points, the women experienced difficulties as a result of the gap between their views and those of their organizations. As mentioned in the introductory chapter of this book, some of the women of this study worked within a dedicated gender unit or position in organizations with a wider remit. This shaped the ways in which they could act on their feminist convictions in their work. Kate, a German woman in her forties, who works in Brussels for a humanitarian aid and development association, for example, compares her previous work with her current workplace:

I presume for me working on gender is not so easy within [this organization]. I have been working in [a feminist network] before, so that is different when you are working within the women's movement or women's organization. When you are working on gender in mainstream organizations, you have the whole debate there, and basically you have the same difficulties, debates, constraints as you have with doing your advocacy work in EU institutions, also within your own organization.

For Kate, in contrast to those who work for explicitly feminist organizations, there is no clear separation between the politics inside her organization and the world of politics outside in terms of feminist gender awareness, since the battles she engages in are very similar. Kate's position can be understood in the context of feminists' strategic decisions to enter mainstream institutions, as discussed earlier in this chapter. The seeming contradiction between her appointment as a gender officer and the constraints she experiences is likely related to the fact that nowadays NGOs are expected to be committed to gender equality, at least on paper, while the political will to critically evaluate the operations of the organization and the financial and social support is often absent (White 2006; Harcourt 2009). Piálek's analysis of Oxfam showed that despite the adoption of gender mainstreaming and GAD approaches at the institutional level, there was no direct reference to feminism. One of the employees he interviewed told him that he liked working for Oxfam, as it addressed gender issues, but was at the same time "not 'one of those feminist organizations'" (Piálek 2008, 289–290). Smillie (2000, 90) quotes a staff member of Oxfam's Gender and Development Unit (GADU) remarking: "When GADU started, many people laughed; one or two called us lesbians, dikes; that is no longer acceptable. Now the most difficult problem is one of people pretending they agree." Dedicated gender experts in organizations with a wider remit often face not only a lack of support in their organization, but also criticism from feminist activists outside the mainstream institutions (Harcourt 2009).

Laura, a thirty-two-year-old woman working on gender in a Northern European country for a development NGO, presents her feminist commitment as, at times, an obstacle to her job:

Being a feminist, an outspoken feminist—that is not a requirement for my job, and I think that sometimes it is also a hindrance. I am not very diplomatic lots of times. I was telling you before about this situation where this man was making comparisons to the animal world when I talked about men and women. For example, in that particular situation I should have chosen to not let myself be provoked by it, [but] I did, and I think if I had not been such a convinced feminist myself, if I would be more professional, or both, I could just let it slide. And I did not, I got really pissed and I yelled at him. This was not very strategic, and it did not make his organization change in any way and it did not make him change either.

Though Laura's understanding of gender power structures is key to her ability to do her work, with "gender" being one of the focus areas of her position, her feminism here is identified as a "hindrance." Laura claims that if she were "less feminist" or "more professional," the situation would not have escalated, as she would have been able to be more diplomatic. This implies that responding to sexism with feminist outrage is associated with being less professional (and hysteria?). "Professionalism as being strategic" is juxtaposed with "feminism as being emotional or out of control," and the demands of so-called professionalism force her to curtail her feminism. In the next chapter, I discuss in more detail the relation between the personal and the professional. For now it suffices to say that in this extract, technical, conceptual, or strategic engagement with gender issues gets foregrounded over normative, activist positioning, and the professional is seen as apolitical.

Catherine, on the other hand, who works for a women's network with a broad thematic remit, explains that in her organization there are some basic expectations with regard to the political convictions of the staff: "It would be difficult for somebody who is against abortion ... to work here, that would be impossible. The person would not even be employed, I guess." At the same time she indicates that there are some issues, such as the headscarf, on which her organization has not taken a position, because it could not find consensus among their members. Listening further to Catherine, it is clear that contentions arise at other fronts as well, when she recognizes that the member organizations of her organization would not all identify as feminist: "Some of them would not call themselves feminist, which is quite funny." Catherine's use of "funny" distances herself from those who are not comfortable with the label "feminism." As a white Western European feminist, she also fails to acknowledge the history of the problematic connotation of the term "feminist," arising from the dominance of white, Western, middle-class women, and its complicity with colonialism and capitalism, as discussed earlier in this chapter. Women in postsocialist Eastern Europe, who are actively pursuing a politics that challenges gender relations, prefer not to call themselves feminists, as this is associated with "a specific western European version of women's emancipation" (Sperling et al. 2001, 1168; cf. Ghodsee 2004; Roth 2007). In *Feminist Theory* bell hooks argues for an avoidance of the phrase "I am a feminist" in favor of "I advocate feminism," suggesting that this frames feminism as a political struggle rather than a lifestyle choice and leaves open the possibility of supporting other political movements as well (hooks 2000, 31). In a similar spirit, black feminist Alice Walker (1984) coined the term "womanism" instead of black feminism to mark it as an alternative approach to what is perceived as ethnocentric feminism. With the term "funny," Catherine depoliticizes these struggles.

Elizabeth Spelman identified the challenge of defining "women" without excluding difference as "the paradox at the heart of feminism" (Spelman 1990, 3). Spelman's observation was a response to the critique by black and lesbian feminists that they felt excluded from the generalized understanding of the category "woman." Radical and cultural feminism have been associated with an essentialist take on "woman," and poststructuralist, postcolonial, and black feminism with challenging this essentialism (Alcoff 1988; Jaggar 2005). The more recent debate on the inclusion or exclusion of transgender people from the women's movement touches upon a similarly fundamental critique of "sex" and "gender."

Fay's organization, a migrant women's organization, considers whether they would hire transgender employees: "We are a women's organization, so it is clear we employ women, [but] what about transgender women? . . . It is something you could start thinking about. So we are a women's organization; that means we also define who is a woman." Fay's comment serves as a reminder that while the notion of a women's organization seems to depend on an a priori definition of the category of "woman," this remains a category "in the making," which can be open for negotiation according to a nonessentialist perspective. For Fay, this discussion is linked again to feminist generations, where she expects the younger generations, among whom she counts herself, to be more open to inclusion than her older colleagues. In the interview, she connects this to a general skepticism toward new "fashions," such as "queer" and "postcolonial theory" among her older colleagues. However, acknowledging that organizational pressures do not allow her and her colleagues in general much time to reflect on and develop new approaches, she disrupts a simple division between older and younger feminists.

Naomi's international Geneva-based organization decided to only have female staff as an explicit political choice. Decisions to employ female staff only, also without explicitly tackling the question of what "female" is, still frame what "womanness" means. Naomi, a forty-year-old in a relatively senior position, aligns herself with the organization's policy, in contrast to Gill, who wished that her organization included men. Naomi:

> I am still a big proponent of having also some spaces that are women's spaces, not being in a mixed organization, and it is something that we are continually

questioned about and have to justify. But I do believe that no matter where you are in the world, when you look in at the levels of violence in even what is considered the most developed of countries, the shocking levels of violence against women, that there is still need for supporting women to be empowered to be independent women, to be able to live a life in dignity and free of violence.

Naomi implicitly frames "womanness" with reference to gender-based violence and foregrounds gender over other axes of inequality. The privileging of gender and the hierarchies between "developed" and "developing" countries, which have surfaced here again, will be further unpacked in chapters 5 and 6.

While the deliberate decision for a women-only organization draws on the legacy of the separatism of radical feminism, women of other organizations indicated that they "involuntarily" have only female staff, since all whom they regarded as suitable job candidates have been women. Stacey also experiences the contentious position of a women-only organization, which Naomi already described when she said that they "are continually questioned." Hence, for strategic reasons, Stacey calls upon men to apply to work at her international organization to silence the criticism they are facing as a women-only department and the delegitimization of her own professional position arising from this homogeneity.

> We hear it all the time: [our department] is like the "girls club," and we had to respond very strongly as to why that is and that we would be very happy to hire men if they were qualified. . . . And we don't also do [this job] simply because we are women, it is not because I have a uterus that I am allowed to do this work, it is also because I have formal training in it. And the assumption that people give when they say, "It is just a group of girls that are doing something"—and literally that has been said—is a way of discrediting what we do.

Stacey uses the discourse of professionalization, "I have formal training in it," with its associated value of neutrality, to counter delegitimization. This resonates with the narrative quoted above where Laura contrasted being feminist and being professional; this will be discussed in more detail in the next chapter. Stacey's story of struggle has to be placed against the background of a dominant narrative in which (a) gender (perspective) is equated with sex (the uterus rather than socialization) and with women. With the adoption of GAD policies, female employees who had previously raised gender issues in their work were often endowed the status of "women officers"; sometimes also wives of male staff members were offered that position (White 2006). The derogative term "girls club" that Stacey hears recalls how WID and GAD work became known as "women's work," with all the accompanying "negative associations for status that this carried" (White 2006, 59).

CONCLUDING REMARKS

In this chapter I have provided a historical overview of women's mobilization around global issues in order to contextualize the ways in which the women interviewed for this study narrated their own feminist biographies. I have argued that the narration of the transnational history of women and development has become canonical in its form, with each account repeating the same benchmarks and debates. While not being silent on the tensions within the transnational women's movement, this story leaves out particular regions and dimensions and reinforces the separation between development and migration. Therefore, this chapter has connected the issues discussed in this global gender-and-development narrative, with the correspondent debates within women's movements in the global North.

In a subsequent section, I have contrasted the experiences of the younger generation of research participants who entered an already existing field of "gender and development" with those of women who have been part of carving out this field. Together the interviews build a picture of the different generations of women, and their relation to different feminisms and the institutionalization of women's and gender issues as a work field and academic discipline. In general, the oldest group of women recognized in their youth and through engagement with the women's movement, that their personal experiences were political; the second group, somewhat younger, made sense of their experiences by drawing on gender perspectives acquired at university; and the third and youngest group tended to recognize the merits of feminism, but understood their personal experiences, in postfeminist mode, as partly "beyond gender." At the same time the interview narratives presented above invite us to qualify and disrupt this neat image by observing that the women's feminist perspectives are dynamic, evolving in response to organizational surroundings and new insights, such as the importance of intersectional approaches, or experiences, such as motherhood. Moreover, since particular moments that have a historical precedent in the transnational women's movement—such as defining "woman"; the experience of motherhood; (re)defining feminism against negative stereotypes—are repeated and reappear as pertinent for subsequent generations, this introduces a certain cyclicality, which disturbs a linear, progressive picture of feminism. The next chapter will discuss the women's motivations for their work as well as their positioning as committed professionals.

CHAPTER 3

Global Responsibilities

This chapter will offer an analysis of articulations of global responsibility. I examine the ways in which the women interviewed articulated their felt sense of responsibility and their positioning as professionals. As outlined in the previous chapter, transnational feminism has been discussed as a prime example of global civil society engagement. The relatively new notion of "global citizenship" that often accompanies discussions on global civil society is commonly associated with working for NGOs and intergovernmental organizations (Carter 2001; Dower 2002; Hutchings 2002; Urry 2003). In this chapter I argue that theories on global civil society and global citizenship, as well as feminist interventions in this field, are instructive in analyzing the motivations that the women saw as underpinning their work. I will also employ these theories to develop an understanding of the ways in which they navigated the overlaps and divisions between their personal passion and professional role. The final section of this chapter will highlight the experiences of those women who do international work to support women in the global South and are based in European capital cities. I will look into how decisions related to location are explained and justified by the women I interviewed in the light of a broader discourse that ascribes normative assumptions to distance.

I combine debates on global citizenship and global civil society because they are intertwined. Some perspectives present "global civil society" and "global citizenship" as the same (Carter 2001, 93), while, according to other perspectives, global civil society plays a key part in the *formation* of global citizenship (Desforges 2004). Armstrong makes this conceptual confusion about the relation between global citizenship and global civil society explicit by stating: "There is an odd slippage in the literature, however, on the question whether global civil society *expresses* the emergence of global citizenship, or in fact *engineers* that emergence. Here prominent accounts of global civil society become somewhat circular" (2006, 352).

Citizenship and civil society theories have become increasingly globally oriented in the last two decades, reorienting themselves from their original national focus (Falk 1994; Amoore and Langley 2004; Anheier et al. 2004). Attempts to translate citizenship and civil society theory to the global level have not been without pitfalls. Since both have been conceptualized in relation to the state, a key barrier for a transfer of those theories to the global level is the absence of a global state. At the same time, it is important to keep in mind that the relation between the state and civil society has always been contested (Anheier et al. 2001).[1] Shifting from a national to a global focus also challenges the assumption of a territorial inside and outside, as well as related notions of foreignness and otherness. As this chapter will demonstrate, this has implications for (re)thinking rights, responsibility, and solidarity.

OPPORTUNITIES AND PRIVILEGES

In this section I will discuss responsibility in relation to power and privilege, taking the ambiguities in global citizenship theory as a starting point. The 1990s and 2000s heralded a combined interest in globalization, global civil society, and global citizenship. While notions of world citizenship and the relation to the universe can be traced back to the Stoics and the ideals of cooperation and tolerance for diversity to cosmopolitan thinkers such as Immanuel Kant or, more recently, Martha Nussbaum (Carter 2001; Dower 2002; Bowden 2003), the addition of the adjective "global" to civil society and citizenship is linked to the phenomenon of globalization. John Urry argues in this respect that "globalisation appears to be changing what it is to be a citizen" (1999, 312). Theories about global citizenship have indeed introduced a qualitative difference in relation to national citizenship. Whereas national citizenship emphasizes rights and duties, global citizenship is associated with global "responsibility" (Grewal 2005). As April Carter asserts in her book *The Political Theory of Global Citizenship*: "Participation in global social movements or in agencies offering relief or aid, is at present the most obvious expression of active global citizenship" (2001, 223), thereby casting the women this book engages with as potential "global citizens."

I will argue here, inspired by the critiques of the exclusionary dimensions of national citizenship that have been articulated by feminist and critical race scholars, that it is important to recognize that global citizenship is also a privileged position with racialized and gendered underpinnings (de Jong 2013). The notion of "global citizenship," commonly associated with normative, globally oriented, justice-seeking imperatives, involves paradoxes and ambiguities at a number of junctures. As this chapter will demonstrate, these are relevant when analyzing the interviewees' motivations. The first complication occurs over the idea of responsibility, since global citizenship is presented not as a mere geographical extension of national citizenship, but is rather imbued with aspirational notions of global justice (Falk 1994; Duffield 2007, 233 on "international citizenship"). As Oxfam writes on its website: "Global Citizenship is about understanding the need to tackle injustice and inequality, and having the desire and ability to work actively to do so. . . . Global Citizenship is a way of thinking and behaving. It is an outlook on life, a belief that we can make a difference" (Oxfam 1997).

Richard Falk (1994), for instance, claims that the global business elite do not deserve the label of global citizen by virtue of their mobility only, as they lack a sense of global responsibility. He contrasts traditional national and global citizenship by arguing that the first functions across space, while the latter operates across time, "reaching out to a future to-be-created, and making of such a person 'a citizen pilgrim,' that is, someone on a journey to 'a country' to be established in the future in accordance with more idealistic and normatively rich conceptions of political community" (Falk 1994, 139).

The emphasis on the normative dimension of global civil society and global citizenship in terms of responsibility can be considered a promising shift away from the mere rights and duties associated with national citizenship. Yet this responsibility appears to be based on an implicit assumption that there is an elite of global citizens, such as NGO workers and transnational feminists, who care for the "weaker" Other, the "nonglobal citizen," rather than that all are global citizens with a reciprocal responsibility. Indeed, the second ambiguity in the notion of global citizenship concerns the relation between global citizenship and alterity. On the one hand, global citizenship is seen as an extension of national citizenship, and hence it carries the connotation that it can only exist in opposition to an Other. National citizenship implies membership of an in-group that is part of a clearly delineated area, which differentiates itself from outsiders excluded by these borders. Bowden (2003) even goes as far as suggesting that universal global citizenship is impossible in the absence of such an outsider. On the other hand, the notion of "global" could be universal, applying to all citizens of the world. Dower, for example, holds that "all human beings are global citizens in virtue of rights and duties which we all have as human beings" (2002, 40).

Hence the notion of global citizenship is inscribed with notions of both *exclusion* and *inclusion*. Kimberly Hutchings (2005) argues that the global citizenship debate has overlooked the fact that citizenship has always been a privilege and depended on coercive powers, which were both enabling and restricting. The notion of responsibility of the global citizen hence articulates itself simultaneously through otherness and through sameness; the global citizen should feel responsible for others by virtue of her *sameness* (i.e., inhabiting the same globe) but *can* only act as a responsible global citizen because of her *difference* (defined by being in a comparatively privileged position). In the context of volunteer tourism, Harng Luh Sin has effectively captured this "paradox," as she calls it:

> The call for responsibilities based on universal justice, or "sameness," between people despite the distance, is itself continuously placing the "same people" into distinct categories of the "rich" and therefore ones who need to assume responsibilities; and the "poor" and therefore ones who will always remain on the receiving ends of responsible actions. (Sin 2010, 988)

This ambivalent identification in relation to responsibility becomes very obvious in a story that Liz, one of the women interviewed in Brussels, recounted. To illustrate to me the connection she feels with those that her international work supports, she recalled a holiday in India. There she had the impression that for most Western tourists, their holiday was a refuge from work. Liz, however, contrasts herself with them by saying that she realized that what she experienced during her holidays made her keen to return to work:

> Because there, you know, I mean I am very lucky that I got these opportunities. And the fact is that I wanted everyone that I met, men or women, to have that opportunity as well: to swim in the water, to have a vacation, for women to walk around—the possibility that life can be enjoyable as opposed to that life is drudgery and just waiting to get to the end of it. And so this is the only way I can explain it, that sort of makes me connected to sort of everybody and so that everyone has these opportunities.

Liz explains her motivation for her work on women's political participation and her felt connection to the people whom she seeks to support simultaneously through sameness (all people would like to have vacation, to enjoy life) and through difference (she has these opportunities, while those that her work engages with do not [yet] have these opportunities). This difference is hierarchical: "Compassion creates asymmetric relations: it is born from a feeling of superiority (I feel relieved that I am not this other who suffers)" (Korf 2007, 370). Liz's ideas about difference and sameness are also based on assumptions of homogeneity. She wants everyone she has met to enjoy the same opportunities, assuming that none of these people has had these opportunities yet. This is also reflected in the binary contrast she sketches between enjoyable life on the one hand (the reality for her) and drudgery on the other hand (the reality for the people in India). While at other points in the interview she explicitly expressed that she is concerned with providing people with opportunities and choices rather than dictating what they should do or want, at this point she assumes that what is attractive for her is desirable for everyone. While recognition of differences between her and the women she encounters on her holidays serves as a motivating force for her, it lacks acknowledgment of the diversity and complexity of women's and men's lives in the global South.

At another point during the interview, Liz again emphasizes her opportunities as the foundation for her feeling of global responsibility:

> Because I have had these opportunities, I would wish that others have these opportunities. And one way to do that is to focus on projects where I feel that through these processes, at the end of a very, very long road and with other projects focusing on all kind of different things, there is the opportunity that there will be the possibility that these people have these opportunities. Not because they got lucky, but because of their constitutions, because of their legislations.

Basing their sense of responsibility on recognition of the opportunities they enjoyed was common among the women I interviewed. When I asked another research participant working on reproductive rights for an international member organization from a Northern European country why she cared about others far away, Frida, responds: "Why would I care? Why would I not care? I have energy and every opportunity in life that I can use, I guess."

The anecdote told by a young, white, American woman, Tess, who is based in Brussels, where she is the interim director for a gender and security advocacy network, reflects a similar line of thought. Tess tells me that while she studied in South Africa, she consciously left the more comfortable American-style spots to work in a township. This corresponds closely to the ideal-type global citizen. Her mobile background has set her up for this privileged identity: being born in the UK, she grew up in the United

States; her parents now live in England again, and her sister, who is also in the field of development, lives abroad. When I ask Tess why she forces herself out of her comfort zone, she explains this by reference to a professor at her US university who involved her and her fellow students in a research project that took place in a hosiery factory in a rural area close to where she grew up. For her assignment Tess had to interview the people working there. They told her that they did not have enough money to finance their children's college education.

As Tess explains,

> My professor made the link to say that these people are all paying taxes and all this tax money is going for my education. So effectively they are paying for me to go to university when they can't pay for their own kids to go. And so what she said was that because we are given this privilege just by accident of birth, that you have a responsibility not to waste that. And that does not mean . . . I mean you can go off and be a businessman, making lots of money and also continue to be someone who does service in the community . . . and that is still giving back. Or you can be out in townships in Bolivia feeding the poor, and that is another way of doing it. But just that idea that it has been an accident of birth, that I was given the fortune to grow up in a stable family and go to university and always have enough to eat. It is really just because of where I happened to be born and not everybody is that lucky. So I can't waste it by doing nothing.

As presented above, Tess, Liz, and Frida each establish a link between having opportunities and being responsible for others. I argue that this link relies on a liberal assumption that opportunities can be increased for all without affecting other people's (or their own) opportunities. So Tess's response to observing the poverty of the factory workers who indirectly support her university studies is not to swap her college place with their son or daughter, or, more structurally, to rally against an inadequate redistributive tax system. Rather Tess translates this into a felt responsibility to do "something" for global justice. In a study about gap year student volunteers, Simpson identified a similar tendency of the students to "ascribe some form of lotto logic" to the inequalities they were faced with (Simpson 2004, 689; cf. Heron 2007, 42). Simpson (2004) found that the student volunteers, similar to Tess, interpreted the inequalities they were confronted with by reference to differences in luck (for example in location of birth) rather than with structural explanations about (neo)imperialism, racism, or capitalism, which they themselves are complicit in. Alternative views emphasize the *relational* dimension to privilege and argue that privilege is inherently dependent on the underprivileged circumstances of other people. Crewe and Harrison, for example, raise the question whether it is actually "possible for some to be empowered without disempowering others" in the light of the relationality of power differences in an unequal world (Crewe and Harrison 1998, 562). Postcolonial perspectives show that "responsible action is never free of its locational imperatives and its identifications so that the responsible agent is always tainted: there is no pure space from within from which responsibility can be enacted" (Noxolo, Raghuram, and Madge 2012, 422). Hutchings uses the language of global citizenship when she states: "The capacity to identify oneself, be recognized and act as a global citizen is parasitic on the dramatically undemocratic and inegalitarian nature of the global order in general, both institutionally and normatively" (2005, 97).

Gaining Opportunities through Work

As I have argued elsewhere, Hutchings's observation about the relation between the claim to global citizenship and the undemocratic and inegalitarian global order can be complemented by a postcolonial perspective. This underlines that those who claim global citizenship enjoy privileges linked to complicities in historical processes, which have exacerbated current inequalities (de Jong 2013). For those working for non- and intergovernmental organizations, the privileges that form the motivation for engaging in such work are often also the precondition for acquiring positions. For example, common criteria for a job in the sector include being able to afford a period of full-time voluntary work (Roth 2015), gathering experience with traveling and living abroad, and fluency in English. These are based on the wealth accumulated through colonial relations, on the hierarchically dominant position of whiteness, and on the supremacy of the English language in the colonial and global world order. The likelihood is higher that a white middle-class person from a former colonial power or settler country can fulfill these criteria and therefore act and be recognized as a "global citizen" (de Jong 2013).

I further suggest that while the women commonly justified their interest in working for a normatively based organization on the basis of a sense of responsibility that derived from acknowledging the opportunities they had enjoyed, their professional roles provided them with new opportunities of various kinds. It is interesting to see how this was expressed by Sonia, a young Latin American woman whom I interviewed in Geneva. Moving from Buenos Aires to the Netherlands for her second academic degree, she relocated to Geneva as soon as she graduated to improve her French, in order to get an international job. Sonia is currently a coordinator for the organization where she started as an intern:

> I know I can have a job where I can do something good for someone else, and that is the reward beside my salary. In fact I worked for six months without being paid, and I still love it. So that's the reward, to be doing what I always wanted to do.... This might sound stupid ... [but] I was in New York because of this job, and we were walking by ... a Sephora store [a luxurious beauty chain], and there were some women working to get [labels] off boxes, and I passed by and I thought, "Oh my god, I am so lucky." There is nothing bad with that job, but I would not like to have to do that. I am so lucky, I am working in what I want ... and being paid and even traveling and meeting all these people and having all these interesting things to do. So I guess that's my commitment. I realize that I am so blessed ... like, "Oh my god, I have this great opportunity, why would I let it go?"

Sonia describes her love for and commitment to her job simultaneously by reference to the "doing good for someone else" and by mentioning the opportunities the job itself gives her, in terms of being able to travel, "do interesting things," and meet new people (cf. Roth 2012). The fact that she could afford to work for six months without getting paid prior to securing a paid position is evidence of a privileged situation. Nancy Cook (2007) notes in her research on female volunteers for Voluntary Service Oversees (VSO) in Gilgit in Pakistan that one reason to take up volunteer placements was for career advancement. The women Cook interviewed were able to have authority and responsibilities that they did not have access to in their home countries (cf. Goudge 2003; Baillie Smith and Laurie 2011; Verma 2011; Leonard 2012). The gains of the job do not necessarily have to be financial—and many might say that with NGO work it is unlikely that they are—and can vary from further career opportunities to travel, from meeting people to "leaving a legacy." While this applies both to working at a local level with women from the global South and to international work, the higher status of the latter reinforces the benefits for women working internationally (i.e., those I described in chapter 1 as constituting groups 1 and 2 of my sample).

The following examples reflect that the benefits should not be conceptualized as purely financial or careerist, but also include excitement as well as having a sense of "mattering" to the world. Ruth, who is working for a small organization that advocates for reproductive rights internationally, says:

> So, I think part of it is that it gives me great satisfaction to be able to do something that adds to more than just me. And I guess that is something that most people feel. And of course what it gives me personally is that I have an interesting life and that it is very diverse. I mean it is very challenging . . . and that is something that I like.

When I asked Birgit, who is working for a women-and-peace organization in Geneva where her sense of global responsibility comes from, she told me:

> It is a moral obligation in a lot of ways, and I don't quite know where that comes from or what it grows out of. But I can't imagine not doing this. When I did not work in this field for a short period of time, I was the most dissatisfied person in the world. [I asked myself] "what is this leading to, what is my legacy?" I'd say there is some ego. What is the legacy I leave for the future, have I made a difference, have I made the world a little bit better than the world I came into?

The word "ego" that Birgit uses is conventionally understood as the opposite of altruism. Her impassioned account, however, illustrates the possibility of the simultaneous articulation of the two. I will discuss this seeming contradiction in further detail below.

False Binaries

Critical feminist scholars have observed in various geographical contexts that the proliferation of NGOs has impacted the women's movement (Lang 1997; Menon 2004; de Alwis 2009; Nazneen and Sultan 2012). As Lang (1997) notices for Germany, these structural and ideological changes have shifted the focus to professionalization. This entails "a conviction that voluntary work and engagement should be replaced by paid labor" (Lang 1997, 114), which potentially results in political commitment being replaced by a desire to sustain the organization as employer (de Alwis 2009). I argue that the discussion that evaluates professionalization in the women's movement negatively (cf. Rao and Kelleher 2000) sometimes fails to consider the gender pay gap, women's high involvement in reproductive labor, and women's lower participation rate in the formal labor market. This negative discourse will be discussed in more detail in the next section of this chapter. What is important here is that the principles associated with women's movement activism are partly shared by ethical expectations in development work. From the 1970s a specific personal comportment, in terms of self-effacement, restraint in consumption, ethical living, and acceptance of low salary with long working hours, came to be expected from NGO workers as a token of their commitment to their work (Hopgood 2006; Duffield 2007; Fechter 2012). In her comparative study of international NGOs rooted in respectively France, the UK, and the United States, Stroup (2012) observed that in the European cases voluntarism and noncorporatism were central to the (moral) identity of the organizations, in contrast to a more professionalized, standardized, efficiency-led organizational setup in the United States. The critique of professionalization of NGOs can also be linked to the critique of the representative function of such organizations, which will be further discussed in the next chapter. This is expressed in questions raised by Silliman: "Who [do] such professionalized groups represent, who [do] advocacy networks include and exclude, to whom [are] they ultimately accountable [?]" (Silliman 1999, 40).

More recently, others have responded to the negative evaluation of NGOization and professionalization of the women's movement, telling a more nuanced story. Saskia Wieringa sums up the ambivalences in Dutch women's NGOs' development:

> In the course of the 1980s we managed to get state funding for many of our activities. ... On the one hand, a measure of professionalization was made possible that could never have been achieved on the backs of over-exploited part-timers; on the other hand, the state now set the agenda. When state funds dried up many of those initiatives folded (2009, 25).

Srila Roy (2011), writing about Indian feminist groups, points to a discourse in which the "career feminist" is negatively evaluated by the (often older) generation of feminist activists. She observes a feeling of nostalgia for times when feminist activism was practiced after regular work, in the evenings, and on a voluntary basis. Jonathan Dean similarly argues that there is "often a sense of what we might call post-second-wave melancholia, in which the acknowledgement that the institutionalization has brought certain gains is offset by a sense of loss of the early radicalism and autonomy of the movement" (2008, 285).

Despite these more recently introduced nuances, I argue that it is only possible to understand how the women in this study presented their motivation for their work and their sense of responsibility for global others in relation to a persistent discourse which frames activism and altruism as incompatible with what are seen as selfish, career-focused choices. Elsewhere, I have deconstructed in detail what I have called a "false binary" of altruism versus selfishness (de Jong 2011). Some of the following examples will illustrate the dominance of a discourse that considers selfish motives as contaminating what are considered pure altruistic motives. At the same time the narratives presented below will show that the women were conscious of (and sometimes self-conscious about) what they could gain from their work.

Nora, a Dutch woman who works in the Netherlands in a paid job with trafficked women and, besides that, in a voluntary position for an African national community organization, states:

> I only can do these things—this sounds very egoistic, this sounds selfish—if I get something back from it. For example, with my voluntary job, I learned how to write proposals, project proposals, how to get money for an organization, how to be an independent foundation. So all those things I learned. So in that way, I mainly saw it as helping myself.

Teresa, who works in Brussels on gender issues for a faith-based international network of development organizations says: "Motivation to do the work ... I am earning money here, and I have an interesting job. In these NGOs you have perhaps also more flexibility than in some other organizations. And you work on issues that I do believe in."

It is striking that a justificatory tone appears in Nora's narrative. This can be identified in the phrase "this sounds very egoistic, this sounds selfish," which anticipates a negative response from the interviewer. At the same time Teresa appears deliberately provocative to counter the romanticized discourse in which justice work should not be combined with career strategies. And indeed, while my reaction was not negative, in retrospect, listening to the interview again, I realize that initially I had not anticipated such a response, since I similarly operated with an unreflective assumption that "moral work" and instrumentalist careerism do not go together. Unconsciously I had associated the first with altruism and the second with selfishness and, following dominant understandings, framed these in binary terms "in which the first is considered desirable but rare and the latter is considered common but immoral and undesirable" (de Jong 2011, 36).

The dominance of the discourse in which careerism is seen as incompatible with altruism can be noticed most clearly when interviewees explicitly defended themselves. While I, as the interviewer, neither hinted that financial (or other) benefits might be a motivation nor expressed judgment either way, many of the women responded to such prevalent discourse. This is, for example, apparent in the response from Rachel, who works in Geneva in the field of gender and health:

> The motivation for doing this work [is] ... my own personal social convictions to equality and to justice, and specifically with respect to women.... Because my motivation for doing this work is not financial, it is not based on professional aspirations. It is really based on a personal commitment to ensuring ... opportunities for equality for women in various settings.... My personal responsibility, I think is, I can't imagine doing anything else. So in that sense the personal responsibility I feel is [such that] I am not quite sure what I would do if I did not have this personal responsibility.

This account is not only exemplary in reflecting the prevalence of (responses to) the negative discourse around professionalization, in stating specifically that "it is not financial, it is not based on professional aspirations." The other main theme that runs through this extract, namely that Rachel cannot imagine doing something else, to the extent that this sense of global responsibility defines her as a person, was also shared with other women. I relate this not only to the fact that some indeed experience the question of how to position themselves in an unequal world as existential, but also to the prevalent discourse presented earlier: to be a "good" NGO worker, one is supposed to completely identify with the work.

Frida, who works from a capital city in a Northern European country on reproductive rights, expresses some doubt concerning the importance of the "right" motivation (cf. Hindman and Fechter 2011, 7), moving from a Kantian ethics to a more utilitarian view in which the act itself rather than the motivation for the act is central. When I ask her why she cares about others far away, Frida continues, after answering my question: "I assume your next question will be, 'Does it make me feel good?'" She says that she becomes angry and is quite tired of encountering people who "are in it for ... that they become very 'good people.'" However, Frida then proceeds to think aloud: "I am thinking about that a lot, and maybe that's okay. I have been switching. Who cares about the reason ... if they do the work?" When I ask her why it makes her angry, she replies: "It just annoyed me a bit, because if that's the case, they are not doing enough, the world sucks so ... and it is not fair to do it for that reason. But they are doing it, so why not? We need more people that do it." This raises interesting questions about whether "doing good" requires "being good," or whether "doing good" means "becoming good."

In the beginning of this section I argued that global citizenship is articulated simultaneously through sameness and through hierarchical difference, the latter referring to being in the position of relative privilege to "d[o] the helping" (Grewal 2005, 142). Subsequently, I demonstrated both that a sense of global responsibility is often articulated through a reference to opportunities that the women have enjoyed, and that the work itself provides new opportunities. I have conceptualized this in relation to a dominant discourse that is critical of the changes introduced by "NGOization." The following account of Nora, who works for a local organization, however, explicitly challenges the assumption that work to "help" others should *not* contain an element of self-interest (de Jong 2011). As Nora coordinates a buddy project for trafficked women, in that role she is also responsible for the application interviews with prospective buddies.

After Nora tells me, as quoted above, that she only does her voluntary work when she gets something back from it, she tells me that she applies the same principle to the buddy program that she coordinates for her paid job:

> If they come to the intake, to the first interview, I also ask them, "Okay, what, why this group?" And if they say, "Oh, I saw a movie on television about trafficking and I thought oh, wow, how exciting what happened," then I don't think you are a good buddy. But also when they say, "Oh, I really want to help these women," then they really have to convince me that they would be. . . . Because it is not equal, but we try to do it as equal as possible, this relationship. But actually a lot of women, a lot of volunteers say, "well, I live in . . . a multicultural city but I don't have any person of color in my social network, so I would like to learn from another culture." . . . Or "I am also new in [this city] . . . so I need to [get to] know the city as well; maybe we can explore it together."

Here Nora displays an awareness of the way in which "helping impulses" and compassion, following the sameness-difference logic discussed earlier, can rely on attributing to the "objects" of compassion a lower hierarchical status. This applies both to international North–South relations and to support relations inside the North or South. Richard Sennett observes in relation to social work that "compassion can be intimately linked to inequality" and that a more distanced approach can "make compassion work," making the discomfort of the inequality more bearable (Sennett 2003, 20). As will be discussed in chapter 6 in more detail, postcolonial feminism has criticized the construction of the poor, victimized, Third World subject. In the particular context of trafficking, feminist critics have spoken out against the prevalent victim discourse, which is also persistent within feminist circles. They have underlined the ways in which rescue narratives elevate the status of (Western) women who act in feminist antitrafficking campaigns, legitimize security measures detrimental to migrant women, and silence the voices of Southern and Eastern migrant sex workers (Doezema 2001; Augustín 2005; Andrijasevic 2007). Nora acknowledges that the buddy relationship can never be completely equal, but she aspires to make it "as equal as possible." She attempts to maximize this equality by encouraging volunteers to consider what they can gain themselves. Personal gain is presented by Nora as a way to narrow the power gap between the person in need and those supporting. This example unsettles the idea that personal benefit in such role is morally questionable and that gaining something always means widening the gap between the "helper" and those "helped, through increasing privilege.

As I argue that the selfishness-versus-altruism binary is false, I propose that we need to move away from categorizing practices and motivations as either the one or the other, and instead "critically investigate *under which conditions* altruism takes place" (de Jong 2011, 37). I also suggest that a stronger challenge against notions of benevolence or noblesse oblige lies in the acknowledgment of historical and contemporary complicity in global inequalities, which I have begun to unpack in relation to "global citizenship." This would mean that those who are on the margins are owed support rather than that it is benevolently bestowed on them, in the spirit of reparations rather than aid. Elsewhere I have in more detail suggested that a responsibility based on privilege and benevolence should be replaced by a responsibility based on a social connection model, as proposed by Iris Marion Young (de Jong 2013). This social connection model conceptualizes mutual obligations of justice, not on the basis of shared humanity, but by reference to the current and historical connections between people, which are shaped by injustices that structurally disadvantage some and advantage others (Young 2006). I hence suggest that personal experiences, such as those of Tess, the young, white, American woman who recounted her confrontation with rural factory workers who paid taxes toward her college education, provides rich material for reconceptualizing responsibility through a social connection model.

BEYOND PUBLIC/PRIVATE DIVIDES

Earlier in this chapter, I presented interview extracts that emphasized the passionate commitment of the women to their work and the way their sense of responsibility links to their sense of personhood. In this light, I will now continue to show the interplay of the professional and the personal in relation to responsibility. I will do so by setting up a dialogue between women addressing the professional/personal, and feminist political theory on the divide between the public and private spheres. The conceptual pair professional/personal showed its significance in two moments: first, in explicit comments by the interviewees about the challenge to separate the personal and professional; second, implicitly, when the women chose to speak about their personal experiences, while being asked about their work. I will argue that the binary that is created around the professional versus the personal relies on distinctions similar to those produced in the division between the private and public spheres. As I will discuss, each of these spheres is associated with a different kind of morality.

The public/private divide features strongly both in global citizenship and in global civil society theory. Together these bodies of theory—in particular the feminist interventions—help to uncover a number of contradictions related to the public/private divide. While the public/private divide is a central defining feature of the concepts of citizenship and civil society, different theoretical frameworks show that this relation is ambiguous. Political theory is ambivalent on whether civil society is part of the private or the public sphere, depending on, respectively, a liberal or republican perspective. While a liberal understanding situates civil society in the private sphere and the state in the public sphere, a republican understanding places civil society in the public sphere as the meeting place for deliberation between citizens (Squires 2004). In a liberal view, politics is exercised by the administrative state. The public sphere is understood as the realm of the public (state) interest, and the private sphere is associated with private interests, which get articulated in civil society as well as in the market (Weintraub 1997). A republican view understands civil society as the public realm of political community and debate, in which the people voice their interests as citizens in contrast to the sphere of both the state and the market (Benn and Gauss 1983). Inevitably, the interpretation of politics shifts with the republican understanding, namely from the authority of the state in the liberal understanding, to political debate, discussion, and decision-making.

The traditional republican understanding of the public nature of citizenship has been challenged by more recent, alternative interpretations, such as "intimate citizenship." Intimate citizenship, as conceptualized by Plummer (2003), demonstrates the interplay between issues deemed private (e.g., sexuality, gender, family life) and the public (e.g., legal or media) discourse. Plummer therefore maintains that the separation between the public and the private spheres is untenable. As he argues, the public and political sphere is "actually constituted through a network of passionate human beings engaging with each other, often in highly personalized ways" (Plummer 2003, 70). This argument is highly significant in the understanding of the experiences of the women and their reflections on their work. Their experiences can be better understood as the actions, thoughts, and reflections of passionate human beings than as disembodied citizens. James Tully's (2005) distinction between what he calls "modern" and "diverse" citizenship, two parallel and sometimes conflicting forms of citizenship practice, offers another way to rethink the relation between the public and the private. According to Tully, "modern citizenship" is the dominant form of citizenship in the West, associated with laws and constitutions, while "diverse citizenship" has been exercised on the margins by those who were denied modern citizenship (Tully 2005). He thus associates diverse citizenship with critical approaches to governance and oppression. Diverse citizenship is exercised in the private sphere, since those that practice diverse citizenship are denied access to the public sphere. The political participation that is demanded through diverse citizenship takes recourse to marginalized identities, such as "women" or "immigrants." Hence this form of citizenship includes (what is regarded as) the private and the personal. Feminism is one example of the articulation of diverse citizenship.

Feminist political and IR theory has been more successful than traditional citizenship theory in capturing the complex convergence of the public and the private, the personal and the political. The public/private divide has long been central to feminist thought, and it has been argued that the feminist challenge to the conventional distinction between the public and the private is one of the most important contributions of feminist thought to political theory (Elshtain 1981; Pateman 1983). More specifically, feminist theory has managed to make the separation of spheres explicit in order to counter the invisibility of the private (domestic) sphere and has simultaneously challenged the rigid divide. Carole Pateman's work (1983) uncovered the successful integration of patriarchy in liberalism, which functions through the separation of the private and public spheres. She argues that while in the first instance liberal and patriarchal doctrines might seem opposed, since liberalism emphasizes individualism and egalitarianism, while patriarchalism advocates a natural hierarchy, the doctrines are reconciled through excluding women from citizenship and hence discounting them as free and equal beings. The division between the public and private spheres depends on an even more complex (sub)division. When the state is viewed as public and civil society as private, civil society is subdivided again in a public (social, political) sphere and a private sphere of personal life (Pateman 1983; Squires 2004); I will return to those nested divisions in my analysis below. As Judith Squires puts it, "Civil society is cast as private when opposed to the state and public when opposed to the personal" (2004, 25). A third way to conceptualize the private is as the domestic sphere. Hence "private" can denote civil society, the personal sphere or the domestic sphere (Squires 2004). Women's association with the domestic sphere and their initial exclusion from the public sphere of the state delegated them in multiple ways to the private sphere (Weintraub 1997; Squires 2004). The private sphere as the domestic sphere has often been imbued with a distinct morality associated with love, relations, emotions, and altruism. In contrast, the public sphere (in terms of both the state and civil society) has been associated with an ethics of rationality, instrumentality, accountability, and transparency (Benn and Gauss 1983).

It is important to note here, as Kimberlé Crenshaw has pointed out, that the interest in the separation between the private and public spheres as an "ideological justification for women's subordination" was particularly central to a Western feminism, which was constructed around the experiences of white women, and "offers little insight into the domination of Black women" (2000, 221). Moreover, critiques from the global South as well as from women in (post) socialist countries of Western feminism have emphasized that the private realm is not merely a site of oppression, but a political space as well (McEwan 2001; Roth 2007). McEwan cites the activities of the Argentinean Mothers of the Disappeared and Islamist feminists as instances where women "have sought an empowering 'private' function" in contrast to some Western feminist conceptualizations of motherhood and home as oppressive (McEwan 2001, 98).

Professional and Personal Lives

The most prominent way in which the public/private divide surfaced was when the women addressed the fact that the nature of the job combined with their commitment to the work made it hard for them to separate work from their private life. As Charlotte, a Western European policy director who works for a European-wide umbrella organization with a broad thematic remit, comments:

> It is sometimes difficult to be so much in [the work], because it has an impact on—I cannot read anything or I can't watch TV or see any movie without looking at it from a gender perspective.... When I see anything, I always count the number of women..., so sometimes I have to stop myself because it is getting a bit too much. That is also why I can't really see myself being extremely active in another organization in my free time. I mean I could do environment or I could do human rights or animals or Tibet or whatever in my free time, but I am usually not doing women, because that would be too much.

I will unpack the meaning of communicating this encroachment on work in private life in more detail later in this section. First, I want to attend to the ways in which the interview material presented conflicting understandings of "the political" and "politics," which were tied to understandings of private and public. I was surprised, for example, when Charlotte continued by saying: "I would not like to be in politics because that is really too much, but I am doing politics in a different way." When I remarked, "I would say that you are in politics," Charlotte replied,

> No, but in an electoral position, because I think that is really hard. I mean my job is eating on my private life in my head. I am not talking about time; this is a different issue. But if you are in political life, in terms of being an elected person, it ... does not seem that you can be at the same time an elected person and a normal person anymore. It is a bit like being a rock star or something.

Charlotte's understanding of the "political" is connected to parliamentary politics in the realm of the state (or the EU), and hence in the first instance she defines her work, associated with civil society, as not being politics. The state is defined as "public" in both liberal and republican accounts. Interestingly, as a consequence, she then considers being an elected politician as more intrusive on private life than her current work (cf. Frantz 2005), which does "eat on her private life in her head" because one's private life is negated by being a "*public* persona." Sperling, Ferree, and Risman (2001) observe that participants in civic activism (predominantly women) often do not define their engagement as political. As institutional state politics is male dominated, and as this sphere is conventionally defined as political, they argue that "politics itself is defined on a gendered basis" (Sperling et al. 2001, 1170). Hence, the feminist questioning of the binary public/private cannot be understood in isolation from debates over competing understandings of the "political" (Enloe 1989). This situates the practices of women who work on women's and gender issues in a complex relation to the public/private divide, which merits further exploration.

One of the main struggles of feminism has been to make public and political the situations and experiences in the domestic sphere. Jean Elshtain, for example, has argued that all different strands of feminism "share at least one overriding imperative: they would redefine the boundaries of the public and the private, *the personal and the political*" (1981, 202, emphasis added). The famous radical feminist slogan "The personal is political," coined in 1968 by civil rights and feminist activist Carol Hanish (Lee 2007, 1), underlines the fact that issues that were traditionally understood as "personal," taking place in the private sphere, for example, domestic abuse, are tightly connected to a public sphere in which women are devalued. The slogan encouraged a politicization of these issues. In feminist IR, Cynthia Enloe has reversed the claim, as "the political is personal," and extended it to "the personal is international" (1989, 195). Through interrogating the distinction between the private and public spheres, feminist theory has redefined the notion of the political in liberal democracy. Squires pushes this point by stating that the feminist challenge to the dichotomy, if taken to its extreme, "would eliminate the boundaries of the political altogether" (Squires 2004, 23). Once politics is understood as the circulation of power, politics is not constrained to one sphere but is ubiquitous.

The account of Charlotte, who does not regard her work as politics, can be contrasted with the narrative of Rana, another woman I interviewed, whose local-level organization supports migrant sex workers and who considers her work very political. This rather corresponds with a republican understanding of politics as taking place in the sphere of civil society. Rana explicitly contrasts apolitical acts of welfare with political activism: "I do not see myself as helping others; as I said, the spine of this whole thing is the political." She initially seems to follow the same intuition as Charlotte that politics is linked to the public rather than the private sphere: "I am passionate about being political, but at the same time it is also very personal for me." Instead of understanding the *but* in "but at the same time it is also very personal" as a strong juxtaposition with the first part of the sentence, a more convincing reading is to understand this as indicative of a broader feminist understanding of the political as going far beyond state politics. It is relevant to read this interview extract in light of the fact that Rana herself shares her migration background with the women she supports in her work. Her father comes from a country in the global South, and her mother from an Eastern European country, where the family lived in the first years of her life. Her advocacy work on behalf of racialized marginalized women can therefore not be separated from her own political claims to an equal status in society. When the two interview narratives by Charlotte and Rana are juxtaposed, the reference to the "private" in the first quote should be distinguished from the "personal" in the second; the first alludes to private time outside working hours, while the second addresses the existential core of the woman interviewed.

Returning to the first strand, the relation between private and professional life as brought up by Charlotte, the following narrative of Birgit, who works in Geneva for an international women-and-peace organization, is equally exemplary:

Yes, it is very difficult to separate [the private and the professional life], and I think it is something that I think is an ongoing challenge. It is also work that is done a lot of times by volunteers, so it is a big part of somebody's life. And I think, not only for me, but also for a number of others that I talk to, the separation is almost impossible. I have seen it burn people out as well, which is rather unfortunate but it happens.

This example clearly indicates that the separation between private life and working professional life is seen as impossible and as necessary (for one's sanity) at the same time. Birgit's account corresponds to Moghadam's observation that a lot of the work by women's organizations is still based on "labor of love" and that, as a result, there is a "tendency toward overwork on the part of a core of members, sometimes leading to burn-out" (Moghadam 2005, 95–96). As Duffield observes in relation to aid work in Sudan, the separation of professional life and private life is very fragile. The division may be enforced in a spatial way, with the fortified aid compound becoming "a place of refuge" for a shower, a beer, and some television (Duffield 2010, 468).

The just-quoted narration of Birgit is worth following a bit further, as it touches on a range of issues, representative of how the women connected to the public/private and personal/professional divide. In addition, her narration reiterates some of the points made earlier in this chapter about the critical discourse on careerism in NGOs and the women's awareness of and reaction to this discourse. At some point in our discussion on this topic, I said to Birgit: "I actually don't even know if I was thinking about this theme before I started doing the interviews, but having talked to people, this is just a theme that comes up every time." She then replied as follows:

Oh yeah, and I would say, probably as you go through you will find this is something that will come up almost every time.... You know, a lot of people, and myself included, live what you call "hand to mouth." And so we are not doing it for monetary gain. We are doing it because we are following a passion. We are not doing it because we have a lack of skills or intelligence, but because we are driven by a passion. And once you are driven by a passion, it is hard for it to not to become everything. It can be quite difficult to balance. Those who are in this field who work professionally, who have children, I know some people—not a lot of people to be perfectly honest—who do, but I do know some and they had to take breaks from their professional careers for a few years because they can't balance or manage the separation.

Birgit's narration includes a reference to combining family life with a career in NGOs, which was a theme that persisted in many of the interviews with those working in Brussels and Geneva. For them, their job had required migration. When commenting on the challenge of combining such career with having a family, some women referred to hardworking, career-minded female colleagues who in their forties suddenly found themselves without children and often also without a partner. Frequently this image was used as a reminder to themselves that they did not want to be in such situation. Roth's research (2015) on humanitarian aid workers supports the impression that the nature of some NGO work, for example when it includes frequent relocation, can have an impact on family planning (cf. Nowicka 2005; Hopgood 2006). Unsurprisingly, she identified a gendered dimension to this finding, with women NGO workers being less likely to find partners willing to move with them than their male counterparts (Roth 2015, 112–116).

For Ruth, who is based in the Netherlands and whose international work on reproductive rights requires certain periods of international travel, having a family is instrumental to maintaining some boundaries between her private and professional life:

> I think [the private and professional] is very connected, but I have now a family since a couple of years; I have two kids, and that is my private life. And I take time for it and I enjoy it and it is important. And I also have friends that are not connected at all to this [NGO] world and what I am doing, and it is very important to also have another view on life from other people.

In Ruth's case, the fact that she has founded her own organization, rather than working within the constraints of an organizational framework less amenable to family life, provides her the space to consider her children and her social life as a welcome change from her demanding job. While Ruth experiences the opportunity to separate private life from work through spending time with her family as a positive change, it is clear that in (high-level) NGOs and political jobs this separation has not always been, and is not always regarded as, positive, having the effect of diminishing women as suitable for demanding international jobs. In 1989 Cynthia Enloe still referred to statements by UN member governments in response to the Ad Hoc Group on Equal Rights for Women in the UN, which lobbied to appoint more women to senior positions of this nature:

> Women can't be put on their own in a world where late-night meetings and cocktail parties are *de rigueur* [and] single women's presence in such an environment

could produce embarrassments, while married women do not enjoy the mobility so essential for UN work; they are likely to get pregnant; they are *diverted by family responsibilities*. (Enloe 1989, 121; emphasis added)

Meaning Making with the Public/Private Divide

While the narratives above serve to illustrate the prevalence, poignancy, and interrelatedness of the themes private/public, professional/personal, and the political, it is important to make sense of some of the contradictory understandings that emerge. I propose that Susan Gal's understanding of the distinction between the public and the private as a "communicative phenomenon—a product of semiotic processes" (2004, 261) is a productive analytical frame in this context. Gal aligns herself with the conclusion drawn by feminist theorists that "the public/private distinction is an ideological one, hence not susceptible to empirical counter evidence" (2004, 262). Gal's conceptualization of the public/private divide as a communicative phenomenon is a helpful counterresponse to common arguments that the terms public/private are employed in contradictory ways. She argues that a semiotic approach to the usage of the public/private divide demonstrates that the distinction is not blurred and that there is in fact a discernible logic attached to the pair. Her semiotic approach implies a rejection of the idea that the public and private are fixed to certain places, practices, or institutions (Gal 2004). Rather, public and private are (1) "co-constitutive cultural categories," (2) "indexical signs that are always relative, dependent for part of their referential meaning on the interactional context," and (3) a "fractal distinction" (Gal 2004, 264–265). This latter characteristic, the fractal distinction, means that the private and the public are continually subdivided or submerged in broader categorizations. Gal (2004) presents the example of the space outside one's house and the home itself, where the outside is classically categorized as public and the home as private. Within the home, however, a subdivision is made, with the living room being public and the bedroom a private space. Similarly, the street, commonly labeled as public, can have a private element to it. For instance, one might be responsible for removing snow from the pavement in front of one's house.

Gal's suggestion to understand the distinction between the public and the private as a "communicative phenomenon" first resonates with a particular type of exchange that I had a few times during the interviews. When asking certain questions, for example about their feeling of responsibility, the women would very explicitly draw a distinction between their personal and their professional views: "My professional responsibility? Or my personal responsibility?" Because it was hard to make sense of the distinction outside their particular narrative and because I was curious about the distinction the women themselves would make, I usually replied "Both!" They then continued to address what they regarded as two separate realms. I argue that Gal's semantic approach is most productive for understanding what these small exchanges were indicative of, namely the women's attempts to (re)draw the boundaries of the public and private spheres. Her suggestion avoids what in my assessment would be an incorrect conclusion, namely that the boundaries of the private and public are meaningless, as they are unstable, or that the categories of the private and the public collapse into one another. Rather it stresses the significance of the categories in creating meaning.

In order to demonstrate this, I propose to return to some of the interview narratives quoted above and reread them with Gal's semiotic frame. In the first extract, Charlotte indicates that she feels that her work life penetrates into her private life when she finds herself analyzing her leisure time activities from a gender perspective. Hence, she explains, it would be "too much" to also engage in other gender activism in her "private time," though she could imagine working on other issues, such as environmentalism. That means that within her private time, she makes a division between a "public" part, where she maintains her gender perspective, and a "private" part, where she could engage with justice issues in different fields. Therefore, this account displays features of the third characteristic, the "fractal distinction," following fractal formations in nature that repeat the same pattern inside a pattern: "The public/private distinction is reapplied and now divides into public and private what was, from another perspective, entirely 'private' space" (Gal 2004, 265).

Birgit's earlier statement ("Once you are driven by a passion, it is hard for it to not to become everything"), which emphasized that her work is not fixed to the public sphere, but also very private, has the effect of foregrounding (the morality of) passion over money. Birgit knows that work, as part of the public sphere, is normally associated with monetary gain and careerism. I propose here that her assertions only "work" when one takes into considerations the assumptions that underlie the pair public/private. For Ruth, time outside regular working hours, which is conventionally labeled as private, was still occupied with work. However, since she has had children, Ruth feels that the distinction between work and private time is clearer, as she has recreated a space, the domestic, within the larger category of "private time." This recalls Judith Squires's (2004) observation that the "private" can denote three things: civil society, the personal sphere, and the domestic sphere. On a more general level, Gal's conceptualization supports an understanding of the naming of public and private as a meaningful, meaning-giving practice, vital to the self-presentation and self-understanding of the women in this study.

The reply from Birgit also included a reference to volunteers, for whom, according to her, it might be even harder to separate work from their private life, as "it is a big part of somebody's life." In this context, it is interesting to shift to two instances of local projects where the task of volunteers consisted of "befriending" the intended migrant beneficiaries of the organizations. In both cases the women involved in these local organizations, in one case the volunteer coordinator, in the other case the volunteer herself, talked to me about "drawing boundaries." When I ask Susanne, a volunteer who is a retired teacher, "where befriending stops," she replies:

> Once the [women asylum seekers] start telling you their stories, and they tell you their struggles and talk to you about their problems, you cross that line of being somebody who helps and volunteers to run the session; you befriend them.... So I find keeping that sort of "me and them" very hard, that sort of separating. And I don't think I would try to be honest; whether that is right or not I don't know, probably not.

Since there is an interesting tension between mentioning that she would not attempt to keep the separation and at the same time saying that this is probably "not right," I asked Susanne: "Why do you think, probably not?"

She then replied: "A lot of people would say that if you are in a volunteer role, that you have to keep your boundaries. And my response to that would be that I have my boundaries and I know what my boundaries are, and that being friends with people does not cross my boundaries."

It is telling that in a situation where the boundaries between the professional and the personal are potentially less clearly drawn, for multiple reasons (the work is voluntary, unpaid, conducted in "private" time, and in addition to that, the nature of the work, befriending, is normally a personal affair), the response of the outside world is a warning to "keep your boundaries." This reflects a fear of the pollution of two realms deemed separate. Both republican and liberal accounts of the private/public divide contain "narratives about the dangers of mutual contamination by public and private spheres" (Gal 2004, 261). Anne-Meike Fechter similarly observes that shifts to increased professionalization of development work have led to a greater reluctance to consider the "role of the personal" (Fechter 2012, 1391).

In the context of the interview I suggested to Susanne that she might set her boundaries in different ways, for example by not disclosing personal information from the outset. Susanne, who is a white woman, then answered:

> Initially you would not ask people up to your house. It is only when you get to know people you invite people into your home, and that has nothing to do with color, has it? This has nothing to do with color or race or anything. Sometimes you do invite people in. But on the whole you ask people in when you know them, because your home is your space, isn't it? It is your space. No, I have no problems having them in the house.

The interview extract shows a redrawing of the private/public divide, which introduces a new nested division within the private space of voluntarily "befriending." Only those women with whom a "real friendship," a personal over professional befriending, has been established are invited to Susanne's home (classed as "private"). Susanne continues meeting the other women in her private time and under the personalized label of "befriending," but in public spaces. Striking in this narrative is also Susanne's unprompted mentioning of color and "race." I read her assertion that it is not important as linked to the fear of being accused of racism (cf. Armbruster 2012, 54). Susanne's account of boundary-drawing in the context of work with migrant women in the global North has strong parallels with the legitimation of distance from local populations among expats abroad, who are similarly keen to assert that this does not have racist grounds (Schondelmayer 2010). Responses of this nature will be further discussed in chapter 6, which addresses postcolonial configurations in relation to the women's work. The spatial separation—and perhaps the coding of the house as white—also maps on to an Us versus Them distinction that will be unpacked in that same chapter.

In the specific circumstances of this befriending project, which was discontinued because of a lack of funding, Susanne is forced to consider if and how these professional "friendships" mediated by her organization and forged in the public setting will continue privately once the project is over. The social, legal, and economic inequalities that cast her in the role of the "befriending volunteer," and the other women in the role of "being befriended," of course persist beyond the project. Reflecting this, Susanne tells me: "I think it is going to be me that is going to have to do it, because I am the person with the car, I am the person who can afford to say, 'Let's go out for a cup of coffee.' They can't."

The public/private dynamic surfaces in a different way when Susanne compares her own relation to the women she supports to that of the paid coordinator of the project: "She is paid, so she has to toe the 'party line' a bit more than I do. I can do what I like because I am a volunteer, even though I am answerable, obviously [to the organization]." Here her narrative suggests that being unpaid implies more autonomy since a paid position is associated with accountability. This neatly maps onto what Benn and Gauss define as the "agency" dimension of the public/private divide: following this logic, the public is distinguished from the private depending on whether the agent acted on her own accord or publicly (Benn and Gauss 1983, 7). As they put it, "A public official has special duties . . . which greatly circumscribe his [sic] freedom of action in comparison with a private citizen. He [sic] can be accountable in ways in which a private citizen cannot" (Benn and Gauss 1983, 10). In this short quotation from the interview with Susanne, she first focuses on her space for maneuvering, when she says that she "can do what she like[s]," but then immediately qualifies this by saying that she is obviously accountable to her organization. I read this in the light of two seemingly competing discourses of morality associated with respectively the public and the private sphere: the first is associated with impartiality and accountability, and the latter with emotional commitment and passion. This leads to what I call a private/public "double bind," in which the women feel compelled to situate themselves in both. Within this short and seemingly contradictory statement, Susanne can align herself with both types of moralities. Before elaborating on this public/private "double bind" with further examples from the women who work internationally, I will quickly discuss the second instance of a local project that enlists volunteers to "befriend" the intended migrant beneficiaries of the organizations. This will provide further insight in the distinction that Susanne has drawn between paid and voluntary positions.

This reflection on voluntary work comes from Nora, who is trained in social work and psychology. In her paid job, she coordinates a local "buddy project" for women who have been trafficked in which volunteers provide additional support to the client that is not offered by the paid staff; this ranges from participating in leisure activities to accompanying the client to a bureaucratic service. Nora persistently stresses the importance of drawing boundaries for the buddies:

> We train the buddies also, mainly in setting boundaries for yourself; what can you do as a buddy and what can you not do as a buddy and what do they have to tell us and me or my colleagues if something happens. Well, we try to make the

lines very clear, what the project is and what they cannot do with the [clients]. And the lines are sometimes crossed, because we always have some volunteers who think they are becoming friends.

In Nora's account the paid, professional staff is responsible for drawing and maintaining "the boundaries" in the relation between buddy and "client." In case of "trespassing," the professional staff needs to be consulted, to enable them to intervene. In this narrative, professionalism entails the capacity to judge whether there is a "real friendship" or not. This thread continues when Nora says: "They say they are friends, but I think that it is very—that is really up for discussion. Because how can you be friends if the relationship is not neutral [and equal]? Because it is not."

She then recalls one exception:

> But there is one couple which I met, and within four months the client called and said, "I really like [my assigned buddy], and we have such good contact it does not feel right to be in the buddy project anymore, because we are really becoming friends." So I called the buddy and she also said this was true. So they stepped out of the project and they still see each other as a matter of fact. But that won't happen much.

Here again the professional needed to "license" the friendship, more or less formally checking with both parties that there was an "authentic" friendship developing. However, both buddy and "client" explicitly addressed the way the boundaries were drawn and, given their affective relation, decided to withdraw from the formal, that is, public space of the project, which was seen as incompatible with their friendship. This "public" space was defined by formal rules; for example, lending money was not allowed because of reported incidences of "abuse" by befriended clients. The buddy and the "client" resisted the drawing of the boundaries within the project by the organization and decided to move the relation into their private sphere to avoid official scrutiny. Here again I argue that it is not a question of "unstable or fuzzy boundaries"; "rather, the intertwining public and private is created by practices that participants understand as re-creations of the dichotomy" (Gal 2004, 267). The fact that the volunteer and buddy were conscious of these boundaries is expressed in: "It does not feel right to be in the buddy project anymore." The buddies were defined as "public" agents with accountability, but because they are also private subjects who have their own moral conscience, "what they perceive as the duties of their office may conflict with the demands of their private morality" (Benn and Gauss 1983, 10).

Committed Workers

In liberal understandings of morality, morality is rationally defensible behavior, which can be universally shared and agreed upon. It therefore belongs to the public sphere: "All morality must be in principle public; it cannot have the private standing of 'gut feelings'" (Benn 1983, 155). As the attentive reader might recall, the issue of private versus public morality speaks to the third and final strand in the account of Birgit, when she stated that the public and private are difficult to separate, as people like her do the work "out of a passion" and not for "monetary gain." The narration of Joan, a young American woman, speaks to this passion or commitment in even stronger language. Joan is now based in Brussels, where she works for an international advocacy network. Prior to this job, Joan worked for two years in a conflict situation in Haiti.

Joan replies as follows when I ask her about her work-life balance:

> [This is] extremely difficult. It is definitely easier now. I think when I was in this mission, there was a lot of restrictions on movement, so to be honest, you could work or you could go home and you could read books. And that kind of thing was what you were trying to do. But the volume of work was really quite intense, so I failed miserably at work-life balance at least the first year that I was there. Here it is a bit easier. . . . I think since moving to a place that has restaurants and rock climbing clubs and a nice park, there is a lot more motivation to leave the office, also because the kind of work that we are doing. . . . We are not saving lives here. It is not as if there are a whole lot of things that are really justifying killing yourself in the office.

In Joan's narration, space and place are significant in understanding the contrast between the personal and the professional, similar to Susanne's decisions about whether or not to invite people to her home. Whereas the Haitian context allowed only "home" to be private, the move to Brussels has increased the range of places where Joan can enjoy private time; what are regarded as public spaces, such as parks and restaurants, is now being included among the places that she can reclaim for her (private) self. In the contrast that she sketches, it becomes clear that not only the volume but also the nature and the location of her work have had a strong impact on her ability to separate her working life and commitment from her personal free time (Fechter 2012; Roth 2015). The stronger the impact of the work, the more time needs to be invested, seemingly diminishing the right to claim private time. The metaphor of "killing yourself" at work to "save lives" of others does not only sound poetic, but has explanatory force in showing how far the boundaries can potentially be pushed and recalls the previously mentioned references to colleagues who work themselves to burnout.

Joan continues to explain why she worked particularly hard in Haiti, leaving little private time:

> When you are young and you don't have a lot of experience yet and someone puts you in a position where it is slightly beyond what you have been doing and slightly beyond your capabilities, there is a lot of pressure to really not screw up. And I was definitely in that situation of feeling like I needed to prove myself as well.

When I suggest that it might then be strategic to put these kinds of people in such situations, she says:

> Oh, completely, yeah. I mean from the hiring point of view, when you have people like that, you know that they are going to work themselves to the point of exhaustion. I mean when you are starting up a mission, you want people who are going to really work hard. And I think—and this might be one of my prejudices that I developed here—you also see a lot of people who are very comfortable working for a big organization, or a UN agency or something like that, where they are quite comfortable in their job security and then end up actually not really doing much. And I think that people who are working on the kind of projects we were working on, they would rather have a young person with lots of energy who they know is going to do the work than perhaps someone with a bit more experience who they worry might not actually do the kind of work that is necessary.

This extract draws lines between young and junior people who work hard to prove themselves versus older, established colleagues who have become complacent. Joan aligns herself with the first and does not just present the latter as having a different attitude, but also suggests that this (lack of) work ethic is problematic. Whereas she originally might have expected everybody in this kind of work to be committed, Joan now indicates that since she has been in Brussels she has developed a prejudice about those who are "too comfortable." Reading the two extracts together, we see that Joan links hard work not only to age and desire for career progression, but also to passionate commitment to the cause. The hard-working, (over) committed worker is the good professional who undertakes the necessary, required work. This introduces a tension in using young age/lack of seniority as the sole explanatory factor for working hard, as she indirectly suggests that she still wants to maintain that commitment (and thus be a good professional) when getting older.

It is interesting to see how Joan reconciles her aspiration to be a "good" professional, that is, committed worker, with her own decision to move to Brussels, the location where she encountered colleagues whom she considers too invested in their job security and lacking dedication. Joan motivates her relocation with the high level of stress she was under in Haiti: "[Being in a conflict-ridden area] you can only do that for so long. At a certain point you either become one of these people who go from disaster to disaster and, I would consider, lose perspective on what is normal life, or you would have to take breaks from it."

I suggest that the main points of interest here are not Joan's evaluation of her senior colleagues—which also reveals some of the generational tensions discussed in the previous chapter—or whether in order to remain effective in conflict areas time out is necessary. Rather, what I want to highlight here is the work her narration does in constructing the "good professional" as passionate, committed, yet able to see things in perspective. Again, this combines two types of moralities normally held apart through the private/public sphere division. There is a different (gendered) morality at stake in the private and domestic sphere than in the public sphere, with the emphasis in the first on "empathy, relationality and caring" and in the latter on "autonomy, individuality and justice" (Squires 2004, 28). Feminist scholars have sought to challenge this divide; for example, Raia Prokhovnik argues for an "interconnexion" (1998, 97) between the private and public spheres to enable the "non-instrumental" experiences, which are conventionally associated with the private sphere, to inform citizenship practices that are usually placed in the public realm (Prokhovnik 1998, 85). As the interview narrative demonstrates, Joan wants to live up to the ideal of a committed worker who bridges public and private moralities. To do this, she makes a (spatial) double maneuver; on the one hand, her account of being in the field, where she "is" her work constantly, is a token for her care and passion, and on the other hand, her relocation to Brussels underlines her ability to be rational and objective and thus have a "professional perspective." Joan positions herself by disassociating from the two negative sides of the poles related with, respectively, the private and the public: the overpassionate worker who loses perspective by moving from disaster to disaster and the distanced, disconnected worker in a comfortable job in Brussels.

The significance of this positioning as a committed and professional worker is further illustrated by the narrative of Ruth, who is the founder of a small organization in the Netherlands with an international reach. In response to my question whether the fact that her work is concerned with justice makes it personal, she says:

> Some people are just not very good at separating their private lives from their professional lives, and that is because they do what they passionately care about, but that does not need to be justice based. I know really a lot of people that don't work on justice, that are architects or artists, or whatever they do, they are as passionate that they have as little separation in their private life and their work. But that is because they really love what they are doing and that's about them [and] what they are doing.... And I also know a lot of people in NGOs that just really do their job and get paid for it. And there are a lot of NGOs that work for justice but actually that have become so much part of this funding, foundation, money [system] that a lot of the work that they do is based on where you can get money and not what needs to be done.

Ruth's reference to NGO colleagues who follow the money rather than needs resonates with the (skepticism about) "professionalization" of the feminist movement discussed before (Menon 2004; de Alwis 2009, Lang 1997). Menon laments in the context of Indian women NGOs: "Freely available funds also attract people with no great political commitment, for whom feminism is often a temporary profession" (Menon 2004, 220). While in a superficial reading of this interview extract it seems as if Ruth also negatively evaluates "not being good in separating the private from the professional life," it quickly becomes clear that this is presented as proof of her passion, care, and love for her work. This recalls the statement of Susanne, the volunteer who is befriending migrant women discussed earlier ("So I find keeping that sort of 'me and them' very hard, that sort of separating. And I don't think I would try, to be honest; whether that is right or not I don't know, probably not"). Here similarly, by alluding to something that "she finds very hard," Susanne actually manages to present herself as "good," distancing herself from detached volunteers. This narrative of Ruth shares with the story of Joan, as well as with other women I interviewed, the gesture of distancing herself from those who consider their work not a vocation but "merely" a job.

Yet again, I argue that in line with the ideal worker, Ruth also discursively needs to "prove" her professionalism in terms of her objectivity and rationality—moralities associated with the public sphere—in the same way that Susanne, the volunteer, did this by reference to her knowledge of where her boundaries are, and Joan could do this by reference to her decision to leave Haiti in order to maintain a healthy perspective. Earlier in this section, I quoted an interview extract where Ruth achieved this by reference to family life with her two children and social connections with people outside the NGO world ("It is very important to also have another view on life from other people"). This follows the same pattern that is visible in Joan's insistence on maintaining "perspective on what is normal life," due to permanent exposure to a conflict situation.

Because the private sphere is commonly associated with a morality of "empathy, relationality and caring" and "real" feminist commitment, in contrast to the careerism and "individualism" of the public sphere (Squires 2004, 28), I argue that the women are under pressure to "prove" their commitment to their work by situating it in the personal sphere and letting work encroach on their private lives. Simultaneously, in the context of professionalization trends in aid (Stroup 2012; Roth 2015) and its associated values of impartiality, rationality, and accountability, the women feel equally compelled to position their work in the public, professional sphere. Gal's (2004) conceptualization of the private/public distinction as a communicative and meaning-making strategy is an effective way to analyze this public/private "double bind," since I can show that the women's seemingly contradictory and shifting statements are active positionings.

As feminist scholars have highlighted, the spheres and associated values are gendered: "The [conventional] model of the professional is that of 'rational man,'" in contrast to the emotional woman, much in the same way as the public sphere is occupied by rational man and the private realm by emotional woman (Kleinman 2002, 277). This means that there is much at stake for women working on gender and women's issues in claiming professional identities. This was already very clear in the previous chapter, "Feminist Trajectories," in the interview narrative of Laura, who contrasted her emotional reaction based on her feminist convictions with professionalism, illustrating the "double bind" and the burden that comes with it: "For example, in that particular situation, I should have chosen to sort of not let myself be provoked by it, [but] I did. And I think if I had not been such a convinced feminist myself, if I would be more professional, or both, I could just let it slide. And I did not, I got really pissed and I yelled at him."

Without discrediting the important claim that there has been an NGOization of the feminist movement and that the concomitant professionalization has a number of detrimental consequences, I argue that it is important to simultaneously consider the flip side of this phenomenon and critically assess the situation in which work commitment invades private life, as many of the women described. Hence I read the interview narratives about "killing yourself in the office" and the burnout of colleagues as an important warning against the romanticization of the underpaid, activist work that leaves no personal/private space intact. This inclination to overwork should indeed also be recognized as a "drawback to [feminist] nonprofessionalized organizations" (Moghadam 2005, 95; see also Hopgood 2006). I therefore argue, in light of the (negative) attention that has recently been given to the NGOization of the feminist movement, that when work in this context is not "sufficiently" seen as a job but "too much" as a vocation, this can also lead to exploitative situations. This merits further critical reflection. For example, in light of the increased neoliberal disciplining of the self, there is a need to think of alternative ways to show passion and commitment than overwork, which critical assessments of the "nine-to-five feminist" (de Alwis 2009, 86) do not offer.

This nine-to-five, disinterested worker still looms in the background of the interview narrative of Liz, a young Brussels-based woman from Canada working on engendering constitutions. However, her musings give an affirmative glimpse of what Prokhovnik's feminist interconnection between the public and private spheres and, mapped on to that, the personal and professional could look like. Liz:

> I feel I finally reached the point where I am quite happy with the work that I am doing and what I am doing, which is a very new experience for me.... I think I am finally at a point where, okay, that I am not stressed does not mean I am not working hard enough. I can imagine a world now ... where what I am working towards is not that all women feel the amount of stress that I felt when I was in school, but rather another kind of feeling: you can be liberated from these cycles of neuroses, ... where the work that I do can also be a sort of philosophy for my life, but that stress does not need to be part of that. I guess I like the fact that the work I do is also something that I want to live my life by. It is not the kind of job where I go nine to five and then I completely shut that off and then go live my real life.... What I want to work towards is something that I want everyone to feel and that I want myself to feel.

NEGOTIATING LOCATIONS

This chapter started out with looking into the motivations of the women for their work and its relation to privilege and opportunities. In this section, I will single out a subgroup of the sample, namely the group of women who are working for international organizations with offices in Geneva and Brussels, and focus on their rationale for working from these Northern centers of international politics on gender and women's issues in the global South. In this chapter, I have so far suggested that the discourse on global citizenship and global responsibility is highly moralized, with the women navigating their position in response, desiring to be recognized as committed professionals. In the previous section, Joan explained why she moved from Haiti to Brussels, where she has more private time, justifying herself with a need to sustain a healthy professional perspective, which dissolves during long exposure to a conflict situation. As I will further demonstrate below, the theme of distance is loaded with moral meaning, which affects the ways in which women speak about their location.

Anna, who is Brussels-based and who works as a consultant for an international organization on women's participation, explains:

> I can hardly say that I work at a grass-roots level, I just don't. If I visit that town for a few days, that is just not the work that I do. Although I guess there is, as I am trying to explain this to you, there must be a certain amount of guilt that I feel towards not being able to say, "I work at a grass-roots level," which is why I am trying so hard to explain why I do what I do.

The fact that Anna mentions a feeling of guilt links directly with the discourse in which fieldwork is more positively valued than what is regarded as bureaucratic work in capital cities. There are a number of (moral) assumptions regarding space, place, and distance in relation to NGO and aid work. The increasing technocratic approach in NGOs is associated with a growing lack of field experience among the younger generation of development workers, who instead received academic training in the new discipline of development studies (Duffield 2007). Fieldwork is romanticized, in contrast with bureaucratic work in the office, linked to valuing "getting your hands dirty" over "staying high and dry." This theme is sometimes mapped onto a logic in which grass-roots organizations are presented as "unproblematically good" and international institutions, such as the International Planned Parenthood Federation, as "unproblematically evil" (Waterman 1993, 10).

Many have, however, observed that development workers who live in the places where they work often occupy safer and better housing (such as former colonial houses) and live in expatriate neighborhoods or even "fortified aid compounds" (Duffield 2010, 461; cf. Smirl 2009; Harper 2011; Verma 2011). As Schondelmayer (2010) demonstrates with her analysis of interviews with development workers and foreign correspondents, the distancing of staff "in the field" can be expressed both spatially and emotionally. Hence, despite geographical proximity, they are isolated from the communities they support in their work, "detached" in their "ghettoized existence" or "social cocoon," "imprisoned within a narrow world" with communication being restricted to short carefully monitored visits and satellite phone calls (Rajak and Stirrat 2011, 167–170). This highlights that proximity does not guarantee close contact. Most importantly for the argument of this chapter, the negative evaluation of distance is maintained (an exception is the explicit critique of development workers on the ground as intrusive; cf. Goudge 2003).

When I ask Anna in Brussels to speak to the guilt that she refers to, she offers a very rich reply:

> Yes, I think that I feel a certain amount of guilt. And again I think the guilt is related to the fact that . . . to a certain extent I do like the academic path, I do like intellectual work. Not that it is necessarily—they are not mutually incompatible. You can do both, but in order to do a job that is both personally satisfying and that I feel can be of benefit of others, I feel that the work I do at this moment combines both elements. . . . I guess more generally in the type of rhetoric that we hear about NGO work or civil society work, "This NGO work is good and that NGO work is bad." I guess the other thing you get used to in Brussels, . . . I mean it is the center of advocacy and policy, . . . You might visit the site for a week or something like that, but in another way you are totally disconnected from these people. And you get used to using the language of like, "Oh, I am not a field person, I am a head office person." And it is accepted in Brussels in a way that perhaps in other milieus people would just automatically say, "What the hell are you talking about, you are a head office person, you are not a field person. What does that mean?" But we don't always pose these questions to ourselves, because Brussels is such a unique environment.

Anna, as well as other interviewees, justifies being located in Brussels in two ways: first, by stating that this is the "kind of work that she likes" and, second, by arguing that this is the way she can make herself most "useful," which links back to the notion of responsibility. Brussels, in contrast to the work on the ground that is "hands-on," is associated with the head, the academic path. Anna describes directly what she calls the "rhetoric" in which certain NGO work is seen as "good" or as "bad." She also indicates that being in Brussels to some extent "sanctions" the focus on the policy and advocacy level, as that is the dominant strand of NGO work there. Naomi, who is based in Geneva and works on women's leadership, stresses the importance of the contact with her member organizations in the global South in order to still connect to "reality." This is necessary, according to her, since "Geneva is not such a[n] in-your-face kind of place; it is a very nice environment." Brussels and Geneva have a distinct quality, similar to what Nowicka (2005) has described in the case of the large multinational city Atlanta. These global cities have a certain "'stickiness' . . . as places of settlement" for expats (Farrer 2012, 24).

The division between "field persons" and "HQ persons" that Anna describes for Brussels was also made by Joan, who told me that "there is a certain tension . . . between the people who are very much EU institution focused and the people who have more field operations and who are more field focused." The binary presented by Anna and Joan contrasts those working in the "field" in the global South and those in advocacy/policy positions in capital cities, predominantly in the global North. The practices of organizations in the global North that work directly with migrants from the global South are left out of this categorization. Given the fact that international staff's career paths mostly move between these two locations, rather than taking the "side turn" of working for national organizations that work with migrants, this is not surprising.

I suggest that the narrative of Rana, who works for such a national organization supporting female migrants from the global South, can nevertheless be situated in the discourse that evaluates distance negatively. Rana, who is familiar with international lobbying platforms, talks about the struggle of her own smaller national organization for funding, and the pressure she experiences as a result. Rana indicates that despite the fact that these international organizations have more resources, influence, and prestige, she nevertheless cannot imagine working for them. They lack the rootedness that she considers essential to her passionate commitment to her work:

> I understand that on an international level there is much on the agenda . . . and you are trying to influence decision-making on a very high level, . . . but it is a huge spectacle, a theater play. . . . Of course there have been results sometimes. Sure, I mean I believe that all the UN women's conferences and all this have been important and valuable things. . . . It is very interesting work, it is very "Wow, you travel to a lot of places, meet a lot of interesting people, and so on," but I don't know if you can do just that and still be passionate about something. Because what would it be? Or where would it be, if you have no kind of home base? Or if you work within the UN, even worse, because what would you then be passionate about if your organization is not something that has this emotional connection to you?

Rana's statement conjures up the image of the traveling businessman presented at the beginning of this chapter, disqualified by Richard Falk (1994) as a "proper" global citizen because of his superficial relation to the places he visits.

While Anna has described herself as a "headquarters person," defending herself in a discourse that critically evaluates the geographical distance to the women she seeks to support, other women I interviewed were less convinced that their strengths lay in the field of policy and advocacy. They had rather made decisions for practical reasons, such as needing to "put down roots" or leave the stress of living in a conflict zone. Joan's narrative can be contrasted with Anna's. Joan:

> When you are used to being able to be working on the ground with beneficiaries and seeing the impact of your work, really at the level where it is most needed, then to make that transition to the Brussels-level advocacy where you are talking about "toolkits" and "communications" and "conclusions" and things like that, you do get a certain amount of frustration of "Well, this is good, but what does it actually mean for people on the ground?"

Joan's expressed frustration with abstract advocacy vocabulary, which seems to bear little relation to what happens on the ground, resonates with Rana's earlier reference to international advocacy as a spectacle or theater play. Both can be understood in the context of the professionalization of the NGO sector, making it "common for humanitarian purposes to be overtaken by the institutions and professional practices which express them" (Kennedy 2004, xx). Joan's negative assessment of distance that comes with working in Brussels, which prevents her from clearly seeing the impact of her work on gender and security, leads her to conclude that she wants to return to "working in the field" in the global South again. Joan's argument draws on the same two strands that Anna articulated earlier: that you should work where, first, your strengths lie and you can be most beneficial, and, second, you most enjoy working. Joan:

> I don't think [this institutional work] is the kind of thing that I need to be doing, or it is not where my strengths are. So I think I would be better suited for going back out to the field for a while.... I don't think I am bad at it, but in terms of where my enjoyment is, I like being in developing countries. I like being able to have as part of my work visits to schools ..., to meet with communities to see the impact on the ground. That is what I need to feel like I am accomplishing something.

Joan and Anna use the same set of arguments to justify their positions, though their conclusion about where they are "best placed" is different. Joan points out that to foster her motivation, she really needs to witness changes "on the ground," echoing other NGO workers who moved away from the field to manage funding, to lobby, and to work on policies, who "have [experienced] alienation from the values with which they came into development and a loss of sense of purpose" (Eyben 2006, 46).

Maureen managed to bring a sense of purpose from her previous fieldwork in the global South to her office in the global North. Despite the fact that in terms of organizational context, Maureen's position in Geneva working for a UN agency is far removed from Rana's work for a small national NGO targeting migrant women, I suggest that Maureen's considerations can be read in dialogue with Rana's evaluation of international work as disconnected and therefore hindering passionate commitment. Maureen consistently emphasized throughout the interview how important it is for her to be in close contact with the women whose lives the programs she coordinates seek to improve. She has also explained that her previous work was grass-roots and community based. When I asked Maureen about her decision to take up this job away from "the field," she said that she had previously been frustrated as well as puzzled by how the UN functioned. She told me that she evaluated its practices very negatively, but at the same time felt incapable of "taking them on." This has striking similarities with Rana, who said that "the UN is a huge organization. Of course the issues are important, yes, it is women's rights. But I don't know, I just don't see it, you know."

Maureen explains how she initially accepted a short-term contract with the UN:

> And I thought to myself, "[In] eleven months I can at least figure out . . ." I literally thought of it as going into the belly of the beast. And I thought, "I will figure out what is happening for myself, not for any other grandiose reason but just for myself." It was like there was a tension within myself, coming from political science, and believing in political structures and believing in the overall goals of the UN and at the same time being so severely disappointed in the results and outcomes. I could not overcome it myself and felt like, "I am at a crossroads now; I can continue what I am doing and feeling that I am making piecemeal progress towards something that I believe in, but I do not have the ear of the government. And I do not have the position even to represent the groups I was working with to go to the government. Certainly not as a young woman, certainly not as young brown woman in certain contexts." And so on a personal level it was important for me to understand how the UN worked and to understand why there was such a disconnect. Not with any grandiose notions of changing the world, but how can I position myself better to contribute to what I want to do, which was to ensure better living conditions for women and girls.

Similar to Rana, Maureen recognizes that international organizations have more resources and influence. Unlike Rana, who decided to remain in her local organization, Maureen decided to engage with the UN, rather than turning her back on it. She sought to figure out its logic and work through it rather than be paralyzed by it, because she recognized the power of the institution and its strategic position. "Going into the belly of the beast," as Maureen describes it, is a powerful metaphor for an attempt to engage in a productively complicit way with an institution that she sees as firmly embedded in the unequal power structures that she seeks to address. I have suggested elsewhere (de Jong 2009) that this act can be read with Gayatri Spivak's notion of "constructive complicity." Spivak introduces constructive complicity in the following manner: "Our sense of critique is too thoroughly determined by Kant, Hegel and Marx for us to be able to reject them as 'motivated imperialists,' although this is too often the vain gesture performed by the critics of imperialism" (Spivak 1999, 6–7). Hence, in the same way that Kant, Hegel, and Marx cannot be simply dismissed by virtue of their universalization of the West—but should invite a critical (deconstructive) reading precisely because they shaped Western imperialist thought—Maureen decides she cannot reject the UN without critically engaging with it. Or, as Ilan Kapoor, postcolonial development critic with a background as development consultant, translates Spivak's intervention to the level of international politics: "Thus, for instance, the World Bank and IMF may well be 'imperialistic' organizations, but they are too important and powerful to turn our backs on; instead, we can engage them unrelentingly from all sides to try to make them accountable to the subaltern" (Kapoor 2008, 55).

Maureen speaks of a very clear goal—"ensuring better living conditions for women and girls"—and subsequently analyzes the power of the UN as well as her own positionality and decides that under these circumstances, her taking the position is warranted to increase her impact. Much of what Maureen says here echoes the short memoir by Kirsten Timothy, one of the founders of the Association for Women in Development (AWID), who describes in "Walking on Eggshells at the UN" how she decided to join the UN in the 1970s. As she recalls, she was "worried about 'selling out,' about becoming an insider in a large multilateral bureaucracy, albeit one that stood for justice and equality" (2004, 53), reflecting broader concerns among feminists about co-optation (de Jong and Kimm 2017).

Maureen's emphasis on her specific positionality as not only young and female, but also "brown," deserves some further attention. Following a constructivist instead of a structural approach to intersectionality, I suggest that rather than understanding people to be "passive bearers of the meanings of social categories," we can view processes of subject construction as simultaneously "subjecting" individuals *and* constituting them as subjects (Prins 2006, 280). As can be shown with her narrative in which she describes her decision to work for a UN agency based on her careful evaluation of her positionality as a "young, brown woman," Maureen is not a passive recipient of her identity. She justifies her move to an organization about which she initially had and continues to have significant reservations, by referring to her realization that in her earlier role she was not heard by powerful institutions. Maureen is "a subject with a sense of self in *complex complicity* with and *resistance to* the matrix of forces that ma[ke her] possible" (Haraway, quoted in Caraway 1992, 2). To continue with the metaphor of going into the belly of the beast, Maureen recognizes that she has become part of the beast as well, functioning according to its logic. For example, she realizes that there are certain things she cannot say as a "bureaucrat," which she would have expressed when she still had an activist role in her former grass-roots organization. However, for the moment these trade-offs are compensated by her sense of political effectiveness in view of the larger political structures in which she operates as an individual situated in and constituted by unequal social conditions.

CONCLUDING REMARKS

In this chapter I have set up a confrontation between the narratives offered by the interviews and two contested issues in citizenship and civil society theories, responsibility and the public/private divide, in order to analyze the ways in which the women explained their motivation for and commitment toward their work. Theories about responsible global citizenship contain a number of contradictions relating to alterity and privilege, which I consider constructive in understanding the position of the women. Underlying these contradictions is that responsibility is premised on simultaneously recognizing one's similarity to the one being "helped," and one's difference, in order to be in the position to provide support. I have illustrated how this conceptual contradiction comes to be embodied in the narratives of the women when they describe their sense of responsibility. I have subsequently argued that their expressed desire to provide others with opportunities similar to the ones they have enjoyed is based on an assumption that opportunities of disadvantaged groups can be raised without impacting the position of the privileged; this disregards global relations between privilege and marginalization. In an apparent contradiction,

I have shown that the very work of creating opportunities for others provides the women themselves with new opportunities and status.

Within the women's movement and in relation to a wider process of NGOization of social movements, there is a persistent critique of the professionalization of NGO work. Here careerism is seen as incompatible with altruistic values. The narratives of the women have clearly shown an awareness of this discourse, either through supporting this discourse, through challenging it, or through justifying their position in response to this discourse. While the incompatibility of altruism and careerism is commonly assumed, I have argued that it should be challenged as a false binary. Related to the selfishness-versus-altruism pair, and equally morally charged, is the public/private binary. I have demonstrated in this chapter that the boundaries between the public and private in the women's narratives get mapped onto those between professional and personal. Observing the shifting ways in which the women draw the distinction between the public and the private, I claim that these shifts, rather than making the public/private divide meaningless, illustrate that the opposite is the case. The interviewed women are constantly engaging in redrawing and redefining what feminist theories have revealed to be gendered boundaries between the public and the private, the professional and the personal. Following Gal's suggestion that the public/private division should be understood as a "communicative phenomenon" (2004, 261), I have proposed that this act of setting boundaries gives meaning to the work practices of the women and is vital for their self-understanding and self-representation. The meaning making through the private/public and professional/personal pairs gets an important impetus from the women's desire to position themselves as committed workers and to distance themselves from the two (gendered) "excessive poles"; on the one hand the disengaged, all-too-comfortable, masculinized worker and, on the other the overburdened, emotional, feminized worker who loses all perspective.

As I have claimed, the result is that they present their work as part of the private sphere to underline the noninstrumental morality associated with this realm (work as a vocation rather than a job), while simultaneously categorizing it as public in order to counter the stress of constant engagement with work outside working hours and to stress their professionalism. As these interview narratives demonstrate, and as also suggested by feminist scholars who have deconstructed the boundaries between public and private moralities, the struggle to reconcile the professional and the personal does not emerge from any real incompatibility between public and private morality. Rather, the seemingly contradictory pressures, which I have called the private/public "double bind," have their roots in the classic public/private distinction, mirrored in the discussion on the NGO career feminist versus the committed feminist activist. I have argued that alongside the critique of NGOization, we need to be attentive to the ways in which (self-)exploitation might come to be demanded of those who are professionals driven by a passionate cause, especially women. In the final section of this chapter I have discussed women's justification for the locations from which they have chosen to carry out their work. I showed that many of the women are conscious of a discourse that negatively evaluates work in support of women in the global South carried out from the global North, by attending to the ways in which they expressed alienation and self-doubt in relation to spatial distance. I proposed that women who justify different decisions regarding their spatial location, choosing to be either near beneficiaries or further away, draw on similar discursive registers to reach different conclusions. The next chapter will continue this theme and discuss dilemmas related to distance and proximity in more detail.

CHAPTER 4

Bridging Distance

This chapter addresses questions around responsibility across distance. It looks at how the women negotiate their relation with beneficiaries, focusing in particular, but not exclusively, on the women who are geographically removed from those who are supposed to benefit from the lobbying, the advocacy, and the project work of their international organizations. In the previous chapter I have already discussed some assumptions about remoteness and proximity in relation to NGO work. The theme of distance is also prominent in literature on representation, for instance in the question whether claims to know the needs of purported beneficiaries can be sustained without closely witnessing their particular circumstances. Hahn and Holzscheiter, for example, draw this link between representation and proximity: "There is the risk that NGOs may perceive the interests of their constituency wrongly. Large international NGOs are far away from those people whose interests they claim to represent" (2005, 8). Distance, space, and the relation between the local and the global are also prevalent themes in feminist theory and practice. Feminist debates echo some of the development/NGO discourse about space and location by romanticizing the site of the grass-roots as more authentic (Naples 2002a; Desai 2002; Moghadam 2005). Relationality and space have also been key in the suggestion to employ the term "transnational feminism" rather than "global feminism," which "conventionally . . . has stood for a kind of Western cultural imperialism" and which had simplistically assumed global sisterhood through universal oppression (Grewal and Kaplan 1994, 17). In addition to deconstructing the unified category of woman and taking account of the variety within and the overlaps between different forms of oppression, transnational feminism should emphasize the relation between the local, the national, and the global (Grewal and Kaplan 1994). Critical feminist approaches also emphasize the relationality between women in a global capitalist system *beyond* spatial distance. As Sara Ahmed has argued:

> The assumption of distance also involves a refusal to recognise the relationships of proximity between women who are differently located in the world. Western feminists are already in relationships with "third world women" given our implication in an international division of labour.... Women in different nation spaces, within a globalised economy of difference, cannot not encounter each other, what is at stake is *how*, rather than *whether*, the encounters take place. (2000b, 167)

Similarly, approaches in critical geography that draw on postcolonial theory argue that "the notion of distance gets altered as all of us are already implicated in each other's presents in complicated ways" (Raghuram, Madge, and Noxolo 2009, 9; cf. Massey 2004). While space, place, distance, and the related (moral) assumptions are clearly prominent themes, the "spatial turn" in research in the social sciences and humanities has been remarkably absent in development studies, as Lisa Smirl (2009) has argued (for an exception see Brown 2011). In this chapter, issues of space, place, and distance take center stage as I explore how the women NGO workers negotiated their relation with the women they supported across distance. I do so against the background of the assumptions about space and distance that are prominent in development discourse as outlined in the previous chapter and above, and draw on critical development approaches, global civil society theories, and emerging debates in geography on care and responsibility (Raghuram, Madge, and Noxolo 2009; McEwan and Goodman 2010; Noxolo, Raghuram, and Madge 2012). The first section of this chapter draws on research that discusses field trips, myths and stereotypes to interpret the women's accounts concerning ways to "deal with distance." In the second section of this chapter, I will suggest that Southern partner organizations, who are the intermediaries between organizations located in the global North and the "people on the ground," serve not only as a "bridge" but also become a "replacement" for the latter. I will look at how this "replacement strategy" plays out and problematizes elements of this partner relationship. In the final section of this chapter I will connect critiques of global civil society's claim to representative status to the women's narratives, in order to unpack the dilemmas that emerge in representation, consultation, and the facilitation of self-representation across and beyond distance.

FIELD VISITS AND STORIES

Studies that have explored the subjectivities of NGO workers have mostly concentrated on the positions of people in geographical proximity to the receivers of support and have therefore not addressed working across geographical distance (Eriksson Baaz 2005; Cook 2007; Charlés 2007; Heron 2007). In these studies proximity was based on the mobility of the aid workers, development practitioners, and volunteers rather than on the mobility of the Other. In this book, however, most of the relations between the women I interviewed and those they supported are articulated across spatial distance, in the case of organizations based in Brussels, Geneva, or other European capital cities. Where there was spatial proximity, this was based on the mobility of the Other as migrants to a country in the global North. The seemingly neutral term "mobility" should not hide the structurally embedded differences between the travel of aid workers to the global South and the journeys of migrants who access NGO services in the North.

Many of the women that I interviewed in capital cities in the global North who worked internationally had had at least some work experience in the global South prior to taking up their current role. I have analyzed in the previous chapter how the women explained their decision to choose a position where they were geographically removed from the beneficiaries despite a discourse that generally evaluated distance negatively. In the next two sections, I will further look into what they considered problematic about distance and the strategies they employed to bridge the distance that they perceived between themselves and the beneficiaries. This encompasses not just the logistical or communicative bridging of the distance, but also the psychological and emotional aspects of reaching across distance. Most of the women from international organizations in European capital cities stressed the importance of field trips for their work. In Magdalena Nowicka's study on the experiences of staff of an international organization, she found that "people desire to know a place through encountering it directly" (2005, 107). She reports that "all the interviewees speak about the need to see things personally" since "being in the country, travelling across it and meeting people ... are necessary to enable the interviewees to achieve satisfaction from work" (Nowicka 2005, 102; cf. Nowicka 2006). While Nowicka's findings are helpful in focusing on the desire of those who do international work and are based in the global North, this statement lacks reflection on the implications of travel and meeting people. Here I suggest turning to critical development scholarship, which has, for instance, problematized development field trips to the global South, in order to contextualize and assess the consequences of those desires.

Chambers has argued that "rural development tourism," by which he means field visits, provides the main source of information, "perceptions and misperceptions," about poor people for many development professionals (2006, 11). He identifies a number of "traps" related to rural field visits, one of which is "the headquarters and capital trap" caused by logistical obstacles (Chambers 2006, 8). For example, Beth, a London-based woman working for a global network advocating for HIV-positive women, told me that she always visits the same locations in the global South: the capital cities, where she is familiar with the café around the corner from the hotel, without knowing and seeing any other areas of the country. She experiences a stark contrast between her current work's field visits and her previous work as a volunteer for another organization when she lived for two years in the community she worked in, learned the local language, and built a social network.

Petra, a German woman who works in Brussels as a policy officer on gender and trade, explains why field visits are important for her:

> It is clear that if you work at a level like here, you are getting pretty far from reality.... If I am traveling and have that [situation of being closer to concrete contexts] from time to time, it makes a huge difference in the way you can learn and can perceive the situation, or reconsider or get insights and a better understanding. It depends on how open you are, but if you are, there you can perhaps hear much more than you were told or see other things which have not been communicated to you.

Petra stresses the value of field visits mainly in terms of the additional information one can extract when one is on the ground, which prevents one from getting too far removed from "reality" and which prompts one to reconsider certain viewpoints. At the same time, she states, "You don't have to be everywhere all the time"; rather, "You need to get in touch with a reality you are working with from time to time." Her stress on "*a* reality" rather than "the reality" could imply her awareness that her view remains partial and incomplete even when visiting the field, including, perhaps, a consciousness of the various ways in which these trips are "managed and manipulated" (Rajak and Stirrat 2011, 173). It could also mean that she considers most circumstances on the ground similar enough to be comparable. The notion of "reality" leaves intact the idea that there is something like a "reality." Feminists have, however, engaged with space and place in relation to knowledge production, advocating for a "politics of location," which should explicitly recognize the situatedness and therefore relative subjectivity of all knowledge (Grewal and Kaplan 1994).

Caroline, an experienced international project officer based in Copenhagen working on reproductive rights, echoes Petra's account when she answers my question whether field visits are important for her work: "Yeah, because otherwise it becomes too administrative here and because we have good discussions on what works, what doesn't work.... So I think it is important to be in the country and sit and discuss because in the meeting you give a lot of ideas. It is not the same by email. It is quite important."

Like Petra she stresses that there are certain things she will not be told when she is far away from the project in her main office: "They don't describe the full development in their reports to us, so it is important to come there."

Caroline is equally aware that even when coming to the country she is perceived as

> very much a donor, but I feel that I get a good discussion, because I have so much experience as I have. So I am very familiar, very experienced in the development administration, but they can also feel that I have a relatively good understanding on what to do when we discuss it. But there is no doubt that my visits are seen as donor visits.... I am the one issuing the money, so they will try to—they will sketch a favorable picture of their progress.

Here Caroline identifies what Chambers calls the "project bias" of field visits; the fact that donors are often taken to "the nicely groomed pet project or model village" where the successes of a particular project are clearly visible (Chambers 2008, 34). Chambers illustrates the problems he identifies with field visits and the pressure on those visited to give the "right" message by sketching an imaginary field visit:

> A self-conscious group ... dressed in their best clothes, are seen and spoken to. They nervously respond in ways which they hope will bring benefits and avoid penalties. There are tensions between the visitor's questions and curiosity, the officials' desire to select what is to be seen, and the mixed motives of different rural groups and individuals who have to live with the officials and with each other after the visitor has left. (2006, 16)

Whereas for Chambers it is important to demonstrate the flaws of field visit practices in order to develop better practices to "offset the biases"

(2006, 3), I claim that field visits serve a purpose for the women beyond their pure functionality as opportunity to gather information. This implies that it is necessary to shift our attention away from increasing field visits' effectiveness in getting to the truth about "reality" on the ground, to the desires that are at stake when people talk about field visits. It is interesting in the above narrative that Caroline claims to compensate what she perceives as a lack of transparency about the state of the project ("sketching a favorable picture"), because of her power position as a donor, with her experience and knowledge about the field ("I get a good discussion, because I have so much experience"). I suggest, in line with critical development approaches, an alternative reading in which her experience rather adds to her power position, and hence increases the power imbalance, leading to a less open dialogue.

Barbara Heron (2005), in an article on social workers' reflexivity about subjectivity, uses a Foucauldian framework to emphasize how subjects are constituted in power relations. She argues that "the constitutive effects of being in a structured position of power over other people would need to be examined," asking "what does this to her sense of self," and what kind of investment she has in maintaining a certain self-image (Heron 2005, 348). With Heron, I therefore propose to understand Caroline's recurrent emphasis on being experienced, which resurfaces in a statement quoted below, as revealing her investment in a self-image as a very experienced NGO worker. When left unacknowledged and unquestioned, this might prevent her from critically interrogating her position. The acknowledgment that she is in a donor position and that this will have an effect on the interaction still situates the power dynamics as "external" to her, namely as related to the organization she is working for rather than to herself. Instead, she presents her own qualities (being experienced) as compensating for this "external" situation.

Caroline says that the difficulties she can encounter as a donor when the partners tend to sketch a too favorable picture of the project are partly resolved when she interacts with partners in the South whom she identifies as similar to her:

> In some of these projects I have the advantage of dealing with women managers, and they are more or less the same age as me, and it makes it easier. Personality wise, we are quite similar, under such different circumstances. They have taken part in these discussions for so many years. We are at the same phase, more or less; they have been developing in their organizations, had a lot of exposure to European countries. It is quite easy, I feel.

This account is testimony to the transnational connections forged in decades of gender and development as well as the significance of feminist generations, as discussed in chapter 2. It also hints at the importance of partners in relation to field visits specifically and in bridging distance more generally, which will be discussed and analyzed in the next section.

Both Caroline and Petra are in a position where they can choose which field visits they wish to make. Caroline stresses:

> I am a very experienced consultant, so I decide myself what kind of visits should I go on. I Should go and see the target group, should I focus on capacity building at the partners, or how do I involve the embassy? Because of my experience I have the freedom to do what I like, and I find that very interesting. Sometimes I do this and sometimes I do that.

From this account it becomes clear that experience indeed comes with the power of selecting whom and what to see and do on a field visit; this authority of selection will be further discussed in the next section of this chapter. These "targeted visits" might on the one hand be more productive but on the other hand contain the risk of overlooking fields and projects that are not on the radar of the specific representative. While Petra and Caroline are experienced staff members with exposure to the countries they work in, Lucia is a young woman in her first paid position in an international organization. Her work targets women in Africa, and she had never been to an African country prior to starting to work for the organization. Since she has visited some African countries now in the context of her work, I asked whether these visits changed her perception of her work or of the women who are the target group of her organization. She replied:

> No, from the moment I started having responsibility here, I started being committed. I am a very responsible person and because I really like what I do, I am very committed and it does not change the fact that I see the people or that I don't see them. It is better now that I know them and now that I see the project moving forward, but it doesn't change anything.

It is noticeable that Lucia understands my question about distance and proximity to be indicative of a certain mistrust on my side concerning her commitment, as she immediately stresses her dedication. Her answer responds to what critical geographer Doreen Massey has identified as a "hegemonic geography of . . . responsibility which takes the form of a nested set of Russian dolls." This assumes that a feeling of responsibility correlates with proximity and that therefore a sense of responsibility for "distant others" only comes secondarily, as opposed to those who have direct contact with target groups (Massey 2004, 9). For Susanne, who works in the global North with refugee women, this hegemonic geography of responsibility is pertinent when she emphasizes that face-to-face contact and personal stories have a very different and much stronger effect than images of refugees on television. Susanne:

> You know about refugees broadly, . . . but your image of refugees is more television viewing, you have seen these vast refugee camps in Sudan or Pakistan. . . . Once you get involved . . ., getting to know people . . . you realize the suffering that these people had. I think that's what has changed for me, the understanding of loss that these people have had.

It is remarkable that Lucia stresses that it does not matter in her work whether she has ever met the people she is supporting, while at the same time she states that "it is better now that I know them." Later in the interview, Lucia indicates she would like to visit the particular conflict-ridden region that is the location of a few projects she coordinates. She explains that initially she did not want to visit the region, as she was afraid of violence, "but I would like to go, to see the things that I am working on, that I have heard of from these women, but that I have not seen with my own eyes." When I ask her whether a visit would be important for her work, Lucia says: "Yes, for my work, but also for me as a person, to see how a human being can treat another human being, what terrible things people can do, but how there are still people that have hope."

Whereas she acknowledges that seeing the situation on the ground could enhance the quality of her work practices, Lucia considers the visit more important as a "life lesson" for herself (cf. Roth 2006). For Lucia, the field visit is not central to her credibility as a committed NGO worker. Rather it is seen as enabling her to gain more experiences for self-development, inspired by a "voyeurism" that characterizes unequal relations, as discussed in the introduction of this book (Hill Collins 1993, 42).

Mediated Stories

Field visits were just one of the strategies that the women employed to make sense of their work in the face of geographical distance. Fieldwork experiences and stories do not merely remain with the person who collected them, but travel further. I therefore argue that in order to understand what happens with fieldwork experiences, it is important to gain insight not only into the circumstances under which field visits are conducted, but also how these experiences get communicated and taken up. I asked Sandra, another young woman, how she maintains a link with the "beneficiaries" of her work, in the context of the geographical distance between them. Sandra worked shortly for the foreign ministry before taking up her advocacy role in relation to reproductive rights for her current international membership organization in a Western capital city. She responds at first by saying that this is the main problem in her position because she works on a very abstract level with human rights documents. Then she continues: "I deal with it by trying to meet with our international program staff, and I try to get their stories. These are of course only their stories. And then when I am in the countries in the developing world, I try to get as many 'stories' as possible."

Andrea Cornwall, Elizabeth Harrison, and Ann Whitehead (2007) focus on the production of "myths" in fundraising, but I suggest here that the notion of myths resonates strongly with Sandra's strategy in advocacy. The term "myth" does not imply that the stories told are necessarily untrue. Rather, what makes stories myths is "the way in which they encode the ways of that world in a form that resonates with the things that people would like to believe, that gives them the power to affect action" (Cornwall et al. 2007, 5). In line with the gendered frames discussed in chapter 2, women of the global South appear in these "myths" of the development discourse "as abject victims, the passive subjects of development's rescue, and as splendid heroines, whose unsung virtues and whose contribution to development need to be heeded" (Cornwall et al. 2007, 4). Sandra uses the term "stories" rather than "myths," as she is referring to what people in the countries of the developing world have told her about their lives, their needs, and their circumstances. Often the stories that Sandra uses are mediated, as she also collects the stories from her colleagues, who work as international program staff. In this process of mediation, of choosing what is told and not told to Sandra, and subsequently selected or left out by Sandra, stories can become "myths." Keith Brown (2011) applies the terms "virtual" and "actual" to understand the dynamics and relations of aid chains across distance. His insistence that the virtual and actual need to be understood as mutually constitutive, with the virtual—for example, a project plan based on a particular image of "the field"—having real, actual effects, is helpful in understanding that "myths" interact with "real" NGO practices and experiences.

When I asked Sandra how she maintained a link with the people she advocates on behalf of, I was initially interested in how she motivates herself when she is far away from her target group, in the way that Joan in the previous chapter suggested that she plans to move away from Brussels back to the field to regenerate her motivation. Sandra, however, indicates that when she calls the distance "the main problem of my work," her concern is only partly her (lack of) motivation when dealing with abstract documents rather than with "real people." Rather, Sandra says:

> I think my worry is more that I am not telling the truth, basically, for example when we talk about the access to condoms and we say there is a lack of access to condoms. And then I met a guy from Uganda and he said, "There is no lack of access to condoms." In his experience, in his community "We have condoms everywhere." [But] now we say there is a lack of access to condoms, [so] don't go around and spread that. So that of course is like, "How do I know that I communicate the reality?" That is a problem. Absolutely!

Here Sandra recognizes the risk that the passing on of stories by colleagues could result in a Chinese whispering situation where the "real meaning" of the testimony and the intention of the informant get lost. Or the "truth" on the ground is misrepresented, "created in the image of the grievance we understand" (Kennedy 2004, xxiii) and "construct[ed as] a world of fantasy that suits politicians" (Eyben 2007b, 38). It is also important to consider here that the storytellers on the ground function only as informants, rather than as partners who share their own perceptions and analysis, as we have seen in Caroline's and Petra's accounts (Eade 2007).

This interview fragment also evokes the question how often (and on what basis) Sandra will update her stories. Indeed, she asks herself that question after telling me about the refutation of the lack-of-access-to-condoms story. At the same time, the exclamation "Don't go around and spread that" (there is no lack of access to condoms) can be understood as a silencing of countermessages that undermine the message her organization seeks to disseminate. Here we can identify a resistance toward revising stories if conflicting accounts do not sit nicely with the stated goals of an organization; the testimonies are needed to give the organization legitimacy. Hence, "the use of particular representations of those whom development seeks to assist are worked into 'story-lines' that come not only to frame, but also to legitimize particular kinds of intervention and forms of knowledge" (Cornwall et al. 2007, 6). At the same time, it rightly or wrongly implies that her organization has better knowledge about the situation on the ground than the people themselves, whose stories function as mere illustration.

Sandra's reliance on selected stories can on the other hand be justified for its strategic use, as policymakers are "likely to be more easily influenced by sound-bite-style headlines, which pressures NGO workers into providing those catchy quotes" (Cornwall and Fujita 2007, 51). Gayatri Spivak (1990) has proposed a "strategic essentialism," a strategic form of identity politics that entails a provisional simplification and homogenization of reality in order to achieve a desired goal. Sandra also recognizes this when she says: "Since I work with advocacy my work is very much linked to hitting emotions of people, and then personal stories become very vital. If I want decision-makers to focus more on sexual and reproductive health, I need to talk about that taxi driver that I mentioned or the young people that I meet." As I have discussed in chapter 2 in relation to the strategic use of gender stereotypes, there is a risk that such strategies to break down inequalities merely reinforce the logics underpinning them. Spivak, after witnessing how "strategic essentialism" quickly became a widely adopted phrase, serving merely as "the union ticket for essentialism," subsequently decided to refrain from using the term (Spivak 1993, 35).

As Chambers has noted, the effect of the international career system with its incentive schemes is that successful development professionals are promoted to urban and international centers away from rural areas (cf. Verma 2011). The result is that those who end up high in the hierarchies of development organizations often base their policies and visions on previous experiences in the "field." Gisela, who works in Brussels for a feminist network on development, manages issues with distance from the target groups of her work by tapping into her experiences from an earlier job. When I ask her whether she meets the women in the global South that she has described to me earlier in the interview, she responds:

> Yes, although I have to say, this is also an office were we have a lot of things on our plate, so we don't always have the time to go into depth with someone. There are limitations to that. But I think it helped me that before joining this organization, in my previous youth organization, the international one, I have done some conferences, for instance, organizing one in India, co-organizing one in Uganda, and I made a lot of contacts there and also some friends. So I know more of these regions and I have an idea how it works there. And I have been there, that also helps.

While she suggests that the work pressure in her organization does not allow her much contact with people on the ground, at this point Gisela does not problematize drawing for current work practices on past experiences with a different organization. However, later in the interview Gisela stresses: "If you are working on North–South relations, you should have had some time in the South. Because otherwise I don't think you can be an efficient policy officer in the North." She indicates that if she continues working in the area of development, she will have to work in the South: "I would need this experience for me. I think, morally, I would need it to justify that I work in that area."

For Gisela, in contrast to Lucia, experience in the global South is tied to her own sense of integrity and credibility in her NGO work. For her, her past experiences have an expiry date. Right now she feels it is justifiable to base her work on previous rather than current contacts and on memories of the field, but in the long term this would be "morally" untenable. Similarly, Leah, who is now based in a Northern European city, but who has worked in the global South before, speaks of the freshness of experiences, which passes after a while.

> I think all of us working in this department have past experiences of working in the field, and I think somehow you rely on that. But that's fresh; it is something that goes away, the feeling of it goes away. So you have to renew it and we know that, we know that we have to travel. Otherwise we will become bitter and depressed.

For Leah, who works for a development aid organization, and for other women in similar positions, the experience of being closer to the contexts that her work addresses is important for motivation, as she feels that change is more easily observed there. Leah's personal circumstances (becoming a mother of two children since she started the job) have prevented her from renewing her experience in the global South. She employs an interesting strategy to compensate for her current lack of possibilities to witness positive change abroad, by drawing on experiences much closer to home:

> I work in a women's shelter here as a volunteer, and I think that has proven to be very helpful for me because that is very, very practical and it is the kind of work where I meet the actual women that have been raped or beaten up. And I can see, meet someone that is changing, so sometimes I feel that I get that there when I don't get it in my work.

Leah emphasizes how her volunteer work gives her face-to-face contact and proximity to change, which is lacking in her formal employment in the field of international development. I propose to understand this as a "replacement strategy": it addresses the lack of practical "hands-on" fieldwork and direct contact with the beneficiaries by shifting the focus from the distant Other to a more accessible group. How this "replacement strategy" functions will be discussed in further detail in the next section.

PARTNER ORGANIZATIONS AS BENEFICIARIES

As I will elaborate in this section, the "replacement strategy" was the most dominant approach among the women for bridging the distance between the target of work and the place of work. In contrast to the example of Leah, who draws on her volunteer experiences in the global North, I argue that most often this took the form of Southern partner organizations serving not only as a "bridge" to, but also as a "replacement" for the target group. While the focus of this section is on the *perceptions* of the women concerning the role of their organizational partners in reaching out across distance, it is imperative to embed this analysis in the structural context of partnerships, as discussed in critical development and postcolonial literature. Since partner organizations can be tasked with the "receiving and entertaining" of visiting representatives of Northern organizations and the provision of "stories and pictures" (Eade 2007, 636; Hudock 1999, 9), there is an evident connection between field visits and stories, as discussed in the previous section, and partnerships.

Many Northern NGOs relate to beneficiaries through a chain of Southern NGOs, who are described as "partners" (Stirrat and Henkel 1997). The notion of "partnership," which came to prominence as a response to critiques of development aid in the 1990s, suggests a more equal relationship, rather than the asymmetric relationship of giver and receiver of funding. Postcolonial theory and critical development theory have criticized the seemingly attractive notion of "partnership" between Northern and Southern NGOs. With many other critics, Stirrat and Henkel note that "partnership is a peculiarly ambiguous concept" (1997, 75; cf. Hudock 1999; Power 2009; Baillie Smith and Laurie 2011). By implying equality and a break with colonial relations, it masks ongoing unequal (paternalistic) power relationships, "the same paternalism the South started to know when Portuguese navigators first sailed down the coast of West Africa" (Smillie 2000, 185). Patricia Noxolo (2006) has traced the historical roots of the concept of "partnership" for development to the pre–First World War British imperial discourse.

One way in which the asymmetry of power between Northern NGOs and Southern partner organizations is expressed is that Northern organizations are often in the position to choose their partners, which logically results in a selection of partners with similar aims. This "donor 'cherry-picking,' treating NGOs like a buffet lunch, taking what they like and leaving the rest," means that Southern NGOs have to spend considerable time writing funding proposals, that they cannot be certain of long-term continuation of funding, and that they have to survive delays in decision-making and money-transferring processes (Smillie 2000, 185). The result of this structure is a weakening rather than a strengthening of Southern NGOs. However, as Eyben (2006) points out, it is important to realize that the binary of donor-recipient obscures the fact that many organizations (including some of the Northern organizations the women that I interviewed worked for) both receive and donate money.

Having presented the contours of the structural critique of partnership relations between Northern and Southern organizations as discussed in critical literature, I will now discuss how partnership figures in the interview accounts, paying particular attention to the aspects of funding, the donor's selection strategies, the burden on partners, and the ambivalences of participation. Many of the women stated that their main contact was with the partner organizations rather than with the beneficiaries of their projects. For example, when I ask Stacey in Geneva whether she has contact with the people who eventually benefit from the projects of her organization in the field of health, she says: "Do I have a direct contact with them? Do I have direct connection? Yes, sometimes. In a mission there is always opportunity for direct contact. The people that I meet though on mission tend to be other partners." Caroline in Copenhagen states: "Right now I am working with other NGO partners . . . and I relate to them, to the partners, not necessarily to the target group in the streets of Uganda or in a hilly environment in Vietnam."

Leah who works on gender in policy perspectives in another European capital city reacts thus:

> Not that much, no. I mean our primary strategy, what we are interested in, is effects in the target groups and in the partner organizations. The whole focus is to work with civil society organizations, but of course at the end of the day what concerns us is that it has some effect on the target group. But we have chosen here to work mainly through the [national] organizations and their partner organizations, which means that our team, we sort of rely on a chain that works. We are not sure all the time how well it works, but we rely on that somehow to work.

Anne-Meike Fechter (2011) has noted that national employees of Southern partner organizations can be seen as beneficiaries, since the work might provide them with new opportunities for developing their careers. In her study on Western humanitarian organizations, Krause shows that partner organizations in the global South are presented as "worthy beneficiaries" in order to justify channeling money in their direction (Krause 2014, 55). While both these observations are helpful in understanding how partner organizations come to be understood as beneficiaries, my argument here takes a different direction, focusing on the function that partners serve in bridging the geographical and psychological or emotional distance that the women need to negotiate. Leah's response betrays some doubts about whether the long "chain" from her organization to national organizations, to partners, and finally to beneficiaries always functions. At the same time, as she says, she needs to rely on this chain to work. Eyben aptly suggests the figure of a "web" instead of a chain to capture "the diversity and complexity of networks and connections of power" between different organizations that are partnered in the aid system (Eyben 2006, 2).

Anna, a consultant in Brussels working on promoting a gender perspective in constitutional reform, similarly expresses discomfort about the lack of direct relation with the beneficiaries of the project:

> I am just trying to think about whether I feel . . . I feel responsibility towards [my organization], I feel less responsibility for the—I can't believe I am admitting this—but I feel less responsibility for the recipients of the project. But I feel responsibility towards the national partners. And so I feel that somehow I feel responsibility towards them, and they in some way take on the mantle of responsibility towards the people. Because I think on some level, it is just impossible for me to feel connected to each recipient.

For Anna, the question of the relation between her and the "recipients," as she calls them, is not only about whether her work is effective when it is mediated through many different parties (as in Leah's account), but it is one of responsibility. There is an interesting shift between "responsibility *for*" the recipients toward "responsibility *towards*" the national partners. She states that she feels more responsibility towards them, and while she tells me this, she expresses her uneasiness with that orientation both through her hesitations and through her insertion of "I can't believe I am admitting this." Anna justifies her lack of feeling of responsibility for the recipients by arguing that it is impossible to feel connected across vast distance to people she might either never or only fleetingly meet, reflecting Massey's (2004) previously quoted observation that a hegemonic conception of responsibility takes a nested form, with the feeling of responsibility correlating with proximity. Anna continued questioning herself and her choice to work in a place geographically removed from the "field" and noted that she must feel a degree of guilt about it as she otherwise would not try so hard to explain "why I do what I do." The justifications offered by women who work from Northern capital cities for international organizations in the context of a discourse that negatively evaluates distance have been analyzed in the previous chapter.

As has been discussed above, Caroline expresses confidence in her own dealings with partner organizations because of her experience:

> I am quite familiar with NGO partners in Africa, in Asia, not these particular partners, but in general. I have so many communications, relationships with this type of partners. . . . It does not mean that I know them deeply at heart, but I am quite familiar with this working relationship.

Here she perceives her partners not necessarily in terms of their specific identity or needs but rather in terms of their common status "as partners." Hence Caroline emphasizes the nature of the working relationship, which she feels is very familiar to her through her experience, over the aims or the quality of the partner organization itself.

Her initial confidence is disrupted when she continues to problematize this relation, joining the other women who have expressed their ambivalence about partnerships, "basically, because there is a constant schism within development work, because you are at the same time a donor with a strong employer identity, but you are also a political partner in development work as such. And this conflict is the main conflict in this type of work." On the one hand, Casey identifies the asymmetric power dimension in the relation with the partners, as she remains the donor, while on the other hand, politically, she views the partner organizations as allies in a common struggle. She even calls this the "main conflict" in the work. I suggest reading Casey's statement with Stirrat and Henkel's argument that the gift is central to the inequality in the relation between Northern (donor) organizations and Southern organizations on the receiving end. They state:

> The gift creates a series of problematic relations, frequently ambiguous in terms of their meaning and often paradoxical in terms of their implications. Most notably, while the gift is given in ways that attempt to deny difference

and assert identity between the rich giver and the poor receiver, a gift in practice reinforces or even reinvents these differences. (Stirrat and Henkel 1997, 69)

The contaminating power of the gift, the idea that the "gift" "reinforces" or "reinvents" differences and inequalities, rather than that these inequalities are present a priori, is underlined by Korf's observation that "Gift" means "poison" in the German language. That is, "gift giving can be a double-edged sword" (Korf 2007, 367). Whereas the term "partners" maintains a degree of ambiguity in relation to the power relations, the term "donor" leaves no doubt about who is at the giving and more powerful end of the relation. However, as Maria Eriksson Baaz rightly stresses, the language of partnership, instead of that of donors and receivers, "does not, of course, imply a reversal of the economic conditions characteristic of the aid relationship" (2005, 75).

Petra, a policy officer in Brussels, joins Casey in her awareness of how money influences the power dynamic of partnerships. Hence, she expresses that she feels fortunate that she does not decide on funding allocation:

> Now, I am in a bit of a privileged position because we are not giving money to any of the partners we are dealing with. So the funding issue is out [of that relationship]. Because I would say, as soon as you have money and funds, it is clear that you have a different position. And the demanding partner can be quite self-confident and know what to do, but as a matter of fact the imbalance is there, because of the dependency on that money.... So what I see with colleagues who are in the position of doing funding, they are in a privileged position because they are important, because they have the money, so you have to credit them, so a partner will relate differently to someone who is their funding-relating partner than to someone else.

Significantly, Petra attributes the word "privilege" both to the position of not having to give out funding and to the position where one does issue funding. She deliberately chooses to use the word "privileged" in the first instance in a counterintuitive way; being privileged here means having less money and thus power and therefore being less entangled in hierarchical relations. However, her second use of the word "privilege" slips back in the conventional use of the term to indicate (funding) power and status. She continues to explain that because she does not issue funding, she could "perhaps engage in a more frank dialogue" with her partners, as they are not forced to take her suggestions on board, in a way that they would more likely be if there were money at stake.

Ruth's organization is not a donor, since it does not get any structural national governmental funding because of its feminist, radical, nonmainstream agenda in the field of reproductive rights. Similar to Petra's ambivalent use of the term "privilege," Ruth uses "luck" in contradictory ways to indicate that the advantage of not getting funding is that their organization is positioned outside the funding competition. Ruth: "Well, we are lucky in that sense that it is really hard to get funding. Well, it is not lucky. I mean of course we are not lucky, but government funding, we never got it and we will never get it, because it is much too controversial what we are doing."

As a consequence of their own weak financial situation, the relation between Ruth's organization and their partner organizations is one where they support their partner organizations with fundraising, diminishing the financial dependency power relation between the Northern and the Southern organizations. Ruth:

> I am not giving them my money . . . and that is nice because they don't have to pay responsibility to me. They have to do it [in relation to] the funders and not to me and I help them; I know the funders so I can [help them]. . . . And that makes it more equal as well. They don't have to say, "You gave us $10,000, this is what we did with it." No, I don't care as long as we have an agreement; this is your responsibility to pay for that, that's our responsibility to pay for this.

This can be contrasted with the position of Isabel, who leads a small international organization in Vienna in the field of gender and security. Her organization is in the position to give the partner organization some funding, and has a policy that if a Southern partner receives money from them,

> they must [also] get involved in fundraising [in their own country]. There is no reason why the countries should not be interested in these issues, so they should be targeted and when they realize that there is [a] co-sponsor, it is an important process, an empowerment process, and whenever you do projects now, everyone asks for cofunding. This is the new world: nobody will give you the full amount anymore.

I suggest that the discourses of dependency and independence (or autonomy) are simultaneously articulated here. On the one hand, it is only by virtue of partners' dependency on their funding that the Northern NGO can compel the Southern partner to seek complementary funding. On the other hand, this is clouded in the language of empowerment: partners should be enabled to get additional funding. This language of partnership and empowerment does not address the power difference between Northern and Southern organizations, in which Northern partner organizations play the role of "disciplinarian" and "provider" of the infantilized Southern partner organization (Noxolo 2006, 260). Strikingly, Isabel equates the countries' "interest in these issues" with ability and willingness to provide funding. Finally, when Isabel says that "this is the new world" in which full funding is no longer provided, she diminishes the differences in position between, for instance, Northern and Southern organizations. This is also expressed in her idea that "there should be no reason" why countries in the South should not be interested in the proposed projects, which ignores specific local contexts. While the notions of partnerships and capacity building of Southern organizations originated from a left-wing political tradition, nowadays, in what Isabel has called "the new world," they are often used to advance a "neo-liberal 'pull-yourself-up-by-your-bootstraps' … economic and political agenda" (Eade 2007, 632). It is important for organizations who use this partnership rhetoric to be conscious of how these competing agendas play out and to realize that the problems that occur in the relationship between Southern and Northern NGOs are "essentially political, not organizational" (Hudock 1999, 31).

Partners and Performance

Isabel states that her organization "always look[s] for strong partners in the region." Southern NGOs have become increasingly important in the development process because of assumptions that "they are 'closer to the people' and share a common culture with those who are to benefit from the activities supported by Northern NGOs" (Stirrat and Henkel 1997, 74). Thus ideas of connection are here based on assumed "sameness" of identity rather than on, for example, shared political goals. By "strong" Isabel means that the partner is experienced and well connected both with the international and the grass-roots levels. The procedures and criteria for selecting partners or members of a network used by powerful organizations, like Isabel's organization, are not without criticism. The EWL has, for example, been condemned by Czech women NGOs for taking an "exclusive and monopolistic" position, which it can afford because of its privileged status (Hašková 2005, 1103). They have argued that the EWL, with its "power to select," excluded feminist organizations with a different perspective on sex work than the abolitionist perspective taken by EWL, while inviting marginal players in the Czech context who are not representative of the Czech women's movement to join the network. In spite of this criticism, the EWL's powerful position led some organizations to sign up for membership nevertheless. As one staff member from a Czech women's NGO pointed out: "We are a bit skeptical about the organization, but we want to be members from the practical point of view. It is better to be in than to be out" (Hašková 2005, 1103). It is important to imagine similar "other sides of the story" when reading the women's narratives about the selection of partners for their own programs and networks.

Like Isabel, Luisa, who works on gender and peace from Geneva, links the issue of working through partnerships with selecting partners: "I think that it is true that this organization does not fully, directly work with grass-roots women; we work with women through the women that we have selected first."

She then continues:

> I think that is also because it is for them to be able to talk to each other better. Like we are at a level probably because of our education that we can talk directly to these women that we have invited.... But maybe it would be more difficult for us to talk to the others [at the grass-roots]. So it is through the [women we invite] that we have to reach the others.
> Interviewer: So the people you are talking to are some kind of mediators almost?
> Luisa: Yes, yes. There are people that can talk to the grass-roots level and at the same time can come here and talk to [highly placed politicians].

Petra similarly argues:

> Because in the lobbying advocacy process you need people who are both; they have to be part of, and distinguished from, their group to be really able to say something valuable or new here. Because if they would only be very closely linked to their context or their broader group and then you put them here in the context [and] you have a policy discussion or debate and there is a particular question which is new to the person, [because] they have different policy debates back home, you would need a person—
> Interviewer: —that can travel both contexts?
> Petra: Yes, they can reflect for themselves and think and give the appropriate answer.... So you might try and spot these people who can [do this].

First, Luisa's use of the word "them" signals a homogenization of people in the global South. At the same time, Luisa distinguishes within this group by arguing that a selected few have the capacity to be in a brokering position between those marginalized in the global South and the political and NGO elite in the global North. What is interesting is that despite Luisa's observation that she and her colleagues might be largely unable to communicate directly with those at the grass-roots, her organization remains the unquestioned center. While Luisa recognizes the qualities of their partners in the global South, she continues to defend the existence of her organization by asserting that the "women on the ground" do not have stable structures, do not have the tools to report back to donors, to design and implement projects, and to lobby the UN, as they lack consultative status. If Northern NGOs continue advocating on behalf of Southern partners, the danger is that the capacities of the Southern partners are diminished to speak on their own terms (Eade 2007). This is reinforced by the fact that Northern NGOs, aided by their good connections and cultural capital, continue to be seen as the most reliable providers of knowledge. As Uma Kothari (2005, 428) argues, the "intellectual distance between donor and recipient" is sustained and the status of donors and expatriate development consultants is maintained through (the constant reinvention of) cultural capital, such as forms of professionalism and experience with new "fashions" in development (such as participatory approaches).

The unquestioned assumption of the centrality of Luisa's organization, for which "issues of communication" need to be resolved, also becomes apparent in that she does not question *why* her organization can demand to work with partners that can "translate" between the two communities and discourses. In Petra's account we can see the same dynamic, where her organization is in the position to select those who "can reflect for themselves and think and give the appropriate answer." In order to be regarded as "contributing something valuable," partners are required to both "be part of, and distinguished from their group." This finds a striking parallel in the findings from two studies on NGOs who support migrants in the global North: first, an in-depth empirical study on migrant and ethnic minority staff in Austrian, Dutch, and British NGOs, who support migrants in their work (de Jong 2016b), and second, a focused discourse analysis of media articles about a Vienna-based project that recruits migrant women as bridges between Austrian majority society and migrant communities (de Jong 2015). There I have argued that migrant and ethnic minority staff are expected to be "exemplary figures," who share their identity with "their" community but are distinct from "their" community by virtue of exceptional traits. I have proposed that these staff members can be seen as contemporary "cultural brokers," sharing similar "desirable" qualities with colonial cultural brokers who were selected to mediate between settlers or colonizers and indigenous communities (de Jong 2015; de Jong 2016b). I suggest that we see a very similar dynamic concerning the role that Southern partners are expected to adopt and the qualifications that are deemed to make them suitable for this position. In the words of postcolonial scholar Homi Bhabha, they need to be "a reformed, recognizable Other, as *a subject of a difference that is almost the same, but not quite*" (1984, 126). This also means that they carry a double burden, unlike organizations in the North.

This signals a wider issue of the demands placed upon partner organizations, which in many cases are short staffed and have few resources. It reflects a peculiar relation in which Northern organizations are often dependent on partner organizations for credibility and "translation" of the needs of women "on the ground," while at the same time their power (sometimes directly expressed in financial power) means that they can place demands on their partners. For example, Catherine in Brussels recognizes this in relation to her organization's national partners working on various gender policy fields:

> The big problem is that they are very busy, so they work at the national level and then we come to ask them for more work. It is really—like we send papers and ask them to comment or ask them to send amendments, and that is really a lot of work. So that can be really difficult, and you have to go back to people several times and respect the fact that they have a lot to do and have little resources et cetera. So that can be challenging sometimes.

Gill, also in Brussels, working in the field of gender, development, and trade, is even more specific than Catherine in her evaluation of her demands and the burden that it puts on the partner organizations in the South:

> I mean, it is very easy for me to get a little bit frustrated at home—"I need this information now from my volunteer in the South, and why doesn't he deliver or why do I get it in a way that I don't understand?"—without really having an understanding of the kind of struggles he or she has to deal with and the difficulties of living there. I mean I know a little bit of this picture, but I think I will need more of this picture to really understand how it is for them to really work in this situation, what are the struggles really, and then it is more easier, I think, to assist them or to collaborate with them in a North–South relation.

Petra stresses the need for learning in the relation with partners:

> If it is a new partner, ... you have to learn about the person, how that person is setting a situation and how flexible they are, and how ideological maybe, or how nonpolitical. What is their mandate or their internal constraints, how far can they go? And I think the better one is understanding the realities of the different actors and accepting that there are different constraints and different flexibilities, the easier you can construct or do something together.

Nicole in Geneva, working with member organizations as partners on women's empowerment, learned about her partners' realities and constraints the "hard way." In order to situate her narration, it is important to keep in mind that not all Northern NGOs choose their partner organizations in the same way, as she explains:

> You know we are different from many global humanitarian organizations or global NGOs who basically pick and choose who their country-level partners are. You know, the Oxfams of this world decide who they want to work with. So they choose the best of the bunch, and if for some reason they are not meeting their reporting standards or whatever, they can just drop them and move on to someone else, whereas we work with our member associations. So that gives a different set of challenges, you know. ... We don't have authority to be able to say, "This is mother [organization's name omitted] talking, and you must do this."

Nicole worked with a partner organization that is operating under a dictatorship in an African country. Her own organization had supported this partner in the South to train women to become election observers. It had also created a platform for them to speak in Geneva about gender-based violence in their country. This partner organization "had the police come in and raid their hostel, and they gathered all the women there, took them to the bus station, and told them to go home." After the elections were won by the ruling party and the dictator remained in his position, the office in Geneva found out that their partner organization on the ground had written a public letter to congratulate the authoritarian ruler. Nicole reflects:

> So that was a case where you know that did not work out so well, because it then also puts us in a bit of a tricky situation. But that also shows the constraints in which they are working, you know. ... While you can think you are all on the same page working for something, that is not always the case. ... If they had said, "You know, in order for us to survive we need to play the game and send something to both sides," then we at least would know, but

we just happened to find out about it, because someone spotted it through an Internet search.

All four narratives quoted here show that the women are aware of the difficult circumstances partner organizations are faced with. However, I suggest that the interviewed women do not fundamentally question the chain or web of partnerships that they rely on. Moreover, I propose that the women who speak here mostly situate the constraints the partners face as located elsewhere, rather than as an inherent part of their relationship. This is most obvious in the narration by Nicole, who had wished that her partner organization had prewarned her about its congratulatory letter, without reflection on the reasons for its silence. Research among Kenyan and Zimbabwean NGOs and their Northern partners found that there was a discrepancy between the ways in which they viewed the partner relationship, with the Southern organizations being much less content than the organizations in the North (research by Carmen Malena quoted in Smillie 2000). In her book *The Paternalism of Partnership* Maria Eriksson Baaz puts this succinctly: "Partners are urged to articulate their needs and goals as if there were no stakes involved. This is, of course, not the case. There are stakes involved, which, among other things, concern access to, or potential access to, economic resources" (2005, 74).

The women sometimes downplayed and at other times acknowledged the tension between the partnership logic that implied a relationship of equality, and the silences of the partners vis-à-vis their more powerful donors or Northern organizations. The example of Gill in Brussels, who described the women working for Southern partner organizations in their network as empowered, capable, and strong, illustrates this. She considers it "good to enable them to go to meetings and offer support, [but] we are helping each other. It is not like we are helping them, it is both ways." Gill places a lot of faith in the organization's network structure as a means to erode North–South power relations:

> You try to build enduring relations with the people in the network. Because they all share the same political vision, they work on the same issues, I think you can then create a collective identity. So then—I mean I don't know what they have thought before they entered that process—but definitely then they see [my organization] also just as partner and not in this North–South division.

Later in our conversation, however, Gill tells me that one of the main challenges she would like to address in her work is to encourage the partner organizations to take more "ownership" of the network. Gill: "Of course time is an issue, also that they feel there is a competence here, that they don't feel, maybe, that their ideas will be that good or that they will be that competent to really contribute, or also that they are not the persons that will really do the implementation." This means that the same women who she called capable, strong, and empowered are at the same time uncertain concerning their competence to contribute. Instead of attributing this contradiction to Gill's personal incoherence, I argue that this contradiction is indicative of the ambivalent discourse on partnerships between Northern and Southern organizations as being equal and unequal at the same time. This was earlier expressed in Isabel's narration about partner organizations "being forced to be empowered through own fundraising."

Anna, who is also in Brussels, and is currently working with partners from Eastern Europe on women's political participation, equally discusses this tension. She more explicitly acknowledges the power dynamics at stake:

> I mean there are downsides as well. The downsides, I would say, are when you focus very much on the sort of participatory approach, . . . you sometimes can get project proposals which sort of just mirror the language that [my organization] would use. And it is hard to know where the national partners' real thoughts are, because what they are putting in there is more a reflection of what [my organization] is putting out there from the start.

Here it is clear that the partners feel under pressure to produce what they expect that the Northern funding organization would like to hear. Charles Elliott describes the "dialogue" between partners as "a dialogue of the unequal" that is characterized by a "reality . . . that the donor can do to the recipient what the recipient cannot do to the donor" (1987, 65). He also stresses, with the term "well-intentioned dialogue" (Elliott 1987, 65), that rather than bad intentions, the issue at stake is the deeply embedded power inequalities, which cannot simply be eradicated by goodwill, as could be seen in the case of Gill. Many Southern partner organizations have developed strategies to deal with the demands of the donor without fundamentally changing their own way of working, for example by using the "right" language (Elliott 1987), or perhaps, in the case of Nicole's membership organization, which operates under dictatorship, by deciding not to inform its Northern partner organization about its letter in support of the authoritarian ruler.

Earlier, Catherine and Gill both presented some discomfort in having to ask the partners to fulfill certain tasks. I propose that the fact that Southern organizations do not always immediately "deliver" (for example, because of their financial limitations, their shortage of staff, or reliance on volunteers) further demonstrates the dependency of the Northern organizations on the Southern organizations: as they told me, the delay causes "frustrations" and "problems"; it is "really difficult" and "challenging." Gill works in a secretariat that is the focal point of a worldwide network. She speaks about the importance of the partners in legitimizing the actions and policy proposals of the secretariat: "Especially in advocacy work, of course, if you don't have organizations in the South fighting against [a] free trade agreement, who are we? It is, of course, good to have Northern NGOs say also, 'Yeah, that is really bad,' but you need the South. It's as simple as that."

As Gill points out, Southern partner organizations are needed to legitimize the work of Northern (donor) organizations. In the mid-1980s Northern development NGOs faced an "identity crisis" when the intervention of Northern development workers on the ground was questioned. This resulted in the introduction of new concepts such as accountability and participation, as well as an increasing number of partnerships between Northern and Southern NGOs (Smillie 2000). In summary, it has become clear from the above accounts that partnerships are not only essential for the legitimacy of organizations and as sources of information, but also, in fact, as sources of motivation for the women I interviewed, who lack direct contact with so-called beneficiaries, in other words, for bridging different forms of distance between the "office" and the "field." Hence, the analysis above suggests two things: there is an obvious *mutual* dependency between organizations in partnership, but this mutuality does not result in a fundamental equality between organizations. Acknowledgment of the mutuality in this relation through the recognition of the value of nonmaterial contributions would alter the understanding of partnerships between the global North and the global South (Sizoo 1996). Once the partnership is conceptualized as a common journey that both organizations embark on, it is clear that the fact that the Northern NGOs "paid to fill up the tank does not give [them] the right to determine the route" (Eade 2007, 637). However, as Kapoor recognizes, "Self-constitution is . . . integral to the gift" (2008, 77). The donor invests not only in another organization but also in its own status and identity. I propose that it is helpful to apply Pat Noxolo's concept of interested "disremembering," which she develops in the context of mutuality in British development discourse, to the narrations about partnership here. She describes "disremembering" as the active act of forgetting and erasing both Britain's dependency on the global South and the "independent agency of third world government [which] is hidden behind the disciplinary agency of the British government" (2006, 261). As Noxolo argues, the gendered dimensions of the language of partnership facilitate this disremembering; the role of Britain as donor is made visible through the paternal figure of the breadwinner as provider of funds, while the role of Southern NGOs and states is feminized along the lines of the invisible role of mothers (Noxolo 2006). Along similar gendered lines, I suggest that the partner organizations deliver feminized "emotional labor" by serving as motivators, stand-ins for beneficiaries, as well as projection screens for the desires that emerge in the context of women working across geographical distance to support women in the global South.

(RE) PRESENTATION

In the introduction of this chapter, I have highlighted that distance is also problematized in relation to representation. Petra in Brussels explained earlier that in her advocacy role for a larger network of organizations in the field of international development, she can get "pretty far from reality." She contrasts her own role of policy officer with the position of program staff: "because in programs you have to deal with the other person in their situation. We basically do not; it is already abstracted. So you add another layer of abstraction where at the end of the day I could do advocacy without caring or knowing about these people." Neera Chandhoke understands distance as exacerbating an already problematic representative role of NGOs: "And when we realize that INGOs hardly ever come face to face with the people whose interests and problems they represent, or that they are not accountable to the people they represent, matters become even more troublesome" (Chandhoke 2005, 362). This chapter has so far discussed the function of stories and accounts of partner organizations as backing up advocacy efforts of Northern-based organizations on behalf of marginalized constituencies. This section will further analyze how the women understood representation, facilitation, and participation in the context of distance, but also in the light of broader issues, drawing on global civil society theory.

Mary Kaldor's classical interpretation of global civil society identifies "a role for global civil society in the representation of marginalised global constituencies and in providing internationalised spaces for a world-wide public to deliberate in" (Baker and Chandler 2005, 6). For organizations working to support women in/from the global South, the issue of representation, *who* is representing/can represent, *what/who is being represented*, and *how* representation occurs, centers on a few contentious issues. Amoore and Langley (2004) argue that the normative aura of global civil society—similar to the positive connotation of global citizenship as discussed in the previous chapter—downplays the very power struggles within global civil society about issues of representation and its relation to the state. Drawing on Foucault's notion of "governmentality," they propose that global civil society should be considered a site of government, "as a place where the global political economy is shaped, regulated or deregulated, disciplined or sustained," rather than a site outside government or the state (Amoore and Langley 2004, 100). This conceptualization opens up further space for debate on the ambiguity and conflicts within global civil society. Global civil society actors might consciously or unconsciously benefit from the positive connotation global civil society carries "as a version of the good society stretched to the end of the earth," for its strategic and rhetorical effect (Chesters 2004, 323; Lang 2014). There are dangerous implications of NGOs' image of moral immunity (Stirrat and Henkel 1997; Hilhorst 2003).

Anderson and Rieff (2004) criticize the desire of global civil society actors to act as representatives and intermediaries without the democratic electoral system of national politics. In order to highlight the tension between representing a political ideology and representing a constituency, they suggest that the work of global civil society organizations should be understood as modern missionary work, an attempt to spread a series of values. They maintain that the reluctance of global civil society organizations to present themselves as missionaries stems from their unwillingness to give up the moral hegemony they have achieved under the banner of "global civil society" (Anderson and Rieff 2004; Roy 2004 on NGOs as the "secular missionaries of the modern world"). Corry (2006), however, counters Anderson and Rieff by arguing that they employ a very narrow notion of legitimacy as necessarily connected to the ballot box. While Corry is correct that legitimacy should be defined more broadly, Anderson and Rieff's criticism still opens up an important discussion on moral hegemony. As long as global civil society is perceived as representing "all the people" and its work is equated with "morally good work," there is little room for critically discussing representation and the underlying notions of morality implicit in advocacy work. The term "missionary" not only serves as a reminder of (post)colonial continuities, which will be discussed in more detail in chapter 6, but is also useful for its subtext of ideology and conversion.

The essential distinction that emerges from Anderson and Rieff's work is between representing an ideology and representing the perspective of a social group. They do not dismiss representing an ideology per se; however, they argue, the ideological dimension should be made explicit rather than clouded in the moral hegemony derived from claiming to be representative of a particular community. The work of Sandra, who is employed in Sweden by an umbrella organization on global reproductive health, would be an example of such modern missionary work from the perspective of Anderson and Rieff. Sandra was quoted earlier in this chapter when she said that she needs people's stories to hit the emotions of policymakers for effective advocacy work. Though Sandra is unambiguous about her agenda here, this raises the question whether her international membership organization, in order to gain credibility and legitimacy, relies on outsiders' supposition of their representability. The following interview extract underlines the complex relation between advocacy of a cause and representation of a constituency, which can neither be conceptually equated nor easily disentangled. When I ask her how she responds when women who are supposed to be beneficiaries of her organization's projects disagree with her concerning the agenda of her organization, she says: "What they often do [disagreeing]! No, I have no imagination that I represent the will of all the women in the world, absolutely not. I represent a political idea and an ideology that some women share and some women don't, and that might be in Zambia or in Tanzania or in Sweden."

Chandhoke, recognizing that access to global civil society is often restricted to privileged groups, asks the critical and pertinent question whether "citizens of countries of the South and their needs [are] *represented* in global civil society, or ... *constructed* by practices of representation" (2005, 362). This question hints at long-standing political debates about whether social groups exist a priori (prior to their presentation "as a group") or become a social group by being presented and recognized as such. In Chandhoke's words, "The expressive ... constructs the experiential" (2005, 362). As the examples below illustrate, rather than a representation and construction being conflicting acts, representation inevitably entails a degree of construction.

One of the women I interviewed, Beth, works for an international network advocating for HIV-positive women. While most of the network's staff members are people living with HIV/AIDS, Beth herself is an exception; hence in her position, representation is a contentious issue. In the interview, Beth presents a contentious example where her organization could be criticized for "fabricating" the needs of those concerned. As she explains, not all women living with HIV/AIDS that her organization works with are necessarily politically conscious about the issue. This corresponds with empirical research dealing with the relation between descriptive and substantive representation, which has refuted the idea that sharing certain lived experiences with other members of a social group automatically leads to loyalty to the group perspective. Not all female political representatives, for instance, seek to promote women's interests, and at the same time, some men do (Celis et al. 2008, 104). Therefore, it makes sense for Beth's organization to organize workshops to discuss and analyze issues facing HIV-positive women. There they can begin to see these issues not as individual problems, but as political issues, around which an advocacy agenda can be developed. Beth recognizes, however, that her organization runs the risk of being charged with imposing ideologies in its workshops, as her organization understands the issues in a particular political light. The issue of representation is further complicated by the fact that although the organization was originally set up as a network, it is now increasingly taking on the structure of an NGO. According to Beth, it has been difficult to maintain the kind of exchange with the membership that the structure of a network implies, because of problems of communication. These are exacerbated by the fact that taboos around HIV/AIDS require that membership details are held confidentially at the office, which hampers direct exchange among network members.

Representation has not only been critically discussed in the global civil society literature, but has also been addressed in feminist theory. Some feminist perspectives have privileged personal experience in theorizing women's oppression and strategies for overcoming that oppression. They have therefore questioned the capacity of women in privileged, dominant positions to speak on behalf of the oppressed (Harding 1991); I have touched on this in chapter 2 when I discussed the critique of global sisterhood. In line with this emphasis on the importance of situated perspectives, Beth understands her own position in terms of facilitating self-representation of network members. She mentions that she insists on refusing to act in a representative role and instead leaves the space for members living with HIV/AIDS, despite the fact that she has recognized that it could be advantageous career-wise. However, this principled stance is challenged in the face of day-to-day dilemmas. For example, she recently felt compelled to go to a conference alone when neither members nor allied activists were available to attend. Also, while Beth seeks to facilitate self-representation and avoid representation, she recognizes that her work, which includes writing publications, developing programs, and supporting conference sessions, inevitably involves a significant representational element.

While extensive membership consultation and self-representation of marginalized groups can address some concerns of fabrication of interests and selective representation, the contextual embeddedness and complex positioning of every person along a range of social axes open a potentially infinite range of situated perspectives that need to be articulated and heard. As Beth describes, while consultation with members about their needs is often feasible, her relaying those needs remains problematic because of the heterogeneity of the group she seeks to support, where being HIV-positive is only one aspect of a person's identity or daily reality; this makes the experiences of person A never exchangeable with person B. Beth's approach has been to understand her task as assuming a political standpoint while at the same time trying to connect this to the women's experiences.

I argue that the tensions faced by international organizations around representation due to internal diversity in the represented group and the political dimension of constructing representation play out similarly in local organizations, as the following account about a women's organization advocating for migrant sex workers illustrates. Fay, like many of her colleagues, shares a racialized ethnic background with the women she advocates for, but not the profession of sex work. She therefore contrasts the moments she speaks on behalf of migrant women with other instances where she is asked to advocate for the rights of migrant sex workers. Comparing herself with some of her non-migrant colleagues, Fay says: "I can say, 'We as migrant women demand this and this and that,' [and] I do not get a political or rhetorical or any problem when I am saying this." Then, moving on to how her organization currently approaches representation of migrant sex workers, Fay explains:

> Sometimes we do special things, a workshop or something when we really want to have space to talk with the women [sex workers]. Because something is coming up or so and we really want to know, "What would you say to this?" But in the end we make a decision, ... because every woman has a different opinion or a different thing that she finds good or not, and when you have ten [women] from ten contexts, they would come up with different things.... We have to make a decision. We have to draw from all these inputs and elements [combined] with our background, and where we position ourselves as an organization.

Oscillating between pragmatic and political justifications, these accounts demonstrate that representation is always and inevitably (politically) mediated and constructed. In her seminal article "Can the Subaltern Speak?," Gayatri Spivak refers to the German terms for representation, *vertreten* (as in political representation) and *darstellen* (to depict, to portray), to underline that "to represent" always contains this double meaning (Spivak 1990, 108; cf. Spivak 1988). It is, according to Spivak, necessary to be conscious of the "complicity between these two things," as "there can be a great deal of political harm" if the necessary and inevitable but contentious relation between those two modes of representation is not acknowledged (Spivak 1990, 109). That also means that it is not possible to maintain a neat distinction between representing a group and representing an ideology. I suggest that the challenge is to make the struggle that inevitably precedes the formation of standpoints visible and to interrogate the negative connotation that "fabrication" carries. Such normative stance is, however, hindered by the context in which many civil society organizations operate.

In addition to the pressure internal to an organization to formulate one clear political position, the demand for a univocal account also comes from the external negotiating partners of the organizations. Catherine, a policy director who works for a European-wide umbrella organization, discusses how her broad-based advocacy organization tries to incorporate the different needs and perspectives of women in its policy recommendations. She then remarks:

> It makes it more complex, also because the policymakers don't necessarily think in those terms. They already don't really think in terms of integrating women, but then when you go a step further, and say, "Well, not only integrating women, but women are not a homogenous group, and you have to go further than this," then of course it gets even more complicated.

Her perception of how policymakers respond to complexity is supported by Eyben's observation, based on her thirty years of experience with aid work, that politicians want "to keep issues simple" (2007b, 37). Alvarez, writing in the context of Latin America, also problematizes representation in relation to its reception, when she states: "Even when feminist NGOs explicitly deny that they represent the women's movement, they are too often conveniently viewed as doing so by elected officials and policy makers who can thereby claim to have 'consulted civil society'" (1998, 313).

At the same time, the question remains how to deal with this external pressure. Fay explicitly criticizes those organizations that downplay their own (political) mediating position:

> We of course allow contradictions in this or [allow] others to have another position. But I know another organization, they always say when they go somewhere, "The women they say . . ." and "The women they tell us . . . ," so they try to make themselves invisible, as if they do not exist, "we only tell you what the

women say". This is not what we do. Because we have a position as an organization and we also have to tell the women what our position actually is.

Ultimately, however, she realizes that some of the problems associated with representation will only be resolved once migrant sex workers represent themselves. As with representation, with self-representation, an insistence on multiplicity, which resists desires for "the authentic voice," is essential. Patricia Hill Collins captures this well in arguing against the black woman's standpoint in favor of a black women's collective standpoint, "one characterized by the tensions that accrue to different responses to common challenges" (2000, 28).

Stepping Aside to Make Room

While sex worker activists have been organizing themselves in different countries, in the country Fay works in, there is no autonomous sex workers movement. As was also visible earlier in the narrative of Beth, who is working for the HIV/AIDS network, Fay is led to reflect on the career impact such autonomous movement would have in the face of her normative convictions. This would mean a move away from a "politics of ideas," which relies on accountability as a measure of fair representation, to a "politics of presence," based on the identity of the messenger, that is, descriptive representation (Squires 2001, 16–17). As Fay explains: "Lately I have been thinking about this, and of course there are considerations, like it is your job and it is also money. But I think if there would be [women] who would come up and say, 'I want to do this myself,' it would be great really."

While this musing is inconsequential at this point, it conjures up knowledge we have about the reluctance of other groups to relinquish vested interests. It also illustrates the relational dynamics of privilege and marginalization, which have been discussed in more detail in the previous chapter in relation to responsibility. From the two interview extracts, it becomes clear that not only the power to represent is subject to a certain privilege, but also that the representative role itself has the potential to reinforce the privileges that come with providing a career. This illustrates the key paradox that many women recognized, namely that successful representation or success in empowering and/or facilitating women from their "constituency" to represent themselves leads potentially to their own redundancy. One of the women I interviewed recalled that she mentioned at a job interview that the ultimate aim of the organization should be to make itself redundant, a comment that she says was met by surprise. This clashes indeed with a common concern of NGOs with their own legitimacy, as identified by Hilhorst, who states that "NGO actions are geared towards legitimation, which means that in order to find clients and supportive stakeholders, NGOs have to convince others of their appropriateness" (Hilhorst 2003, 4; Lang 2014). This contradiction has been observed in different places, as is tangibly described by Duffield (2010, 468): "Despite the aid industry's ethos of transience and working itself out of a job . . . the fortified aid compound is here to stay." Ilan Kapoor employs Gayatri Spivak's notion of "working without guarantees" to argue that this ambivalence and challenge is inherent to development work. This implies that one has to be conscious of the limits of one's own knowledge and "representational systems" in the short term, and of the "long-term logic of our profession: enabling the subaltern while working ourselves out of our jobs" (Kapoor 2008, 58).

Anna, a Canadian woman who works for an organization in Brussels on promoting a gender perspective in constitutional reform, shares her ambivalence about her own position. She says she felt compelled to reconsider her own position in the face of a challenging meeting with civil society and government representatives from the Eastern European region her work focuses on. Whereas the antagonism she experienced in the meeting was partly due to internal conflicts between the participants and their skepticism about a gender agenda, it also had to do with her background and the way she was perceived. As she explains:

> Again it is some young international expert coming to say how to do things [there], and that is still a very, very big challenge, and it should be. Whenever you have someone come in . . . and say, "This is how you could things," you are liable to get people saying, "Well, who the hell are you, what do you know?"

I suggest reading this statement in the context of the "feminism-by-design" interventions that Kristen Ghodsee describes as prevalent in postsocialist Eastern Europe (2004, 731). Ghodsee argues that Western feminists brought in a "cultural-feminist conception of gender," which has largely been unsuccessful and which has been met with resistance by women in these countries, as it lacked acknowledgment of the specific postsocialist context and failed to consider and comprehend class distinctions (Ghodsee 2004, 748). In response to Anna's openness about the fact that she was ignorant about the country context, more questions were raised: "'Who are you? Why are you here? I mean you have no connection with us whatsoever. You don't know us, you don't speak our language. I mean, what are you doing here? You look like you are sixteen years old.'"

What is first presented as a general challenge against repeated foreign political international interference in domestic affairs, in the context of a hierarchies of knowledges between West and East, subsequently targets her personally. In this account it is not clear how far this is a recollection of the actual challenges articulated in the meeting, or whether it reflects Anna's own projected ambivalences about her role. The way in which (perceived) age and gender intersect to delegitimize expertise and professionalism of women will be further discussed in the next chapter. However, it is clear that the challenge here runs deeper and addresses hierarchies of knowledge, the dominance of the English language, histories of foreign intervention, and the privilege of traveling as a global expert, as has been discussed with reference to global citizenship in the previous chapter. It is interesting that the interviewee recounts that her colleagues did not seem disturbed by what she perceived as open hostility. Thereby they also closed the space to discuss the challenges. Anna recounts that this meeting triggered a personal process of reflection about her own role in particular, and about the mechanisms of what have come to be recognized as participatory approaches in international aid work more generally. "I had to make sure for myself that it was really something I was adding to, as opposed to just being in a job where I just get a good paycheck and that was enough to justify [my role]."

The interviews made clear that the apparent paradox of making oneself redundant by being successful in one's work is challenging for those women who are passionate about their roles and who can often not imagine doing other work outside the NGO sector. Further reflecting on participatory approaches, Anna adds a more positive note on the idea of forging her own redundancy:

> I think it is based in the fact that the people you are standing before have the knowledge.... So it is just a matter of pulling it out, and empowering them to use it, which is, I think, very special in a way. If you can do that right, you do make yourself redundant in a way.... I mean what an amazing accomplishment to actually say, "Our work here is done."

Anna's statement follows Kapoor's argument that in working with no guarantees, recognizing your failure (to ever be a true representative or expert) should be seen as success (Kapoor 2008). In light of the fact that I interviewed Anna while she was active in her job, her narrative, however, also implies that despite her almost celebratory account, Anna does not judge the "local" people she supports to (already) have gained that knowledge and position; indeed at another point she describes them as having "basic knowledge." I propose that this judgment cannot be isolated from the power dynamics involved in the relation between international organizations in the global North and local organizations in the East and South. At the same time, the above accounts demonstrate that the women were in general aware of and struggled with the problems associated with representation, as suggested by Chandhoke (2005), by Anderson and Rieff (2004), and by feminist theorists such as Harding (1991). It remains to be seen how this awareness and reflection will materialize when ultimately tested, for example by demands of self-representation.

Burdens of (Self-)Representation

The following example, which takes us back to Catherine, the policy director who works for a European-wide umbrella organization, problematizes what is often considered desirable practice. It shows how extensive consultation with those that are represented can place a burden on the represented group. This becomes clear when she, as a white woman from a Western European country, says:

> We also want to be able to represent the views of migrant women, and the challenge here is that migrant women are not enough organized, so they are not very present in the migrant organizations, or antiracist organizations. They are not always very present in women's organizations. So it is really something that needs to be done to give migrant women a space, to input in policies.

A generous reading would recognize that her organization sees the need for consulting with migrant women and including them as a member organization of the network, in order to adequately represent them. A more critical reading questions the whiteness of the umbrella organization's office and the desire to remain central in representing others. Here the ambition to include the perspectives of migrant women turns into a demand on those women when they are subsequently found not to be enough sufficiently organized. Catherine's organization wants migrant women to be organized *as* a migrant women group since that would give easiest access to *the* voice of migrant women. This project again runs the risk of "conflat[ing] social position and identity with political position and opinion" (Verloo 2006, 222–223). As the earlier examples have illustrated, the mere fact that migrant women (partly) share a social position is no guarantee of a shared political view. Catherine explains that the project of inclusion has been challenging with reference to what she perceives as a lack of organization on the side of the migrant women. This forecloses reflection on the role of exclusionary mechanisms in her own organization, or in other antiracist or migrant organizations, which have not sufficiently included migrant women in the first place.

The dilemmas presented here from Brussels by both Catherine and, earlier, Anna emerged in the context of two examples in Europe and concerned the relation with, respectively, Europe's migrant women population and an Eastern European country on the periphery. I suggest that it is relevant to draw parallels with concerns in development studies focusing on the global South. From the mid-1990s, NGOs and development organizations made an explicit effort to involve their target groups in their interventions and to hear about their experiences and their needs. This has had mixed results, as Neumann aptly argues on the basis of interviews with women in a Nicaraguan village, who are "enlisted" by NGOs to participate in their projects. She observes that the NGOs' participatory approach "exploit[ed] women's unpaid community care labor," making development a "gendered burden" (Neumann 2013, 799). Robert Chambers, as a response to the shortcomings he identified in NGOs' field visits (as discussed earlier in this chapter), formulated the Participatory Rural Appraisal approach (PRA), which suggested strategies for consulting and empowering the poor. Kapoor criticizes the PRA approach for assuming that the subaltern voice can transparently be heard and represented and for ignoring what he calls the "knowledge/power problem," in which every production of knowledge creates power relations (Kapoor 2008, 50). Kapoor takes his critique one step further when he argues that the supposedly participatory safe space functions as a panopticon in which the person who is "empowered to speak" is monitored and under pressure to express him- or herself in a certain way. In addition, he emphasizes that the power/knowledge problem persists beyond the specific speech act, as the narrative of the subaltern is co-opted and presented in a specific institutional framework (Kapoor 2008).

I suggest that these critiques can be applied to a range of situations that have been considered in this chapter so far: from the selection of partner organizations based on their ability to perform in certain spaces, to the additional burdens placed on target communities and partner organizations to deliver stories, information, and viewpoints. What is clear is that these issues arise in a continuum of practices of representation, mediation, and facilitation, and that they cannot simply be resolved by replacing representation with extensive consultation or the provision of a platform for self-presentation.

For example, Lucia, who works for an organization that lobbies the UN to include African women in decision-making processes, states that instead of representing women, she wants to give them the opportunity to speak for themselves. In the narrative that follows, I first argue that a gap emerges between the organizational vision on (alternatives to) representation that might have developed out of a history of (feminist) politicization, on the one hand, and the perspective of a young and relatively inexperienced staff member who echoes the official commitment to facilitation of self-representation without that process of reflection, on the other hand. More in general however, it is necessary to remain vigilant and critical of attempts to move from a representative to a facilitating role according to the logic of participation. For example, as is illustrated here, the process of facilitation can bring to the fore the same recurrent issue that has been identified in relation to representation, namely the challenge of (re)presenting the internal diversity of a group. Lucia recognizes that it is hard to let a diverse group of women express their needs with one voice. Alluding to regional differences, she says: "Between them they don't agree on all the topics, but they have to find a consensus, they have to see what it is that they agree on, to be able to work together. There is a lot of politics and a lot of differences." When Lucia continues, another layer is added:

> We want them to be women, not to be South Darfuri, North Darfuri, West Darfuri.... If you go to the ... negotiation table, ... we want you to represent women, nothing else. You have to forget all the other. But of course, I mean, one thing is saying it and the other thing is actually doing it.

In her narrative it remains unclear whether the push to include women in the decision-making process is motivated by the ambition to introduce feminist ideas, or the interests of women or gender equality (Squires 2007). In this organization, in contrast to the European umbrella organization mentioned before, the emphasis is on facilitating women to speak for themselves rather than representing them. A closer look at this facilitation of self-representation reveals, however, that the demands on the women are actually similar to the European organization's wanting to represent migrant women's perspectives. While Lucia acknowledges the gap between theory and practice and the difficulty in bracketing out other parts of one's identity (their regional background in this case) in order to speak "as women of Sudan," she continues to request that the women foreground their gender and national perspective. This points to an interesting conflict since deciding not to speak for others and letting others speak can lead to imposing a burden on others by demanding a simplified, essentialized (re)presentation that "may structurally disadvantage some gendered identities while privileging others" (Squires 2007, 155). So the engagement with the women is limited to the role they can perform at the peace negotiation table "as Darfuri women," while there is less space for engaging with the complexities and multiple perspectives that intersectional positionings bring, not least in the context of a nation in conflict. Moreover, by expecting the women to foreground their identity *as* women, it is implicitly assumed that women's prior exclusion from the negotiation table is only dependent on their gender and not on their "race," class, ethnicity, or geopolitical location. Lucia's conception of identity is essentialist as it assumes a stable experience of being a member of a particular group independent of time, history, social location, and personal situation, and expects that identities and perspectives neatly map onto each other.

Despite a recognition of the critique of representation and an adherence to alternative modes such as consultation, participatory approaches, and facilitation of self-representation, the above accounts have revealed that many of the women held on to what they regarded a desirable or requisite behavior by the marginalized or "subaltern." I present the following example as an exception to demonstrate what a more radical perspective on the autonomy of women from the global South looks like. Stacey, a racialized woman from Canada who works for an international organization, tells me that the demands of the women in the global South whom she consults are generally in line with her own expectations and political agenda, such as equal access to health services and a reduction of harm and discrimination. Stacey then recalls that she was once surprised nevertheless. She recounts an example from a former position where she worked "on the ground" in India on issues surrounding education and health. When she consulted the women from a community about plans to build a school in their area, many said that they would not want to send their daughters to school. They told her that they did not want to revive the hope in their daughters of a professional future when in practice this was unlikely to happen within the current patriarchal system that would force them to move in with their husbands, become mothers, and be responsible for household chores.

Stacey reflects:

> At that time and at that stage of my own career and my own life I was very surprised to hear that. You know, if you got a school that is going to be built there, why would you not send your kids there? For me I could not figure

out the logic, but their logic makes a lot of sense at the same time. So I was surprised by that, but I was not disappointed by taking off the recommendation to build a school in the village, because in the end, it is not about what I want, it is about what they want and how they can use me as a tool basically to ensure it.

Stacey emphasizes here that she should be "used as a tool," which very much reflects the facilitating role, even though it is not clear here which alternative recommendations were added to the lists based on the input of the women. Despite her knowledge about the positive relation between education and health, Stacey decides to delete the recommendation to build a school based on what the women tell her. I find it interesting here that she emphasizes that in a dialogue with the other women she came to understand their "logic" and that once she had understood this logic, it was easier to accept something that was initially counterintuitive for her. This follows Gayatri Spivak's call to "learn from them, to speak to them, to suspect that their access to the political and sexual science is not merely to be *corrected* by our superior theory and enlightened compassion" (Spivak quoted in Young 1990, 166–167) as well as the previously mentioned idea of "working with no guarantees," which recognizes the limits of one's own knowledge frameworks (Kapoor 2008, 58). It would be speculative to draw a causal link between the perspective of Stacey in relation to the Indian women she encounters and her racialized identity. At the same time, Stacey's biographical experience of being "othered," the experience of growing up as a child of migrants from the global South in a Northern country and the fact that she, as she told me at another point, is sometimes mistaken for being Indian, is likely to inform her perspective. In this interview account the image of the Southern Other not "able" to speak for herself is also problematized, since Stacey presents the mothers she speaks to as very capable of voicing their concerns.

In line with this, Stacey later remarks:

Very rarely do you need to convince women of their own rights. I have found that they know what they need. . . . They know exactly why they are not getting it and they know what they need to get it. . . . They don't need to be told by anyone else what they need; they certainly do not need to be told by me.

This fragment runs counter to assumptions about women from the global South who, because of their oppressed position, would neither know "what is good for them" nor be able to voice their needs. As Patricia Hill Collins has put it in the context of African American women: "People who are oppressed usually know it" and they "produce . . . social thought designed to oppose oppression" (2000, 8–9).

The question is what happens to this knowledge. Spivak's article "Can the Subaltern Speak?" (1988) is again of relevance here. Spivak discusses the paradoxical position in which the subaltern Indian woman is cast in the practice of *sati* (widow sacrifice) by both colonialism and traditional patriarchy. She states: "Between patriarchy and imperialism, subject-constitution and object-formation, the figure of the woman disappears, not into a pristine nothingness, but into a violent shuttling which is the displaced figuration of the 'third-world woman' caught between tradition and modernization" (Spivak 1988, 306).

As refusal of sati will be understood as succumbing to imperialism, while preparing for sati would be interpreted as victimhood of patriarchy; there is no space left for asserting agency. If we translate this to the example above, it is conceivable that the mothers' resistance to the building of the school is simplistically read as a sign of their "backwardness" and unwillingness to provide chances to their daughters to be educated instead of the more complex reading that is narrated by Stacey. While Spivak has been criticized for negating the agency of the subaltern by claiming that she cannot speak, Spivak intended to stress that the subaltern when attempting to communicate is not heard. In the reworked version of the article in the book *A Critique of Post-colonial Reason*, Spivak states this last point more clearly: "It is important to acknowledge our complicity in the muting, in order precisely to be more effective in the long run" (1999, 309).

Therefore the challenge for Stacey is to convey and translate the mothers' concerns within hegemonic terms, to enable them to be heard, without silencing them through a reductive (re)presentation. This is consistent with Spivak's original critique in "Can the Subaltern Speak?," which argues both for the impossibility of recovering the voice of the subaltern and for the ethical obligation to try (de Jong and Mascat 2016). One has to try, rather than be silent, since the decision not to speak altogether in order to avoid speaking for others is a kind of cultural relativism that turns into solipsism, recentering the one who refuses to speak: "I can only speak about myself, or I can only speak about the impossibility of my speaking" (Ahmed 2000b, 166). As Spivak states in the last sentence of the original text: "Representation has not withered away. The female intellectual as intellectual has a circumscribed task which she must not disown with a flourish" (1988, 308).

CONCLUDING REMARKS

In light of the moral assumptions regarding space and distance in relation to NGO work and feminist international activism, as well as the real challenges associated with bridging this distance in the context of power relations, it is imperative to critically interrogate the strategies women employ for bridging distances and look at the wider implications of these strategies. In this chapter, I have first demonstrated how stories and field trips become practical and psychological strategies to remain connected. I have drawn on critical development literature to tease out the consequences of these strategies, such as the "traps" associated with field visits (Chambers 2006) and stories becoming "myths" (Cornwall et al. 2007). I have subsequently argued that in order to understand how the geographical and, arguably, "imaginary" distance between women NGO workers in the North and their final beneficiaries in the South is bridged, it is essential to look into the role of Southern partner organizations in their conceptualization of that relation. While at some points, partners are described as *bridging* the geographical divide, in some instances we can see that they come to *replace* the final beneficiaries in that the latter become or remain invisible. Here again I have suggested that it is necessary to complement the analysis of this function of partnerships for the women in bridging the distance to the beneficiaries, with a structural critique of partnerships, offered by postcolonial and critical development literature. I have connected the interview data with the ambivalences that the benevolent notion of partnership conceals. Subsequently, I have demonstrated that there is a *mutual dependency* between organizations in the North and their partners, in that they need their partner organizations for the provision of information, for moral legitimacy, and for maintaining their motivation through feeling connected with "the ground." However, the continued centering of the Northern partners and the "disremembering" (Noxolo 2006) obscures this mutual dependency. As Maria Eriksson Baaz (2005) has argued, critical accounts of partnership commonly assume that the idea of partnership is merely used by Northern organizations to hide their "real" motives without actual intention to change practices. On the basis of the interview narratives, following Eriksson Baaz (2005), I am equally critical of such a "conspiracy" conclusion. As Eriksson Baaz (2005) writes, the term "partnership" is not reflective of an intended plot, but rather has conflicts, ambivalences. and tensions subsumed under it.

Finally, this chapter has engaged with the critique of the representative role of global civil society, which includes but is not limited to concerns with distance. I have illustrated the ways in which representation inevitably draws on construction—similar to the aforementioned "field stories"—and includes a political perspective. This requires that global civil society organizations be explicit about their position and refrain from claiming moral legitimacy under the pretense of representative status. With the interviews, I have contested the idea that alternative models, such as processes of formal consultation, participation, or facilitation of self-representation, deliver a radically different dynamic than representation and can resolve the contentions of representation. I have demonstrated not only that the women in this study are in a comparatively advantaged position vis-à-vis those they represent, but also that this gap is potentially widened with the representative (or facilitating) role bringing additional career advantages. The women who were critical of the role their organizations played as representatives in the lobbying process felt ambivalent, at the same time, about their own redundancy. Spivak (1988) bequeaths a similar ambivalence in her famous critique of representation, arguing that it cannot simply be discarded while stressing the need to acknowledge our own complicity in silencing the subaltern. The next chapter will further discuss the ways in which the women understood the relation between themselves and the women they supported, offering an analysis in the context of feminist understandings of sisterhood and solidarity.

CHAPTER 5

Interlocking Connections

Sherene Razack's invitation, presented in the introduction of this book, to critically reflect on one's relational position in the light of global inequalities emerges, among other things, from a history of struggle in the women's movement. In chapter 3 I argued that the sense of responsibility for global Others was, in a seemingly paradoxical manner, articulated by the women I interviewed in relation to the Self. It was expressed in reference to their own opportunities or to their desire to leave a legacy, rather than to the Other. This chapter shifts the focus by addressing relationality. It provides an analysis of how the women understand the connection with the women their work seeks to support. It also looks into how they reflected on the implications of their own identities for their work practices, against a history of problematized sisterhood.

Antoinette Burton and others have described how British first-wave feminists constructed their arguments for women's suffrage in Britain around the "plight" of their "'Indian sisters' in the empire" (Burton 1994, 172; cf. Syed and Ali 2011). First-wave white feminism has also been challenged for presenting other feminist voices as marginal, represented only by a few "exceptional" figures like Sojourner Truth (Caraway 1992). As mentioned earlier, second-wave Western feminism has been criticized by black feminists who problematized the universalization of a homogenous category of "woman" (Lorde 1984; hooks 1981; 1986; Carby 1992). This assumed universalism is reflected in the notion of "global sisterhood," employed to describe women's bond of shared victimhood. As black feminist activist Audre Lorde stated: "Today, there is a pretense to a homogeneity of experience covered by the word SISTERHOOD in the white women's movement" (1984, 116).

Deconstructing this homogeneity, black feminists, as well as other women who were marginalized by the white middle-class women's movement, have pointed to the importance of looking at how the categories of gender, "race," class, and sexuality intersect in the creation and maintenance of power relations (hooks 1981; Crenshaw 2000; Lugones 2010). Caraway introduces the alternative term "segregated sisterhood" to stress its incoherence against a history of inequality between women. "In the logic of combining these two terms, each invalidates and cancels the other, rendering suspect the animating symbol—'sisterhood'—of a profoundly transforming social movement" (Caraway 1992, 3). Critical voices also challenged hegemonic feminists to confront their own privileges and to be aware of their complicity in maintaining racism and other systems of oppression (hooks 1981; Amos and Parmar 1984; Carby 1992; hooks 2000). Hazel Carby, in a contribution tellingly called "White Woman, Listen!," calls white women "extraordinarily reluctant to see themselves in the situations of being oppressors." She attributes this to white women's fear that acknowledgment of their role as oppressors will distract from their marginalization on the basis of their gender (Carby 1992, 221).

In chapter 2 I contextualized the women's feminist biographies with reference to developments in (transnational) feminisms. In this chapter I suggest that the women's understanding of their work, of themselves, and the women they seek to support, must be analyzed in light of the challenge against sisterhood as a "natural" relation between women globally. Given that (some) Western feminists have reworked and reconsidered their positions in response to these earlier critiques, it is relevant to investigate in how far the documented tensions within second-wave feminism are present in the women's work today and whether the different critical strategies and understandings of engagement that have emerged have salience in their work. In this chapter I will examine different configurations of sisterhood and solidarity that reconfirm as well as rethink connections between women globally. On the one hand, I will establish a connection between the critique of sisterhood as shared victimhood and women's understanding of their identities in their work, by showing how women perform a "race to innocence." On the other hand, I will argue that some women are establishing negotiated solidarities through a reflexive practice that forms the basis for reimagining women's relationalities.

RACING TO INNOCENCE

As discussed earlier, there is an important link between sisterhood as victimhood and the refusal of privileged women to take responsibility for their implication in systems of oppression, such as racism, classism, and heterosexism. The idea of a universal, shared identity neatly separated white women from racial oppressions by men and masked the divisions between women. In each of the interviews, I asked the women how they considered their own identity to play out in their work. When I asked Casey, a woman in her fifties with a long track record in international development work, about the impact of her identity and explicitly mentioned her nationality, her whiteness, and her gender, she replied:

> The gender part of it is strong. The academic training I have undertaken, my education has played a strong role.... The difficulties I have faced have been related to my gender, but also to my profession, having a nontechnical education. This field in development has always been dominated by men in mainly technical positions, and very little respect has been paid to the work of sociologists. And it is still a very difficult position, I think.

In this reply, Casey chooses to focus on gender and her education, dimensions where she is in a marginal position, leaving out dominant markers such as her nationality and her whiteness, despite specific prompting from my side. She considers her academic degree in sociology as an obstacle, due to the bias in development toward technical studies, without reflecting on the privilege of academic education. That the women I interviewed focused on women's and gender issues in their work, and that most of them were politicized feminists, as discussed in chapter 2, accounts to an extent for the women's focus on their gender identity in the interviews. In contrast, Roth (2015, 118) found a downplaying of gender differences among the female expatriate aid workers she interviewed, who in her case worked in the wider field of aid. I propose that it is still important to attend to the silences on other markers, such as "race," among the women I interviewed, especially in cases where this was explicitly addressed in the interview questions. This silence can be explained with Ruth Frankenberg's (1993) reflections in her seminal study *White Women, Race Matters* on the difficulties she experienced in finding white women who were prepared to talk about "race." She attributes the resistance she encountered to the fact that for white women the only apparent options were "either one does not have anything to say about race, or one is apt to be deemed 'racist' simply by virtue of having something to say" (Frankenberg 1993, 33). I add to this the transparency afforded to hegemonic categories, where dominance means going unnamed, as the title of the black feminist-edited collection *All the Women Are White, All the Blacks Are Men, but Some of Us Are Brave* (Hull, Bell-Scott, and Smith 1982) captured so well.

Borrowing from Mary Louise Fellows and Sherene Razack (1998, 335), I argue that the women's emphasis on gender over other categories needs to be analyzed as a "race to innocence" and that this proclivity forms an obstacle for developing solidarities among women globally. Fellows and Razack (1998) coined this term in dialogue with one another after being confronted with their own and each other's focus on structures of oppression that directly affected and interested them, at the cost of working through their own complicities in other processes of subordination. I find the "race to innocence" both in the women's foregrounding of gender and in many of the silences, for instance concerning whiteness, nationality, and class. The term "identity" in my question generally triggered a reflection on categories linked to subordination rather than to privilege and domination, which remained unnamed and invisible. I suggest that it is no coincidence that this "race to innocence" is especially pronounced among women who consider global sisterhood rather unproblematic.

Observing the frequent occurrence of the "race to innocence" among feminists, Fellows and Razack ask why we are led into the "trap of competing marginalities" (1998, 339), where we compare different types of oppressions, privileging "our" oppressed position. Exploring why it proves so hard to acknowledge our complicity at an affective register, despite the intellectual, theoretical knowledge of multiple oppressions that we often possess, they identify three reasons. First, we fear we "risk erasure" if we are not foregrounding the oppression we experience. Second, attention to the subordination that we feel most affected by often constitutes a first step in our own liberation, "a productive defensive response to oppression." And third, from a dominant position we tend to belittle the narratives of those who are oppressed, since we are utilizing a hegemonic framework to interpret their experiences (Fellows and Razack 1998, 339–340).

Casey, whom I quoted above, further reflects on experiences with gender discrimination in her work:

> In general it is not an advantage to be a woman, because most of the management positions are being held by men. . . . And they have only [recently] grown to realize that sometimes you send out women here with influence and resources which they need to take seriously. So it is only because you have the power that you are recognized. But no, over the years it has not become easier being a woman, only if you have other women to relate to.

Casey explains here that having resources and influence sometimes "compensates" for the marginalization that she faces as a woman. I propose to understand Casey's statement as holding onto what Fellows and

Razack (1998, 348) have called a "toehold on respectability." In line with Burton's previously mentioned analysis of the discourses of imperial suffrage movements, they trace this back to the emergence of the bourgeois, colonial woman whose respectability was sustained by her hierarchical (exploitative) relations with the domestic worker and the prostitute. I suggest that this means, in contrast to Casey's remark in the interview that her womanhood supports her relation with other women, that this relation is fractured by other structures of inequality and can only be the segregated sisterhood that Caraway (1992) referred to. Fellows and Razack warn that "respectability" is an unstable position and can never result in transformative justice. They echo Patricia Hill Collins on the "interlocking nature of oppression," who has argued that transformative social justice requires a collective struggle (1986, 19; 2000).

Elisa, a white woman of the same generation as Casey, with a similar academic background, focuses on her identity as a feminist, in response to the same interview question about the impact of her identity on her work in the field of women's leadership. When I ask a second question related to whether her identity could also form a barrier in terms of relating to others, she continues talking about her feminist identity. To my third prompting, which specifically addresses whether her Western nationality, her whiteness, her age and feminist generation also impact her work, she replies, "Oh, that is very beneficial." She then explains that she decided to organize the international launch of a new project on gender and security not in a country affected by terror, but in Austria: "Vienna is a destination, especially for the women from the Middle East, to reach without problems. Visa problems we can take care of. It is not an issue for them to come here."

When I ask Sarah, a white American woman in her thirties working in Geneva on peace, security, and gender, to give me some examples of how her identity plays a role in her work, she tells me what she calls "an anecdote" about a meeting with a Middle Eastern government official, responsible for human rights issues, trade, and disarmament. After the first introduction and greetings, the following occurred:

> He said, "So what is this young woman, young lovely woman, doing? What can I help you with? We are improving our maternal health programs.... We are really taking care of our young ones." And I looked at him and said, "I think that's great, I am glad that you said that, but no, I am actually here to talk to you about the chemical weapons convention."

Again, in this example the focus lies on experiences associated with marginalized positions. The official's statements about maternal health programs and "the young ones" could, on first reading, be interpreted as a response solely based on gender, and Sarah indeed says to me that her example applies only to her gender identity. She continues her story by relating that she met the official again a year later at a reception, where he remembered how she impressed him with her knowledge on "hard security issues."

> He puts his arm around me ... and he takes my hand and he goes around, shaking my hand, and starts to explain to this group of people that this is the woman who is completely surprising. Because he thought I came into his office to talk about what he called at the time "soft issues," you know, about women's rights and about maternal health and about children's rights. And instead I came in and shocked him by speaking knowledgeably about hard security issues, and that was not what he expected.

Whereas Sarah attempts to communicate with this narrative that she managed to impress him and thereby challenge his gender stereotypes, I suggest that his arm around her illustrates that gender norms and inequalities persisted beyond their first encounter. I also suggest that the gender reading of this "anecdote" needs to be complicated with an intersectional perspective, which serves to upset the "race to innocence." That is, I argue that intersectionality can be drawn upon for its normative and political (rather than "merely" analytical) function, since its conceptual underpinnings undermine the logic of the "race to innocence" in three different but related ways. First, by showing how gender functions in conjunction with other categories like "race," it destabilizes "gender" as a fixed and homogenous category and effectively hinders using (white) gender oppression as a "cover." Second, intersectionality reminds us that positions are the result of the interplay of multiple structures, and thereby makes visible the dominant axes underlying "mixed" locations, such as that of the white middle-class woman (Hill Collins 2000; Yuval-Davis 2006). It thereby draws attention to privilege as well as to complicity in the subordination of others, which a "race to innocence" would deny. Third, intersectionality demonstrates the interdependency of systems of oppression and thereby resonates with Fellows and Razack's claim (1998) that only by addressing systems of oppression together, rather than in isolation, can structural change occur (cf. Hill Collins 2000). Elsewhere, Razack has formulated this in terms that can easily be translated to Sarah's "lovely young woman" anecdote:

> An interlocking analysis reminds us of the ease with which we slip into positions of subordination (for example, the sexually vulnerable woman, the woman with sole responsibility for child care, or the woman without access to managerial positions) without seeing how this very subordinate location simultaneously reflects and upholds race and class privilege. (Razack 2001, 14)

Hence, from such intersectional perspective, I suggest understanding the image of the young lovely woman as one that is coproduced and strengthened through the intersection of sexism and ageism. Being young coupled with being a woman is read as lacking status and credibility (Sarah can therefore be addressed as "lovely"); this in contrast with the combination of youth with maleness, which is often interpreted as a sign of ambition. Also, the attraction and desirability that is communicated with the term "loveliness" functions at the nexus of young and female, rather than old and female. Other structures remain unnamed and implicit here, such as "race." For example, "loveliness" could be underpinned by whiteness. The government official's slippage, assuming that Sarah is an expert on maternal healthcare, rather than on the chemical weapons convention, would likely have taken a different form with a racialized young woman, who might not have been accepted as an "expert" on any issue in the first place. "Loveliness" also operates with heterosexism and implicit heteronormative assumptions, for example about "availability" and "appropriate" women's presentation and dress.

In contrast to Sarah's silent "race to innocence," Laura addresses and reflects explicitly on her own "race to innocence." Laura, a white middle-class woman who is also in her thirties and works in a Northern European city for an international development NGO on gender, says:

> When it comes to gender, I think I am fairly good, and for me that is an immediate reaction: "Okay, there are no women here." . . . But, for example, with class it is different because I am really [a] comfortable, middle-class academic, and I can easily get caught up in discussions and just afterwards realize, "Wait a minute, but all the people I talked to, they were university students, academics, middle-class people" and not having that class consciousness at all in the same way.

Laura is open and thoughtful about her own blind spots, and attempts to take notice of other marginalizing structures. She does, however, fall into the "trap of competing marginalities" (Fellows and Razack 1998, 339) when I ask her why gender inequality rather than other structures of subordination is at the forefront of her mind.

> First of all, I think it is important because I think it [gender inequality] is absolutely fundamental to change as a power structure. I see that it is more fundamental than other power structures. And it is also, it is very personal, it is a power structure that I relate to personally every day and the difficulties related to it, the way I don't do with [other power structures].... In the gender structure, that is where I am in a disadvantaged position, but it is almost the only one. I mean age-wise I am in my thirties, which is a fairly good age to be in—it is better than being twenty-three, for example. And of course although it is not that obvious in [the country where I live now], but I know that had I been in Colombia now, the fact that I have two kids is also an authority in itself. Being middle class, ethnically white, those are all advantaged positions.

And later in the interview, she says:

> I am not sure, but sometimes I get the feeling that gender in that way is so much more deeply rooted because we are forced to produce and reproduce gender roles all the time. You can find settings that are fairly homogenous in other ways with class or ethnicity.... But I mean in almost any environment, in each family you have men and women, so you have this constant low-intensive reproduction of roles that is really hard to get at because so much of it is still perceived as private.

Laura wavers between, on the one hand, acknowledging that her own experience of gender oppression leads her to prioritizing gender and, on the other hand, trying to find rational justifications for this. Treating "one form of oppression as primary" only leaves space for "remaining types of oppression as variables within what is seen as the most important system," counter to an understanding of structures of power as interlocking (Hill Collins 1986, 20). I suggest that this leads Laura to sidelining and reinforcing other forms of subordination, for example, in her heteronormative account of the family or in the suggestion that "homogenous settings" are inherently liberating or free of reproduction of power structures, rather than, for instance, results of segregation. Razack and Fellows's three reasons for racing to innocence—the fear of erasure, the focus on the self as the first step of liberation, and the blindness that comes with a hegemonic perspective—emphasize the individual level and have a slightly psychologized ring. I argue that this analysis needs to be complemented with a structural account of the vested interests at stake in racing to innocence and competing marginalities. This also implies a shift away from a focus on Laura's or other women's individual articulations to the structures and discourse in which these statements are embedded.

Laura's argument can be contextualized with political debates in the United States and Europe. For example, during the 2008 US election contest between Hillary Clinton and Barack Obama, feminist Robin Morgan, whose influential book *Sisterhood Is Global* has been discussed earlier in chapter 2 and will be further discussed in the next section, called on feminists to vote for Hillary Clinton. Morgan (2008) stated: "A few non-racist countries may exist—but sexism is everywhere." In the European context, the EWL, the largest platform of women's organizations in the EU, which I introduced in chapter 2, argued in response to a "European Commission consultation on a possible new initiative to prevent and combat discrimination outside employment":

> Gender-based discrimination is about the structural unequal distribution of power and resources between women and men belonging to all groups in society and thus should be distinguished from discrimination on other bases such as ethnicity, disability and so on. Furthermore, women as a category can be distinguished from other major oppressed groups in that they represent a numerical majority and it is imperative that they are regarded as a basic unit of analysis of social life and experiences and in relation to all other forms of discrimination. (European Women's Lobby 2007)

This is exactly the kind of primary treatment of one kind of oppression that leaves no space for other structures of subordinations than to be subsumed under it, as described by Hill Collins (1986). Kimberlé Crenshaw argued in 1991, when she introduced the concept of "intersectionality," that antidiscrimination policies, which focus either on sex or on racial discrimination without looking at the combined effects of subordination, "cannot sufficiently address the particular manner in which black women are subordinated" (Crenshaw 2000, 209). However, EWL here raises arguments to separate gender discrimination from other types of discrimination. When the EWL states that "gender-based discrimination is about the structural unequal distribution of power and resources between women and men *belonging to all groups of society* and thus should be distinguished from discrimination on other bases" (emphasis added), there is an underlying assumption that gender affects everyone while ethnicity, for instance, does not. This implies that all of us have gender, but only some of us "have an ethnicity"; this makes whiteness invisible. The competition between marginalities also concerns a struggle over interests and resources, as political debates in different European countries on the integration of different equality bodies into one institution have revealed. Andrea Krizsan, Hege Skjeie, and Judith Squires, summarizing the results of comparative research on the integration of equality regimes in different European countries, found "competitive relations between different groups typically in instances of levelling up, when a previously privileged gender- or race-only approach is integrated with other inequalities" and noticed that "different inequality groups rarely appear to perceive a common interest in their struggle with the state" (2012, 226). Feminists have expressed concerns about the incompatibility of different equality lobbies, and fear that the inclusion of other categories in the mainstreaming of different equality strands is an indication of a decreasing concern with gender (Squires 2007; Agustín and Roth 2011). Mieke Verloo (2006) has effectively demonstrated that different structures of inequality, such as gender, sexuality, and class, have different roots and that the social movements associated with them have distinct aims, ranging from appraisal of difference to deconstruction of categories, and from redistribution to recognition. This important conceptual and political insight, which points to the risks involved if the *distinct mechanisms* underlying different forms of subordination are not recognized, does not amount to a justification for a "race to innocence [which] depends on the idea that the systems of domination are *separate*" (Fellows and Razack 1998, 340; emphasis added). In the face of political challenges and struggles over funding, it remains imperative, following the idea that oppressions are interlocking and that emancipation cannot be complete when taking a one-dimensional view, to resist the temptation or the political instigation to engage in a competition among different forms of marginalizations. Hill Collins's critical observation that "the much-bandied-about accusation of racism in the women's movement may be much less about the racial attitudes of individual White women than it is about the unwillingness or inability of some Western White women to share power" (2000, 234) aptly captures which interests are at stake.

DESIRING SISTERHOOD

The women's focus in their work on women and gender issues combined with the contentiousness of the notion of "sisterhood," underlines the relevance for investigating how the women considered their relation with women globally. In this section I will substantiate with different interview narratives my argument that sisterhood as well as its critiques have continued salience. At the same time I demonstrate the heterogeneous understandings of sisterhood. In chapter 2, I have introduced the feminist trajectory of Casey, a white university-educated woman in her fifties, who has been working in the field of development for different public and private organizations since 1985. Recently, Casey began working for an international membership NGO in her home country on reproductive issues. One of the deciding reasons to apply for the job was that she would work on gender issues, which she regards as important for international development as well as for her home country. Without using the term "sisterhood," her narration reflects the idea of connections among women on the basis of common oppression. When asked where her feeling of responsibility comes from that prompts her to engage with the lives of women geographically far away from her, she says: "Because it is part of my own upbringing to have a gender point of view, or gender experience to relate to. For me, it is the same kind of struggle, just a different environment." As her work has a strong international dimension, I further enquired about the international orientation that is present in her work. The idea of sisterhood based on shared experience of oppression is repeated when Casey says:

> The gender orientation is something from my childhood and family upbringing. I would have taken that anywhere. And you may also say that I am carrying out the same struggle just in another part of the world, the struggle that I have with me from home here and I just recognize it everywhere else and act upon it. The international [dimension] would not [necessarily] have been there.

Casey experiences her work field as male dominated, and only sees an advantage in her being a woman "if you have other women to relate to" as representatives of partner organizations or in management.

In a very similar vein, much younger Sonia, in her late twenties, working for an international organization in Geneva on gender, peace, and security, says:

> I would say a woman in need is a woman in need, here in Switzerland, in [Chile], in Africa, or whatever. I wanted to work with something that had to do with gender, and that is probably because of where I come from, because of a very macho culture that we have, and I feel I can do something for women, and I like it.

Both Casey and Sonia emphasize the similarities of women's struggles worldwide. Despite their differences in age and background, both implicitly compare their own experience of being (disadvantaged as) a woman to the experiences of women globally. As bell hooks (2000) argues, this notion of commonality in victimhood can have counterproductive effects, since it reinforces a sexism that regards femininity in terms of vulnerability. It also raises questions about the privilege of focusing on victimhood.

Refraining from speculation about Casey's experiences, we can ask what it means for a professional, middle-class, educated, white woman with a long career behind her, like Casey, to see herself as a marginalized woman in a male-dominated work field. A double irony can be identified in that those who emphasize women's victimhood are often relatively privileged (hooks 2000). In contrast, those who suffer substantial oppression can often not afford to think of themselves as victims, as they have to focus on survival.

Casey and Sonia speak as women about the plight and struggles of other women. Spelman expresses her critique of global sisterhood by calling the phrase "as a woman" "the Trojan horse of feminist ethnocentrism" (1990, 185). It is useful to offer some nuances here that bring us back to questions about essentialism, with Caraway's observation that feminist thought, to some extent, *needs* generalizing: "So, yes, all feminists are essentialists in this basic sense" (1992, 173). The problem, then, does not lie in generalization per se but in its "obstreperous cousin ethnocentrism" (Caraway 1992, 173). I suggest that a subtle but important difference can be traced between Casey's and Sonia's statements. Whereas Sonia sees her own experience in a macho culture as the inspiration for her interest in and commitment to gender issues (here equated with "women's needs"), she does not see women's needs everywhere in the world as emerging out of a macho culture. In contrast, Casey takes her own struggle for gender equality in the country where she is born and raised as central, and subsequently finds it everywhere.

Such comparison between one's own experiences growing up as a woman with the experiences of women worldwide has multiple precedents, for example in Robin Morgan's famous book *Sisterhood Is Global*, which first appeared in 1984. Morgan (1996) compiled gender statistics and women's stories about women's position from seventy countries and argued, with those figures in hand, that sisterhood is global. Chandra Mohanty in her sympathetic critique of *Sisterhood Is Global* argues that while the homogeneity arrived at in Morgan's book is not based on biology, but on "the psychologization of complex and contradictory historical and cultural realities," the bond between women conceived in the book derives in the end from an assumption of sameness in oppression that is ahistorical (Mohanty 1992, 80).

One of the women that I interviewed, who now heads a small NGO,[1] is one of the original contributors to *Sisterhood Is Global*, and, perhaps unsurprisingly, she talked with me about "reviving sisterhood." Speaking about the idea behind one of the projects initiated by her organization, she says:

> I wanted to ... revive this concept of sisterhood, this kind of connection beyond borders that we have something in common with ... women all over the world.... I think that this idea is somehow engrained in us, we feel it emotionally.... But it is something that we have to rediscover; it somehow got lost in transition. And this old concept of consciousness-raising groups ... somehow it got lost. It is not there anymore, and actually it was our strongest tool in the seventies. And it is a very good tool, as women are very curious. And I wonder why we stopped asking questions, why we were kind of quite complacent.

I suggest that her call for "reviving sisterhood," rather than for reforming or revolutionizing sisterhood, gives the impression that the much-criticized notion of sisterhood has remained unblemished for her. My reading is reinforced by the fact that she depoliticizes the disappearing of the concept of sisterhood as something accidental; "somehow it got lost." The contradiction between a natural or, as Mohanty might say, psychologized notion of sisterhood and a political notion of sisterhood is interesting here. On the one hand, sisterhood is presented as something we feel and that is engrained in us, while on the other hand it is something that has been lost and needs to be actively (re)created through participation in consciousness-raising groups. In contrast to Casey and Sonia, who talked in the "I form," in this quote the woman speaking uses "we" and "us." It remains slightly unclear how far "we" and "us" are the white, middle-class Western European interviewer and her or, more likely, include women worldwide.

Conscious-raising groups have both an individual(ist) and collective component; hooks (2000) warns that while the process of consciousness-raising, which encourages women to see their own experiences in the light of patriarchal structures, is an important step, it should at the same time not be the last step in establishing feminism as a political movement. She cautions against the tendency to see women's ability to describe "their own woe [as] synonymous with developing a critical political consciousness," as this means a feminism based only on "incomplete perspectives" (hooks 2000, 26). For example, when a group of relatively privileged, white, middle-class women are encouraged to take the personal as the starting point for thinking about women's issues, it is likely that they will develop blind spots. This cannot be abstracted from the multiple power structures in which women are differentially situated. The interviewee's reference to conscious-raising groups as a space for asking questions, rather than for providing answers, encourages multiple perspectives to be shared and discussed. At the same time, her reference to what she considers the innate quality of curiosity among women alienates, for instance, those who employ gender perspectives that resist naturalizing women's qualities.

I complement and contrast the three statements above with those of other women who explicitly qualified their confidence in a form of sisterhood. For example, Naomi, a senior staff member in her forties working for an international women's organization in Geneva on women's empowerment, states:

> The whole thing [global sisterhood] has been pretty problematic, but I believe we do share common sisterhood in many different ways, in a general, common struggle in being taken just as seriously as a man. Wherever we are, we still have a long way to go, no matter where we are in the world. I mean obviously many of us have huge privileges that most of the other women in the rest of the world don't have, [don't] enjoy.

Naomi's awareness of a critique of sisterhood shows when she says that "the whole thing has been pretty problematic." Also, by recognizing the differences in privilege and by including herself in the "many of us" with substantial privileges, Naomi acknowledges not only commonality, but also inequality. Whether this difference of privilege is here interpreted as a random difference in luck or as relational—with the former being the common understanding among the women, as I have argued in chapter 3—is unclear. Naomi's initially qualified account of sisterhood takes on a different connotation with her later reference to "a general, common struggle." This risks succumbing to the idea of patriarchy as the most significant enemy for all women, ignoring the divisions between women. This demonstrates the continued relevance of Mohanty's (1992) critique that Morgan's book *Sisterhood Is Global*, with its assumption of shared struggle against patriarchy, masks the implication of women in practices of domination like imperialism and ignores the real differences, material and ideological, between women.

Naomi also added that sisterhood is established through motherhood, a recurrent theme that I have briefly touched upon in chapter 2:

> I think that the common bond of motherhood is also something that is very strong that I feel since having had children. Yeah, so I do feel that there is something that as women we have in common. We have a lot of common linkages, but I don't feel that we are a homogeneous group by any means.... Well, it is all part of patriarchy of trying to somehow insist that women agree on everything in order for us to move forward, and of course that is impossible. So while I think that there are lots of things that bring us together, we are still individuals and have different needs and realities. And we need to respect that, that there is no particular group of women who have all the answers on behalf of women.

I suggest that the second part of this rich quote, where Naomi refers to "different needs and realities," is consistent with her earlier statement in which she recognizes dissimilar realities, without explicit reflection on the complicity that women can have in some of these inequalities. Moreover, I propose that the idea that differences need to be respected is ambiguous in its implications; on the one hand, it can mean decentering ethnocentrism, while it can also be understood as naturalizing difference and ignoring the structural inequalities that "different needs and realities" are grounded in. The notion of sisterhood through motherhood potentially supports the bridging of other, for example "racial" or class, divides, but it also contains new elements of exclusion: not all women can or want to be mothers. Also "a common bond of motherhood" ignores that the experience of motherhood is inflected by other structures, such as class, "race," sexuality, and citizenship status.

Elisa's statement illustrates the tensions identified in Naomi's account further, by showing that while "global motherhood" as sisterhood can offer new avenues for connections, it problematically imbues motherhood with universal meaning. Elisa explains how her own struggle with raising a young boy means that she "can relate to a woman who talks about how difficult it is to have a dialogue with a seventeen-year-old with my counterpart in Iraq.... And I realize I can only do it if I strengthen my own situation, my own position, my own status. Otherwise he would not listen to me."

Such universalization is countered by Patricia Hill Collins's (2000) rich account of different practices of mothering, which situates black motherhood in the different socioeconomic structures and ideological frames that women face. Nora, a young woman working on a national level with victims of trafficking, leaves more room for the coexistence of a variety of meanings of motherhood. She does not align womanhood and motherhood; in fact, she feels that her identity as a woman has very little impact on her work, except that when she became a mother, she grew more focused on the needs of children of the women she supports. She also recognizes that her clients related differently to her, taking her "more seriously," either because of the status of motherhood or because they perceived her as older and thus more senior, in line with the frequent complaints of the young women in this study that they are not taken seriously.

Thirty-two-year-old, white, middle-class Laura, like Naomi, expresses an ambivalent relation with sisterhood in her international development work, which is worth quoting in more detail:

> For me [the whole notion of sisterhood] has been a journey. It has been complicated for me. I was never part of female groups or gatherings where you could feel that solidarity because we are women. And for me it has more often than not been a question of competition with other women. And I think that for me to feel this, it is one thing to want it in your head, like I want sisterhood so much, but then the other is to feel it immediately. I felt it a lot in Colombia when it related to security. That became very obvious, that I felt more secure in any environment where there were women present.... I was in a really, really ugly robbery, an armed robbery with five guys. After that I got really scared, and I almost could not continue working, because I got really paranoid when I went out. And it was really scary.... But all the time in Colombia [I would] walk where women were walking.... That became a strategy of security, which has nothing to do with reality, except for the fact that most violence is conducted by men, also in Colombia, but it was not really less likely that I was going to get mugged.

Laura talks here about her desire to "feel sisterhood," a desire that arose from her feminism, but that was challenged in situations of competition rather than cooperation between women. The notion that patriarchy hinders the bonding of women or their mutual recognition as being part of the same social group with common interests is a well-known feminist argument (Morgan 1996). An analysis that goes beyond a focus on gender can extend this, for instance, to the role of capitalism, in promoting competition. Laura eventually finds an alternative form of sisterhood, one that is based on a (she calls it "false") feeling of safety. In this particularly challenging situation of fear of being a target of robbery, Laura's usual privilege in relation to other women in Colombia is reversed, as her whiteness and visible Western identity, signaling affluence, make her a more likely target. The sisterhood that she finds in the company of other women in Colombia lies in her assumption that women are less likely to attack her, rather than in their shared vulnerability. Still I suggest that this alternative sisterhood does not amount to the building of a collective political spirit, which for example could develop in the context of working together to construct safe spaces for women.

I argue that this collective spirit could be found in the strong expressions of sheer pleasure and admiration by many of the women when they were talking about working with women from all over the world. This was recounted irrespective of national or international location, work remit, or generation.

Ruth, for example, says, "I must say that I am thrilled with all the wonderful and the remarkable women that I met through the last ten years."

Catherine finds it motivating to meet the members of her organization's network, "because it is great to have feminists, for most part, from all over Europe, from all ages, meeting and sharing and that is quite motivating."

Sophie finds motivation for her work in that "you meet wonderful persons in this work, people that struggle and that have political fights and do service delivery in countries where it is really impossible, and they sacrifice a lot in their work, so I guess the motivation comes from the people that work in countries that are so much more difficult than [here]."

Naomi says: "Working with women from all over the world is just a really fantastic and really enriching experience."

The energy that comes from the mutual inspiration and admiration can be a source to draw on when constructing more sustainable forms of solidarity than a sisterhood based on common victimhood.

BUILDING SOLIDARITIES

In the final section of this chapter, I will look more closely at instances of self-understanding and relationality that go beyond, respectively, racing to innocence and sisterhood as common victimhood. The aim of this section is twofold: first to offer an interpretation of the range of ways in which the women understood their connections with the women their work targeted. Second, the goal is to draw some individual and collective components from these narratives that, as I suggest, can foster solidarities beyond sisterhood. I will argue that the following four building blocks are relevant and discuss them in turn: resisting divisions; establishing connections through experience; recognizing the instability of one's own position; and solidarity as a process rather than a given.

Resisting Divisions

The critiques of global sisterhood presented in the first section have problematized dynamics of a particular invocation of relationality, namely shared victimhood, without wanting to dismiss the linkages between women worldwide. I therefore return to Casey's narration that I quoted at the beginning of the chapter about finding her struggle at home in other places in the world. While she problematically centered her own experiences, her emphasis on linkages and parallels between different locations offers a positive contribution in disrupting the divisions created by (interlocking) systems of oppression. As she explains, she contrasts herself with people who look at "climate or immigration issues as something specific that is not part of their everyday life," whereas she sees herself as "part of the global village [as] it is so evident that most political issues on a global level are part of my daily life." This brings to mind Cynthia Enloe's (1989) twist on "The personal is political," mentioned in chapter 3, that "the political is personal."

In a very different way, Stacey in Geneva also resists the divisions between herself, the partners, and the final beneficiaries within the field of gender and health in which she is working. When Stacey highlights the ways in which she, the partners, and her colleagues are also affected by gender inequalities, she neither equates their experiences nor draws on her own personal victimhood. Rather, I suggest, she challenges a division between those that are perceived as in need of development and those that are seen as already developed, equal, and empowered. Instead, she understands herself and her colleagues as implicated in gender struggles without presupposing anything about the specific ways in which these play out in different contexts:

> People assume that those of us that work in international institutions, that work on gender equality and women's empowerment, don't have to deal with these issues ourselves. That assumption is very, very clear, and that has played out, for example, when once someone asked me to review footage of some film clips that they were planning on showing in last year's international women's year event, which was around ending impunity for violence against women in emergency and conflict settings. And there was no warning that the material I was about to open was very graphic, very difficult. . . . the fact that that had not been thought through, that not only the women also the men might have gone through something just as traumatic, may have experienced gender-based violence in their own life, whether through physically experiencing it or through supporting someone else through it. . . . And that aspect of my identity, in terms of being not only somebody that works on an issue, but also somebody that can have experienced an issue, is often ignored. . . . But I think it is important for institutions [like ours] to think about.

Stacey makes a very similar statement about the "local" partners she works with:

> I think often there is an automatic assumption that people that are working in gender are not affected by gender relations, which is completely not true. . . . Inevitably the people that I meet along the way who are in what some would consider positions of power in their own communities are still very much

affected by gender inequality, still live the norms, roles, and relations that affect everyone and not simply marginalized groups.... So for me the women that we work with in that sense are very much also a part of my target audience. It is not only the women that are coming to health centers for services, but it is also women who are making decisions as to how these health centers work.

I suggest that Stacey's narrative also challenges the notion of distance, discussed in chapters 3 and 4, as the distant and near here are linked to each other through lived experiences (Massey 2004). In this narrative, Stacey collapses the distinction made between Northern organizations, Southern partners, and target groups by stating that her female colleagues in the North and the Southern partners *are* effectively (one of) her target group(s). There is a dominant assumption that the women who are working in her field are an "emancipated" elite with experiences very different from those "on the ground." Stacey, however, emphasizes the continuity between the gender struggles of all women, and also of men, in the sense that all face related structural inequalities, or, as she puts it, "norms, roles, and relations that affect everyone and not simply marginalized groups." While Stacey's explanation relies on institutional observations, her own biography as a child of migrants from the global South might have sensitized her to the continuities between the global South and the global North. I suggest that it is important for building sustainable alternative solidarities, that the gesture of resisting divisions is complemented with an understanding of how interconnections play out. Following Casey's terms, the question is how the global and local interact in her as well as in others' everyday lives, and under what conditions she resides in the global village compared to her "neighbors" in that same global village. Patricia Hill Collins captures this interplay with the term "matrix of domination," denoting "the universality of intersecting oppressions as organized through diverse local realities" (2000, 228).

Establishing Connections through Experience

The second building block I turn to are connections built on and through one's own experience of marginality, without centering those experiences as primary or as universally valid. The three examples that I present here have their distinct dynamics, but they have in common that experiences become a source for reaching across boundaries. Strikingly, none of these experiences center gender. Susanne, a retired teacher, who works as a volunteer with refugee women in Britain, grew up with Welsh as her first language. She explains:

> They are always very interested in the fact that English is not my first language. That is a very good point of contact, especially for those who don't speak English as their first language. The fact that I learned to speak English when I was five or six, they find that really interesting and they want me to speak Welsh to them ... which is actually a point of similarity between us. Even though obviously for me learning English, it was more like being brought up bilingually. So it is not the same as arriving as a foreigner in a country and not knowing a word and trying to make sense of a totally different culture. It is very different, but as far as they are concerned, it is a little point of contact: "She knows what I am talking about!"

Gisela, whom I have described before as a white woman from a poor background working for an international organization in the field of gender, trade, and development, draws a link between her own experience of being marginalized and how she responds to others:

> To have the experience of how it is to be in a more marginal position ... makes me more modest in my own ideas in that I don't think I will know. . . . I am confident about my work, but when someone wants to do it differently, I am easier with saying, "Okay, you do it your way, and you have your reasons for it, and I try to support it." I think if you really try to be respectful to people and really try to see where they are coming from, and really see them on the same level, then they will also feel that and respond to that in the same way. I think it is about being honest and being really open towards other people. It sounds a bit more general, but it is difficult to explain.

Finally, Viola, a white woman in her early sixties, discusses her motivation to set up an organization that provides a meeting point for women who have migrated from different countries. Viola grew up in Germany and spoke German as a child; she moved to Scandinavia not long after the Second World War had ended. She explains: "I have a very strong sympathy for those who [are told,] 'You should not really speak your language.'" She speaks of how her mother benefited from finding church networks after she migrated, being able to maintain contacts in German:

> I don't know how religious she really was, but she could come and they would be talking about lots and lots of things. And that is really very strong, to see what it means to have people around you. They would have been very different in their

education, and how they were living, and how much effort they had to make to understand their children.

Viola herself also traveled to America when she was young and tells me, "I thought I knew English, but one thing is to know it on school level and another one to sit down and speak with people. And after a week I could not just sit there and read, I had to get out, and that was another eye opener."

These instances diverge from each other in a number of ways. Whereas Susanne speaks as if the shared experience of foreign language acquisition is discovered by the refugee women she supports, rather than introduced by herself, Viola and Gisela tie their own biographies more explicitly to their (modes of) engagement. While Viola is explicit in drawing connections around experiences of migration and foreign languages, Gisela establishes a general link between her experience of marginalization and a certain modesty and openness toward other lifeworlds. Susanne and Gisela talk about ways to facilitate relationships, whereas Viola talks about what experiences inspired her to found her organization. I argue, however, that they share an affective expression of global interconnectedness, drawn from experiential knowledge. While it might be tempting, especially in the light of the predominant eloquence of many of the women in this study, to dismiss Gisela's statement as naive or superficial, I propose to read the moment that Gisela gets stuck in explaining what she means—"It sounds a bit more general, but it is difficult to explain"—as illustrative of affect grounded in an alternative epistemology of experience (cf. Hill Collins 2000).

Recognizing Instability

In order to counter the risk of reification of (gendered) experience, I propose that the destabilization of positions is a complementary building block for alternative solidarities. This destabilization is to prevent assumptions of sameness and to underline the contextual and shifting effects of interlocking systems of subordination. Kate, an experienced, forty-something German woman in Brussels working for a humanitarian aid and development association, challenges the idea that gender produces a stable effect and instead draws attention to the way in which contexts shape the way her gender is read and plays out. She is also explicit in highlighting the ways in which gender roles are not fixed to sex and that sexed bodies can take on different gender performances. This also challenges simplistic notions of sisterhood through (perceived) commonality in sex. Kate talks here about how her womanhood impacts on her contact with women from partner organizations in the global South:

> It creates boundaries and it may ease others. With a woman I might have less [boundaries], but it does not have to be.... What you mentioned before is a bit old school, that there is a woman and therefore there is the [connection]. I think that's not anymore true, if it ever has been true. Presumably not, but it might not anymore be so helpful.... I can nowadays, at least in NGOs, ... as a woman, I can take on a gender role that is masculine or feminine.

Kate continues to suggest that within the global South there is possibly less flexibility and fluidity concerning gender roles and status, but then immediately seeks to disrupt the hierarchy she seems to introduce:

> In those countries, they [women] still face fierce opposition. But if you are, for example, a woman whose children are big, then you have quite a lot of status as well, so it also changes according to age. I am not sure—it would be interesting to compare a young woman, middle-aged, professionally active, and an older woman in developing country A with one here in our countries. It could also be that at some point, it is more equal and then perhaps you are in a better status when you are an older woman in a developing country than in ours.

She relativizes the difference between the global North and the global South, which she first noted with reference to other examples from the global South where gender does not unequivocally determine position and status, but functions in a more complex interplay with other factors, such as age and motherhood. Kate also reverses usual hierarchies between the global North and global South (often framed in terms of progressive and less progressive gender regimes), suggesting that the position of an older woman in the South might be "better" than in the North.

Sylvia's reflections on how being a woman affects her work with gender issues similarly traverses between the different meanings that she sees being attributed to her gender, depending on the context. As she, a white, middle-class woman who works internationally on gender and security, explains in a long narrative:

> That gets a bit difficult sometimes, being a woman and working with gender issues, where there is a certain type of frustration, as it is generally very much white women who do things. I find that going into a room and seeing a whole bunch of people who look like me is just depressing and gets a bit frustrating. I mean frustrating and disheartening in terms of what are we actually

accomplishing. If it is just the same people talking to the same people, then we are never actually moving anywhere.... [When] it is more likely to be with people from the same background and other women, [then] my identity as a woman seems less important, because we are all women. Whereas I think my identity as a woman working in a postconflict situation where nine times out of ten I was the only woman, then it became much more important. Because then I had to assert certain things. There I had to be almost like "the representative woman." And there was a lot more stress . . . of having to make sure that the woman view comes in. But also there is more of a reason sometimes to be less of a woman and be one of the guys in order to fit in.

In this extract, being a woman who works with gender issues takes on many different meanings and is navigated in various ways. First, her professional meetings with other women from similar backgrounds to talk about gender equality make Sylvia conscious of her own whiteness because of the overwhelming whiteness of such meetings. In addition, she feels that the significance of being a woman is less obvious in all-women or all-feminist company. In contrast, while working in international conflict zones where she is often the only woman, she experiences a pressure to be "the representative woman" who is supposed to give a gender analysis or the (generalized) "women's view." At the same time, being in a predominantly male environment, she feels the need to adopt a "masculine" gender role in order to adapt and be accepted. While whiteness as well as other privileges are noted here without explicit reflection on exclusionary mechanisms that might lie at the root of the homogeneity of the people in the room, the instability of the meaning of gender in this narrative prevents an easy sliding into victimhood or innocence.

The final narrative that I present as an instance of the third building block, the instability of gender, is Stacey's reflection on the shifts in how she is perceived. Stacey has earlier described how she deviates from the "norm" in more than one respect, because of her religion, her "race," her social class, and the way in which her childhood experience of being the only non-white child in her school has been formative, as discussed in chapter 2. She emphasizes, however, that currently "being a young woman is perhaps the identity that is the hardest to deal with here." Stacey observes that in the international organization she now works for, "it is no longer the challenge of being the brown girl." Stacey:

So I mean, that is the wonderful thing about working in an international organization: that everyone is from everywhere else. But that does not mean that there are no assumptions about my identity. There are assumptions that automatically brown means Indian; brown can usually never mean Canadian or [where my parents come from].

As this account shows, the intersecting categories, shaped by structural forms of discrimination, take on their specific meaning within particular locations, institutional settings and times (Farris and de Jong 2014). The signification of categories shifts according to the context in which they are brought into play. Stacey's brown skin is "read" differently and takes on different meanings depending on the situation. Sara Ahmed (1997) uses an autobiographical narrative to illustrate the multiple, shifting readings of her body in an encounter with the police as a fourteen-year-old in Australia. In their short confrontation her bare feet and brown skin are first read as deviant Aboriginal and hence as a threat to the safety of the neighborhood. Then, when she tells them which elite school she attends, she is seen as a middle-class white girl with a sexy sun tan. Neither interpretation does justice to her "real" origin, in the same way that, according to Stacey, "brown can usually never mean Canadian" or where her parents come from. As Ahmed asserts elsewhere, black feminists have drawn attention to "the processes of identification which produce contradictory and unstable subject positions, where subjects are addressed or 'hailed' in many different ways" (Ahmed 2000a, 112). Patricia Hill Collins, listing her ascribed and self-identified subject positions, states, "I am all of these things some of the time, but none of these things all of the time" (Hill Collins 2012, 14).

Solidarity as a Process

Finally, I suggest that the analysis of the interview material, as well as a discussion of what can be drawn from these narratives in respect to establishing alternative connections, presents a fourth component. I have labeled this "solidarity as a process rather than as a given." Caraway proposes solidarity among feminists as an alternative to sisterhood, as a "sign of our political maturity" (1992, 201). According to her, solidarity, in contrast to sisterhood, "allow[s] for greater differentiations [of] the roots of oppression" and should be created through the practice of political struggles rather than being taken as natural. This also means that alliances and coalitions are shifting with different contexts and topics (Hill Collins 2000). For example, Ruth's small international radical organization often works with other women's organizations on reproductive rights, but sometimes finds allies in young people's groups. It is clear from her account that she does not take a shared experience and approach among women for granted, when she says: "It's a tremendous fight for everybody. So everybody does it in their own way and sometimes you can find a common ground on which you want to work together and it is really nice."

Ruth emphasizes the hard work required and the exceptionality of such common ground. It is possible for women to find and share common visions; however, we need to be constantly aware that we cannot take for granted commonality or consensus and that this requires effort (Caraway 1992; Roth 2003). Sarah's account of how the international unit of her organization in Geneva works together with the national sections is a powerful example of such negotiated solidarity:

> Yes, it is challenging. The challenges though are also opportunities and strengths because while it is challenging that we have varying opinions, it also means that we pick critical looks at what it is that we are doing. And when we do come to consensus, that consensus includes so many different perspectives, that we know it is a well-thought out impressive consensus.... A lot of times we don't get there, and we continue debates and discussions for years before we can achieve a consensus. And that too, because we are exposed to all these different opinions, it informs the work that we are doing and makes that work more holistic. When we issue statements from the international level, we are very clear that we have consulted quite broadly and we have consensus on those decisions. I think, as opposed to the UN, where you get the lowest common denominator, because of the challenges we put to one another, we are more often challenging each other to make a stronger and more powerful statement.

Similar to Ruth's account, in Sarah's narrative coalitions become intensive, challenging, time-consuming, but ultimately rewarding. Sarah's reference to discussions where they cannot reach consensus, which she positively values as informing their work in other ways, resonates with hooks's (1986) suggestion that commitment to feminism as a political struggle entails a preparedness to productively engage with conflict in order to develop mutual understanding. Even when no consensus is found in the short term, the mere exposure to alternative viewpoints becomes (self-)transformative. Spelman aptly calls a shared viewpoint "a difficult political achievement" (1990, 13). I argue here that the energy many women gain from their admiration of and inspiration by other women, as I discussed at the end of the previous section, is a productive source to draw on in times of working through solidarities-in-progress.

While the examples of Ruth and Sarah have spoken to collective efforts, I close this section with discussing the individual "work" that is needed to underpin the building of coalitions that are more sustainable than a sisterhood based on shared victimhood. For this I return again to Laura, whose narrative I presented as an instance of the trap of competing marginalities and who said that she desired sisterhood, but found it difficult to find. Ruth Frankenberg concluded from her study of white women talking about "race" that being subjected to one type of marginalization does not necessarily lead to awareness of other subordinations. Importantly, however, she also recognized that "liberatory movements" could provide "specific tools" that help to develop antiracist approaches (Frankenberg 1993, 20). Laura indeed explains that she "sometimes do[es] the exercise to translate [her ideas about gender structures] into one of the other power structures," where she is in the dominant position.

She gives the example of the sessions on masculinity that she facilitates as part of her job and which she thinks should be compulsory for all boys and men. Laura then asks herself:

> Does that mean that I also think that I should be in groups with white people talking about racism and whiteness and how we reproduce these power structures? Of course it does; that would be a logical way of dealing with it. If I expect that from men, then I should also expect that from myself, and I don't. And I could always say, "Yeah, but I have chosen to focus on working with gender and feminism," but that is also my easiest choice, that is my disadvantaged position that is also where I have something to gain. For me working with my whiteness is a lot less rewarding, so of course I am not better than someone else.

Speaking directly to Laura's acknowledgment of her own false excuse, "and I could always say, 'yeah, but I have chosen to focus on working with gender and feminism,'" Fellows and Razack pertinently urge us to ask ourselves, "Where have we positioned other women within our strategies for achieving social justice? What do we gain from this positioning?" (Fellows and Razack 1998, 352). These questions are particularly relevant in the context of NGO work, which has a commitment to forms of social and global justice. Lorde, in the aptly called section "Uses of Anger," appeals in an affective register: "What woman here is so enamoured of her own oppression that she cannot see her heelprint upon another woman's face? What woman's terms of oppression have become precious and necessary to her as a ticket into the fold of the righteous, away from the cold winds of self-scrutiny?" (Lorde 1984, 132).

Laura's awareness and questioning of her own privilege and the acknowledgment of her "race to innocence" shows, however, that she is not "so enamoured of her own oppression" that she shies away from critical self-scrutiny. While the focus on her gains and losses with respect to fighting different forms of oppression speaks honestly to the interests and power at stake, Laura continues isolating forms of subordination.

To further explore the tools that feminist theories can offer for addressing the "race to innocence," I have suggested elsewhere (de Jong 2009) that it is useful to turn to Sandra Harding's notion of "strong reflexivity," which she develops in the context of her famous account of feminist standpoint theory (Harding 1991, 163). Harding's standpoint theory is on the one hand a response to the call of marginalized women that more attention should be paid to the multiplicity and diversity of the category "woman" and on the other hand an answer to the demands of conventional science in terms of truth and objectivity (Harding 1991). Arguing for the "situating of knowledges," she asks researchers to reflect on their own backgrounds, cultural baggage, and, importantly, the relation to the research subject studied. This demands an interrogation of Self and Other that pays attention to the power structures that influenced the research and to the relational aspects of (research) identity. This

> would require that the objects of inquiry be conceptualized as gazing back in all their cultural particularity and that the researcher, through theory and methods, stand behind them, gazing back at his [sic] own socially situated research project in all its cultural particularity and its relationship to other projects of his [sic] culture (Harding 1991, 163).

Despite the fact that the notion of reflexivity is most commonly used within the context of academic knowledge production (Adkins 2002; Harding 1991; Rose 1997), I argue that it is equally relevant within justice-seeking practices, as knowledge production plays an equally central role there. In Laura's narrative discussed above, it is possible to see glimpses of such reflexivity. In response to my question about how her identity plays out in her work, she says:

> I don't think there is a moment in my work where my identity does not matter, of course. And I think I sometimes manage to be conscious and to do a good job anyways, but I also think I slip all the time, I forget things.... I am really prejudiced sometimes about lots of things, but at least I think I am fairly honest with myself and I can see it.

In this example "identity" is not solely associated with Laura's own subordination as a woman, but also explicitly with her domination and prejudice, in contrast to the silences on privilege in the narratives presented earlier in this chapter. Here Laura stresses the importance of recognizing her own position, while at the same time she realizes that she "slips" all the time. She cannot reach a point where her recognition of her prejudices is complete and finished, where she does not risk making the mistake again. I argue that these slips and the reflections that follow are more productive than risking what Rose (1997) and Maxey (1999) have called a "transparent" reflexivity. In the context of so-called reflexive research, this transparency emerges when researchers, after presenting some short note on positionality at the outset of their research, fall back onto universalizing knowledge claims, assuming that the process of reflexivity can be completed, and that by being reflexive they have absolute and unmediated access to their own and the other's position. This is a flight to certainty. When Laura says, "I think I am fairly honest with myself and I can see it," this verges on the transparent reflexivity that Rose warns against. Rose (1997) instead argues for the productiveness and the significance of the uncertainties in reflexivity. I suggest that this is in line with understanding solidarity as a process and work-in-progress. The uncertain struggle and labor for building solidarities ties together the collective and individual attempts discussed here.

CONCLUDING REMARKS

In this chapter I have discussed relationality between women in the context of aid practices, shifting the focus from the self-directed sense of responsibility presented in chapter 3 to an analysis of how the women conceived of their relation with those they seek to support.

I have analyzed their narratives against the backdrop of the controversy surrounding the notion of sisterhood as common victimhood. This chapter has shown the currency of sisterhood as a way to understand connections between women on a global scale, with some women's understandings of sisterhood resembling the much-critiqued assumption of universality of victimhood, and others presenting a more ambivalent desire for and understanding of sisterhood.

In the second section of this chapter I have taken a closer look at the mechanisms underpinning the assumption of sisterhood as shared victimhood, which critics have exposed as ethnocentrism and the refusal to admit to complicities in other structures of subordination. I have argued that this is supported by what Fellows and Razack call the "race to innocence." The "race to innocence" is the move to underline and identify with one's "subordinate identity" at the expense of attention to other structures of domination. It hence encompasses the belief that gender oppression is the most fundamental power structure as well as a lack of critical self-scrutiny in relation to one's own implication in processes of domination. I have presented different instances of the "race to innocence" and have argued that this "innocence" is present both in what is said and in what is left unsaid, reflecting the privilege that dominant positions remain unmarked. I could thereby establish a connection between how the women understood their own identity to play out in their work and the ways in which they saw their relations with other women, a form of sisterhood that failed to decenter their own positions. I have shown that women's privileging of gender structures as primary led them fall into the "trap of competing marginalities" (Fellows and Razack 1998, 339); this obstructed their view on structures of oppression as interlocking. I have proposed to read the interview narratives that foreground gender over other structures not as women's individual failures, but as reflecting wider power dynamics and vested interests that are visible at a discursive and material level.

The final section of this chapter has taken a different set of narrations about relationality as the point of departure for analyzing the women's attempts at alternative positionings beyond global sisterhood. It has also turned to those positionings as a basis for developing an understanding of the building blocks required for constructing alternative solidarities. I have identified four building blocks: resisting divisions; establishing connections through experience; recognizing the instability of one's own position; and solidarity as a process rather than a given. I argue that these building blocks are interdependent and together constitute essential ingredients for establishing coalitions between women in the face of mutually reinforcing and entangled structures of domination. With the interview narratives, I have shown that the strategies assembled from these building blocks are interactive and relational, working from ascribed and self-identified positions. Moreover, these strategies need to be developed with collective as well as individual labor that can be nurtured by the affective components that common struggle and exchange between women can bring. As one of the women whom I interviewed said to me, quoting from the song "Overlap" by feminist singer Ani DiFranco: "I know there is strength in the differences between us and I know there is comfort where we overlap." In the next chapter, I will further probe Self-Other relations in the context of the women's work, shifting the focus to how the "Other" is understood, and placing this in the context of postcolonial continuities.

CHAPTER 6

Postcolonial Configurations

In this chapter I draw on postcolonial theory to analyze how the women I interviewed imagined and understood those at the receiving end of their engagement for national and international organizations across North–South divides. Postcolonial theories can offer ways for rethinking Self-Other relations, in the same way that critical feminist perspectives on sisterhood have offered both critique and alternative conceptualizations of women's connectedness, as demonstrated in the previous chapter. Postcolonial perspectives have problematized at least three components of Western feminism, as Leela Gandhi (1998) argues. First, the prominent motif of "the third world woman" in white Western feminism; second, the history of feminists as imperialists, with Western women being "liberated" at the cost of the "third world woman"; and third, the legacy of "colonialist deployment of 'feminist criteria' to bolster the appeal of the civilising mission" (Gandhi 1998, 83). These intertwined contentions will each be addressed in this chapter, focusing in particular on the Othering processes that unite all three.

Recognizing the continuities with colonialism that persist after decolonization means that the "post" in "postcolonial" should not be read as a clear cut between the current epoch and the colonial era (McLeod 2000; Ahmed 2000a). Rather, "postcolonial" "marks a decisive, though not definitive shift that stages contemporary encounters" (Frankenberg and Mani 1993, 301). It is therefore simplistic to consider development mere "colonialism by other means" (Cooper and Packard 1997, 30). The field of aid and development is often singled out, however, to demonstrate the endurance of colonial structures and logics, such as those that underpinned the imperialist intervention and in its civilizing mission (Stoler and Cooper 1997; Spivak 1999; Kothari 2006a; Cook 2008). Following Maria Eriksson Baaz, placing the identities of development workers in relation to the postcolonial "does not mean that these identities should be seen as an articulation of already constituted identities drawn directly from the 'colonial library'"; rather the "colonial library" is used to make sense of and to give meaning to situations that arise in the context of development (Eriksson Baaz 2005, 72). While the women that are the focus of this study worked on a wide range of issues beyond "development" narrowly conceived, I will show that a postcolonial approach is relevant in the light of the imperative to "help" present in their work and their operation along a North–South axis.

The first section of this chapter addresses one of postcolonial theory's key claims, namely the durability of colonial structures and discourses. I will offer an analysis of those specific fragments in the women's narrations that make explicit reference to colonialism, to argue that their denials of the enduring relevance of the colonial past confirm the contrary. This speaks to Fechter and Walsh's observation in their edited volume on mobile professionals that the colonial past matters to expatriates, though in different ways, "including mobilising it as valuable resource, modelling it to their needs, or denying it" (Fechter and Walsh 2012, 14). In the second section, I will move to discussing more implicit (post)colonial traces by focusing on the processes of Othering in the interview accounts. I will demonstrate that these processes of Othering operate by reference to cultural difference, in which commonly a hierarchy is created between the gendered Self and the gendered and racialized Other. In these interview narratives, culture becomes reified and reflects colonial racial discourses. Cultural explanations also serve to stabilize ambivalences that arise in the encounter with the Other, and as I propose, hamper more complex interpretations that take into account other structural dynamics as well as power differences. In the final section of this chapter, I present the heterogeneity of terms with which the women made sense of Otherness, discussing narratives that exceeded a cultural frame when confronting difference. I observe at the same time the ways in which many of these narratives remain grounded in a desire for stabilizing the ambivalence of difference.

(POST) COLONIAL LEGACIES

It is well documented that a number of development NGOs and governmental foreign aid institutions originated in the colonial era. Also, scholars have shown that Western women's organizations often failed to take a critical stance toward colonialism, and have traced the continuities between white women's colonial philanthropy and postcolonial development projects for women (Kothari 2006a; Confortini 2011; Higgs 2015).

Nathalie, a white Western mobile professional I interviewed, addressed such links directly by explaining the following about the internationally operating organization that she works for:

> There are many [national associations of my organization] that got started in the mid- to late 1800s. So it was really already by the turn of the last century that the [organization] was in quite a number of countries, so that global nature was something that caught on. Now, of course, Britain being a colonial power at the time certainly helped in its development in other places, and certainly India and South Asia. There are a number of [national/local associations] that date back to late 1800s: India, Myanmar, Sri Lanka.... And then with the partition, you also had Pakistan and then finally Bangladesh. But there is certainly a link there to colonial times, where you had British women who had started [national/local associations] who were overseas.... As the empire crumbled, there is also very much a strong push for the [national/local associations] to be run by the women of their countries, so that they are run by indigenous women, if you will.

The organization's current global status and the legitimacy it gets through its alliances with local associations are directly linked to the status of Britain as an imperial power. Though the organization is officially open to women of all different faiths, its Christian heritage and identity and presence in countries where Hinduism and Islam are the dominant religions recalls colonial, in particular missionary, interventions. I was interested in hearing more about the transfer of organizational governance from the British women as the original founders to the "indigenous women" and hence asked Nathalie whether this had been a challenging process. She replied:

> We are talking now what, fifty years ago, or more, so I don't think.... It is not an issue anymore. I think during the whole period during the forties, fifties, sixties when the whole colonial structure was being dismantled ... well, the official colonial structure was being dismantled, and countries were turned back into the hands of the people, rather than being run by colonial powers. [The national/local organizations] were certainly within that period of the forties through the seventies, certainly being run then by women of the country and not by colonial women.

I suggest that Nathalie's narrative contains a tension; on the one hand the colonial period and the decolonization process are firmly situated in the past ("it is not an issue anymore"). At the same time, by qualifying her argument ("well, the *official* colonial structure was being dismantled"), this is disrupted. She defends her organization (against my suggestion that it could have been "challenging") by stressing that the handover of power in her organization was conducted earlier than the handover of power by national governments. This tension between colonial closure and continuity reappeared in various forms in the women's statements, as I will further demonstrate below.

As mentioned above, postcolonial theorists have insisted that the "post" of postcolonialism does not denote closure, but points to enduring structuring dynamics. Postcolonial and decolonial thought have different intellectual heritages, geographical origins, and foci, but share, at its most basic level, a common concern with decentering Western epistemologies and with highlighting that the notion of "the West" is sustained by a violent colonial and imperial history. Recent years have witnessed more efforts to bring together postcolonial scholarship that was originally developed by (diaspora) scholars from the Middle East and South Asia and inspired by literary studies and Marxist thought, with decolonial perspectives, which are grounded in the South American context and draw, among other things, on world systems theory (Maese-Cohen 2010; Bhambra 2014). Decolonial thinkers, equally concerned with finding ways to theorize the lasting effects of colonialism, employ the term "coloniality" to underline historical continuities and "modernity/coloniality" to denote the inseparability of those two, decentering modernity as a European phenomenon (Quijano 2000; Escobar 2007; Lugones 2010; Verschuur and Destremau 2012). Hence both postcolonial theory and decolonial thought, in different ways, have diagnosed the persistence of the dynamics emerging from the colonial era and see their interventions as responding to a denial of these legacies.

It is in this light that I also read the narration of Eva, who talks to me in her European home country about her small organization's aim to work *with* other women in the global South on security issues, rather than *for* these women. When I ask her whether she thinks power differences (still) play a role, which would complicate the claim to be really working *with* the women, she replies:

> I think it is difficult not so much in how we frame the problems, but it is sometimes difficult how you are perceived. Because the women [in the global South] have less access to funds, money, media, whatever, and they obviously want to do something to develop. And in the world there is so much inequality …

At the same time we are not in the year of colonialism, we go there twice and we give back a little bit.

What is interesting about this quote is that on the one hand, the question about power differences prompts Eva to reflect on global inequalities. On the other hand, she places colonialism in the past when she stresses, "We are not in the year of colonialism." The desire for closure is expressed in this contradiction, where her pondering on inequality leads her to mentioning colonialism—which suggests that she recognizes the postcolonial impact of colonial relations—while concurrently the final part of her narrative insists on being beyond the colonial era. I propose that there is another tension in the fact that it is Eva who can announce that colonial times are long gone, despite the fact that, as she said, there is still a perception in the South that colonial continuities play a role. This points to the enduring power inequalities where their concerns can be dismissed and Western knowledge and historical narratives remain centered.

Gill, a Western woman from a former colonial power, relates a similar gap between the perceptions of her own European-based feminist network and those of an organization from the global South about the dynamics of their cooperation. She recalls an encounter with a "group of women that were from Africa." This group suggested that Gill's organization, which is active in the fields of development and trade, should work on a certain policy issue, which Gill's organization had decided not to make one of its priorities:

> They were like, "Yeah, but Africa is not really prioritized." You could kind of feel, "We are being marginalized again," that kind of atmosphere. We tried to be polite and also be open to say, "Okay, we will try. If you have issues, we will pass them on to [a certain] working group, and you are always welcome to contact us, and if you have issues, please let us know." And this is then how you try to resolve it. But sometimes it is difficult if you don't really have the time to go into depth, to really explain from your perspective that they understand it and for them not to feel, "Okay, we are being marginalized" or, "Okay, it is again the Western European imperialists that are telling us what to do." Because sometimes you feel this kind of tension, and they also said something in that direction.

Gill explains that she personally "did not lie" awake over this situation, but that one of her colleagues found the situation challenging. The exchange does not prompt Gill to reconsider the position of her organization; rather, she focuses on making the group of African women understand why they made a certain strategic decision. As she indicates that there "was [no] time to go into depth," I asked her whether she thought that with more time this issue would have been resolved. This is where she introduces partnership—as discussed in chapter 4—as a way to establish an equal relationship: "In one meeting you don't resolve this; this is really something you resolve through a partnership. And even then I heard [such] stories from people, and even then if organizations are not really open to discuss their initial ideas, it cannot be resolved."

When I suggest that another reason why they could not discuss this tension openly might have been the formality of the meeting, Gill says:

> I don't feel this was because of the formality of the meeting, but more if people have these engrained ideas ... , that they are being the poor South, and the people in the EU are not listening to them, and the NGOs are also much stronger than them and they have this perspective. I think sometimes it takes much more time to change that. Maybe if they have the chance to live here for a month and work in this kind of organization, that maybe helps to change their mind, but there is not that. . . . Or maybe even if they keep exchanging with their partners, they would change their mind. I don't know.

Again, the source of the tension is attributed to a misjudgment on the side of Southern organizations and, similar to Eva's narrative, there is a strict division between "them" and "us." At another point in the interview, Gill indicated that she also identified her own prejudices when she traveled to Uganda, and in that sense she sees biases as commonly held. She proposes that mobility, experience in other countries, and contact with other cultures would "change their mind," but recognizes that the average person from the South has a smaller chance to travel abroad than a person in the North and concludes from that that it is therefore hard to rid themselves of prejudices. So while Gill expresses the conviction that people from the global South "cannot help" holding particular views, at the same time she holds them responsible for the tensions in the meeting. In addition, she dismisses the women's claims that their concerns were not being prioritized by framing these as "engrained ideas," rather than as being rooted in real historical practices and material realities. I suggest that the term "engrained" also naturalizes the women's objections. It thus avoids engagement with the imperialist legacies of development and women's organizations and with the fact that the women's objections might have grown out of repeated experiences of not being heard.

Karoline, a white Western woman in Brussels, when speaking in the context of considering the ways in which her Northern organization engages in the global South around issues of development and trade, is very careful in stressing that before acting, various approaches need to be employed to understand different contexts. When I put to her that organizations are now more conscious about trying to engage with multiple perspectives as a response to being criticized for one-dimensional views, the colonial suddenly crops up again—without being named as such—when she replies: "I think the days are over where you can just come and say [that people have to do something a certain way]. If you do that, you just do it because you have money and you are white, but not because anyone would want to listen to you [laughs]." Again, there is the suggestion of a significant rupture with the civilizing missions from the past, while at the same time, the reference to the enduring power of whiteness and capital disrupts that firm break.

Sonia, a Latin American woman whose international work aims at supporting women in African countries, says, when asked whether she thinks her identity has an impact on her work: "Yes, I would think so. But I maybe, I don't know how to explain it, but I guess the fact of being Latin American, that does not make me European, so that does not make me a colonizer." When I asked her whether the women she works with in Africa have made references to colonialism (to explore whether that was the reason for her to foreground her "noncolonizer identity"), she replied that they had never expressed that. If her mentioning of colonialism is neither prompted by the women she works with nor by me, it is interesting that this is one of her first associations. This could be read as a general acknowledgment of the power of colonial discourse. Her stressing of her noncolonizer identity can also be interpreted as a way to deflect attention from her other privileged identity markers, such as her level of education and her (passing as) white(ness), where she would have needed to reflect on her position of dominance (see chapter 5 on the "race to innocence"). Sonia's reference to the suitability of a "noncolonizer identity" for development work, resonates with discourses that link national identity with a disposition for development cooperation. For example, in Irish political debates, development aid is defended with reference to a shared history of colonial victimhood with countries in the global South (Kevlihan 2001). In Austria the idea of a limited involvement in colonialism combined with the country's pretense to be the first victim of National Socialism surfaces in national parliamentary debates as the impulse for reaching out to African nations at the time of their struggles for independence (Pfeffer 2012; cf. Loftsdóttir 2012 about Iceland).

In answer to the same question about identity, Naomi, a Canadian woman working in Geneva on women's leadership replies:

> Coming from Canada, which has a fairly mixed-up culture in terms of it is not like a European culture; the people who settled in Canada are not the original

people in Canada. So I guess I also have that respect for living in someone else's country and being mindful of that, and being mindful of the history of how my country was set up by effectively displacing the original people there.... In Canada, the French were there first and then the British kicked them out. I think that, sadly, that kind of thing keeps going on and on in the world and we are not learning from history.

In this extract I identify again the tension between the fact that Naomi emphasizes that she has learned from the past—as she claims that her awareness of Canada's history makes her more mindful—and her statement that "we are not learning from history" as the displacement of peoples continues. Similarly to Sonia, Naomi understands colonialism in terms of an identity rather than as a persistent structure that shapes North–South relationships and differentiates her identity from that of a European former colonizer. Canada's exceptional status in international politics is a common trope, in particular in relation to peacekeeping (Razack 2004; Whitworth 2005; Heron 2007). As the Canadian NGO TakingITGlobal, which engages youth in global issues, for instance writes on its "Ethiopia Millennium Project" website: "Canadian culture inherently includes being a global citizen. Canada embraces multiculturalism, immigration, and cross-cultural understanding. Canada is recognized internationally as a peacekeeping nation" (TakingITGlobal, n.d.).

Interestingly, Naomi connects the violent history of building a nation through displacement and annihilation of other peoples to the idea that this legacy has provided her with a particular respect. This echoes arguments by ex-colonizer countries, who profess that they have a special responsibility toward their ex-colonies and other developing nations in development cooperation. I therefore argue that similar to women's expressions of "competing marginalities" in chapter 5, the women's individual statements on colonial legacies that I discuss in this section have to be understood in a larger discursive and structural postcolonial context. For example, Tom Hampson of the Fabian Society, Britain's oldest think tank, which is constitutionally affiliated to the Labour Party, argued in the Fabian Society publication *2025: What Next for the Make Poverty History Generation?*: "We need to ask ourselves why it was the British ... who, of all Western peoples, felt the moral certainty last year [in the Make Poverty History campaign] to intervene and proselytise" and "We need to recognise that our role must draw on the benefits of our history of empire ... [and that] we have wisdom in our experience and the responsibility that comes with it" (Hampson 2006, 12).

Such justifications serve to recenter former colonial powers and settler nations, with a veneer of apology and humbleness, and validate new (violent) interventions. Grace, a white British woman who is older than Naomi and Sonia, works on a national level with female migrants, including from the African continent. She explicitly reflects and is concerned about the lasting influence of her upbringing in relation to British imperial discourse:

> For our generation, you know, all Africans wore grass skirts, they lived in mud huts, and they carried spears. Those were the images that you had of Africa. That was what you read in the books. I suppose my attitude has changed over the years, but it has been quite . . . I have not noticed the change, but certainly that is all we saw of Africa. And lions and tigers and elephants. . . . I believe the term that was used in this country was "natives." . . . We have been conditioned to think of certain people in a certain way. And it must be altogether easy for this misconception to bubble up to the surface, possibly when you are least expecting it.

Grace's words and her narration about her upbringing are effective in demonstrating that the colonial past is not as remote as others presented it to be. While some of the images she refers to might not be circulating with the same starkness, they are still recognizable. As Grace underlines, something must have changed, but since these shifts have been gradual, she is suspicious about the traces of these images in her own and others' mental colonial library. By referring to the fact that colonial imaginary appears when you are least expecting it, Grace introduces a gap between the conscious efforts to be antiracist (as will be further discussed below) and the way in which she and others are embedded in and shaped by particular histories. I argue that this gap underpins the women's desire for a closure of colonialism, as expressed in the above-quoted narratives, which often deny the relevance of colonial structures for contemporary work practices, while simultaneously underlining their significance by repeated reference to them. This section has provided some examples of how women described their identities with reference to the colonial; the next section will further explore the relational dimension of (post)colonial identities.

CULTURAL LENSES OR BLINKERS

One prominent theme in postcolonial theory is the relation between colonial Self and colonized Other, and the identity constructions that emerge from this relation. In the previous chapters I have analyzed the women's self-understandings and relationality in the context of their work. In this section, I will shift the focus to women's understandings of those they support with their work. Given that the previous chapters demonstrated that the women's self-understandings by extension also disclosed something about the intended target of their work, I work in this chapter with the reversed assumption that the framing of the Other reveals much about the Self.

For Sonia, a Chilean woman who is working in a junior position on gender and peace in Africa from Geneva, the Other as the "culturally radically different" is both exciting and frustrating, as she describes here in one breath:

> I find it challenging [to relate to other people from different cultures], because I am talking to them, and let's say I have all my culture that they don't know. Particularly when I say I am from [Chile], it is like, "Where? What?" So I know I have a lot of things inside me that they don't know and that they probably would not understand. And at the same time they have the same thing: they have their culture that comprises a lot of things I might not know and not understand. But we can still talk to each other and do something together. I think that is great.

Similarly, at another point in the interview she says:

> I think that the cultural differences are sometimes very challenging and sometimes in a way very rewarding to be able to discover them. I think that I am very lucky that I am able to see many things that a lot of people don't, that just always live in the same place. So sometimes it is difficult. Sometimes, I don't know, I think that you have to help them a lot, you have to really guide them. You have to be there for very silly things.

I suggest that in the first quote, culture is central to both Sonia's own understanding of Self and of Other. In this narrative, there is no obvious hierarchy of cultures present but rather a celebration of cultural pluralism. A potential danger of this particular understanding of cultural diversity is that cultures are still seen as stable "possessions"; Sonia indeed speaks of "having" culture. To learn about cultures then is "not to create a more rich and universal culture, but to imprison us more effectively in a human zoo of differences" (Malik 1996, 150). In the second quote, a hierarchy emerges when Sonia states, "You have to help them a lot," where she is the one in charge of "guiding them." The Other is here, in the words of postcolonial scholar Homi Bhabha, the object both of Sonia's "desire and derision" (Bhabha 2005, 96). Sonia's pairing of adjectives like great/challenging, challenging/rewarding, and lucky/difficult to describe the relation between her and the women she seeks to support through her work reflect the ambivalent relation between colonizer and colonized, which is characterized by a "conflict of pleasure/unpleasure" (Bhabha 2005, 107). In the remainder of this section, I will return to and further elaborate on how the women addressed culture, and especially to what cultural explanations do in terms of providing closure for what is seen as uneasy difference and ambivalence.

Bhabha's understanding of colonial stereotypes is helpful in underlining their complexity. He emphasizes the instability of the colonial discourse and states that precisely because of this ambivalence the stereotype is "needed" to reaffirm a certain image, to fix the Other who in fact escapes easy classification (Bhabha 2005). Closer analysis shows that stereotypes contradict each other and thereby deconstruct a coherent image of the Other. An easily recognizable example of this is the coexistence of the stereotype of the black man as being aggressive and sexually active and the image of the black man's passiveness and servitude. According to Bhabha,

> It is the force of ambivalence that gives the colonial stereotype its currency, ensures its repeatability in changing historical and discursive conjunctures; … produces that effect of probabilistic truth and predictability which, for the stereotype, must always be in excess of what can be empirically proven or logically constructed. (Bhabha 2005, 95)

I follow here Bhabha's suggestion that critical analysis should move from merely identifying stereotypes as positive or negative "to an understanding of *processes* of *subjectification* made possible (and plausible) through stereotypical discourse" (Bhabha 2005, 95). One powerful example of the ambivalence of stereotypes can be traced in how middle-aged white Vita discusses the veil or headscarf in the context of reflections on her work at a social meeting space for migrant women in the capital city of a European country. Throughout the interview, the "scarf" makes seemingly spontaneous, repeated appearances in Vita's reflections. The first time is when Vita expresses her strong disapproval of a political campaign by an extreme right-wing party in her country that uses an image of a female judge in a burka as a way to generate anti-Islam sentiments. Vita shows similar awareness of the topicality of the headscarf when she tells me that journalists approach her organization to ask her: "Can you find [me] someone with a scarf [to interview]?"

The headscarf surfaces again when Vita describes a woman who was supported by her organization:

She has a scarf and she is a Muslim. I can see it when they have a scarf. Otherwise I hardly ask, unless it is important and she tells me: "In our culture, Vita ..." [We] are talking about [the fact that] she has children and she is divorced and this husband, he sees the children, and he helps her—and it appears that in their culture, they are not allowed at all to see their ex-husband. And I am thinking, "Jesus!" It is 180 degrees different from what our legislation is trying and what is common in [this country]: the more the parents meet and are together with the children, the better. And she wants it, because she can see it is good for the children. [But] her parents, her family, their friends, they don't want it and they could even [have an argument] about it. And I am thinking, "What is she going to do?"

Though Vita stresses that she is not necessarily interested in the religion of the women coming to her NGO for support, she does not only notice "the scarf," but also uses it as a main descriptor of the woman concerned: this reflects how the veil has become an "overdetermined marker of identity" (Dwyer 1999, 6–7). Later in the interview it is used in a similar descriptive way as one of the main identity markers of another woman: "She wears a scarf and she is divorced and her husband wants her to come back, not to live [with him], but to marry." Through the image of the "woman with the scarf," a story with a clear "us" (the "host" community) and "them" ("her culture") is constructed with the "woman with the scarf" caught in the middle. In Cook's study of Western Voluntary Services Overseas (VSO) volunteers in Gilgit, Pakistan, clothing and veiling plays a central role for the female Western volunteers in situating themselves in relation to the women in Pakistan (Cook 2005).

The veil has been a contentious issue for feminists both in the global South and in the global North, and there is no consensus around its interpretation even among those whose arguments follow a similar line. For example, in her famous essay "Under Western Eyes," Mohanty (1984) criticizes simplistic readings of veiling as oppressive and calls for a contextualized and subtle understanding of the different meanings of the gesture of veiling as a more productive political strategy. While Razack (2001) makes the same point about the homogenizing features of the critique of the veil, she explicitly stresses her viewpoint that the practice of veiling is oppressing for women. Razack proposes it is more important to interrogate the function of the veil as a "marker of difference," which designates African and Asian women "as bodies to be saved by benevolent and more civilized Europeans" (Razack 2001, 6–7). This occurs in Vita's interview extract by attaching the veil to a juxtaposition of family and parenting practices in "our culture" versus "their culture," where the first is connoted as positive and progressive. The ambiguity of professing disinterest in the headscarf while at the same time reinforcing its significance through repeated mentioning culminates when I ask Vita how she would define "success" in her work. "I would define it when the women get on with their lives, when they stand on their own two feet. Maybe they don't take off their scarf tomorrow—I don't really care, I must say. I hardly ever discuss it with them." Against Vita's expressed indifference to the veil, I suggest that Vita's statement establishes a link between lack of freedom, dependence, and veiling practice, which functions, following Razack, to position Vita as benevolent rescuer.

The final manifestation of "the scarf" appears in Vita's narration of her concerns about a woman who uses the services of her organization: "I keep thinking where she is and how they are. And then she came and her scarf became more and more dark and sort of really black." When the woman appeared at the center the next time,

> She came and she was dark and we were talking and talking . . . . She was fragile and I said to her, "Could I ask you something? You had this very nice blue scarf on when you first came, and now you are so black?" And she says, "In our culture, when people die we dress in black," and there had just been bombs in her home country. And what we see as extreme is culture. And I came to think of my friend—when she lost her girlfriend, she shaved all her head and she dressed black. . . . And I got so much wiser, because that is what they do. And I can understand that instead of thinking, "Aaah." And when the women ask me and we talk about [the headscarf], I say, "It will offend many people, [but] it is a choice."

At the end of Vita's quote the scarf emerges simultaneously as a symbol for perceived oppression and as a sign of political agency, "a choice," even with the power to "offend." The headscarf as symbolic for the stereotype of oppressed Muslim women, rather than simply being "a false image which becomes the scapegoat of discriminatory practices ... is a much more ambivalent text of projection and introjections, ... overdetermination, guilt, aggressivity" (Bhabha 2005, 117). In Vita's reflections the headscarf is a symbol of the political and media obsession with Islam, where it is represented as a threat to "Western values." As a response to that, for Vita, it is crucial for her self-image as a tolerant, liberal woman to consider the veil "unimportant." Yet as a symbol of her professed tolerance it becomes immensely significant and hence resurfaces every time again in her descriptions, reinforcing the dominant obsession with the headscarf. In a climate of Islamophobia, the veil figures in the denial of its importance, like "race," "in which an episode of racial talk is closed by a statement that denies the significance of race" (Armbruster 2012, 54). In Vita's narrative the headscarf symbolizes Otherness, radically different culture and religion. This is disrupted the moment she addresses one of the women directly with a question about the color of her headscarf: the explanation gets incorporated in a discourse of similarity through the image of Vita's mourning friend who shaved her head. This strategy of "translating" behavior seen as "alien" to familiar scripts, as a way to manage intercultural encounters and to claim to "know" the Other, was also identified by Schondelmayer (2010) in her study on development workers and foreign correspondents. I will further discuss this desire for closure of ambivalence in the next section.

Desiring Closure

The above examples have already indicated that constructions of the Other are closely connected to constructions of the Self. The desire to grasp Otherness in a way that brings it into reach rather than remaining "alien" is therefore not (merely) a quest for broadening horizons of knowledge but about securing a sense of Self. The confrontation with Otherness is experienced as a destabilization (Schondelmayer 2006). "Cultural knowledge," and the explanations generated from it, fulfill this desire for closure. In response to early development policies that focused on economics only, anthropologists importantly insisted on taking "culture" into consideration to counteract policies that treated local communities as "empty vessels." However, the notions of culture that were adopted by development discourse were often fixed, as well as outside context, time, and space, and groups tended to be understood as culturally homogenous (Pigg 1997, 263–264). Similarly, in gender analysis, while culture was introduced to resist gender essentialism, the result has often been cultural essentialism (Kapur 2005). Culture is particularly often, though not exclusively, invoked in relation to women in the global South, in a "victims of culture model" (Lazreg 2000, 7). The overestimation of the explanatory value of "culture" has, moreover, led to insufficient attention to other factors, such as the damaging effects of some forms of modernization (Narayan 1997). For that reason, the title of this section is cultural lenses or blinkers, pointing to the ways in which cultural explanations can result in blindness to other structural grounds. Cultural blinkers also have a function in shielding against the disruption of a particular sense of Self.

This is illustrated by the following interview fragment from Eva, a middle-aged woman, like Vita, who is in a senior position in her small organization with an international reach. Eva told me that after the large tsunami hit India, she read some reports that stated that the death toll was much higher for women than for men. Upset about this information, she liaised with Indian NGOs in the region and decided to visit the affected area to investigate the reasons for the number of women casualties. Eva describes this experience as follows:

> What we found on the ground in the South Indian region [was] that the women had no chance in the tidal waves, because of the status of women in society, which is defined as being immobile, not very active.... The whole relation to the body is such that they would never go out of their way and run like mad or whatever, you see. They would never undress, even in the situation of danger. They were just swept away even if they would have the chance, but in the sari they could not move. The men were climbing on the trees. They would not; they were just frozen in time. It was incredible, incredible, so many women drowned. And then we thought that we had to do something. That something was that we came up with [a] swimming . . . project.... And this was in time with a new development, a new stage of the organization. We felt we have to leave mainstream, we have to look into areas that are constantly overlooked and pose the questions in those corners where others don't even go into, because they are kind of messy and untidy.

Here the story about the female victims of the tsunami quickly turns into one about the development of Eva's NGO. I suggest that this underlines the way in which narratives about the Other are intertwined with narratives about the Self. By presenting her organization's intervention as exceptional, as going away from the mainstream, Eva also frames the identity of the organization as exceptional. It should be stressed that immediate relief work often overlooks the distinct needs of women as a vulnerable group and that feminist organizations' interventions are important in this light (Asia Pacific Forum on Women, Law and Development 2005). Eva's organization was not the only one to offer a gender analysis. An Oxfam report did suggest as one of the reasons for the high number of female casualties the fact that women were not able to swim or climb in trees (Oxfam 2005). More importantly, however, a number of other explanations are mentioned in alternative sources, which move away from using "culture" as the sole explanatory tool, for example, that women were particularly affected because they were standing at the beach waiting for their husbands who were fishing at sea, since the women have an important function in the fishing industry, or that the women were bathing in the sea (Oxfam 2005; "Most Tsunami Dead Female—Oxfam" 2005; Asia Pacific Forum on Women, Law and

Development 2005). This raises questions about whether Eva overstates the uniqueness of the organization's findings and intervention as well as about the effect of cultural lenses as blinkers.

It is contentious to reconcile the assertion that these are the messy and untidy corners few other organizations wanted to engage with, with the fact that within one visit to the field Eva's organization found the solution to the riddle of the high number of women casualties. When Eva says that "they were just frozen in time. It was incredible, incredible, so many women drowned," her vivid explanation resembles the account of an eyewitness, despite the fact that Eva was not there at the time. Strikingly, there is no contextualization of how the organization comes to this "knowledge"; for example, whether Eva comes to this closure by drawing on what she considers "objective" information or through local informants, two ways in which development workers try to make sense of intercultural encounters (Schondelmayer 2010). This is not merely an issue of whether Eva's organization's intervention was necessary, justified, or productive, but also of the centrality of Western knowledge production as a postcolonial phenomenon.

Though this narrative might initially sound quite seductive, it is important to take a closer look at the way the problem and the intervention of Eva's organization are framed. Eva's description of Indian women as being immobile in the face of the floods because of the demands placed on them by "their" society is a very literal expression of the persistent idea in development that traditions "hold . . . people back" (Crewe and Harrison 1998, 43). In Eva's story, *all* (South) Indian women are immobile and inactive and have an uneasy and rigid relation with their body that requires them to "*never* go out of their way" and "*never* undress." Eva describes the women as both constrained by the societal role imposed and quite literally by their clothes: "in the sari they could not move." Her description turns the women into passive victims, as there is no account of struggle or resistance, neither in the particular situation of the floods nor against the perceived oppression within society. There is an underlying assumption that women in the West are mobile as opposed to the immobile women of India, both in the sense that Western women would have managed to escape and in terms of Western proactive women flying to India, "discovering" the cause of the high death toll, and then setting up a project for their "immobile" Indian female beneficiaries. It remains a question if knowing how to swim is enough to escape a tsunami. In cases of comparable disasters in Western countries, culture is unlikely to be introduced in the same way as the explanation (do women in the global North also suffer "death by culture"?) (Narayan 1997, 84). Eva's narration therefore reinforces the familiar trope that "'they' have cultural barriers while 'Westerners' are guided by modern rationality" (Crewe and Harrison 1998, 133).

While in Eva's account the contrast between the mobile Western women and the immobile Indian women was implicit though clearly present, in Grace's reflections this juxtaposition is made explicit. Grace speaks here of her direct experiences with a group of women asylum seekers from Somalia who live in the UK:

> Their opportunities for studying English are very limited, because the culture dictates that the man takes priority and the woman's job is to stay at home with the children. And I find it quite hard, actually, because it is something that I find quite difficult to take on board, because it is so different to the European culture, isn't it, where I have my right to go out and have my own job. . . . And to understand these women's acceptance of the role imposed—I would say imposed, they would see it as normal, I see it as a role imposed on them—and they are far more difficult people to get to know, partly because of the lack of English and partly because they are not encouraged to integrate with the English community.

Grace contrasts the culture of Somalia with the "European culture" and also directly personalizes this in a "herself versus them" logic: "where I have my right to go out and have my own job." She includes me as the interviewer in the "us" by seeking confirmation for her statement in the "isn't it?" The women Grace describes are quite literally made mute and passive through the language barrier. Similar to the lack of agency in Eva's account of Indian women, Grace leaves little room for the possibility of contestation from the side of Somali women, by asserting that the women "accept" their role in the household and that "they see it as normal," which is a striking claim to make given that she has not addressed this directly with them. By contrasting her understanding of the role of the women as "imposed" with the assumed "acceptance" from the side of the Somali women, the gap between "us" and "them" is widened further. Not only are the lives of women from Somalia and from Europe radically dissimilar, even their desires are constructed as radically different. Through recourse to a cultural understanding of difference, Grace fails to see connections with mothers who stay at home in Western cultures. Again, these cultural explanations leave little room for alternative reasons such as the costs of professional childcare or the lack of social networks providing informal childcare in the context of forced migration.

Grace told me that as the language barrier restricted the conversation, she had never talked to the women about "their role." When I asked her whether she ever met their husbands, she told me that, as they brought the women to the group that Grace was involved with, to "deposit them," she had met them and that they were more proficient in English. Grace: "I don't feel that I could question the blokes as to why they take this attitude, because I think they would perceive it as intrusive and possibly racist. Because you are questioning their traditions and their standards and their code of practice and their faith almost." She continues:

> Before challenging it, before talking to the men, to their husbands, their fathers, I would need to know a lot more about the culture, about the background and about the particular area they came from. It is not an area I know enough about to challenge. You have to be careful, haven't you, that you don't offend people by challenging a situation that you don't know enough about, because you can say the wrong thing out of ignorance almost.

There is a contradiction between the fact that Grace says that she does not know enough about Somali culture, combined with the fact that she has not spoken to the Somali community members involved, with Grace's explanations of how Somali culture "is" and treats women. Similar to Vita's sudden understanding of the "blackness of the scarf" as a sign of mourning and Eva's realization that "culture" played a role in the high number of women that died in the tsunami, Grace draws a link between (not) knowing and (other) culture. Spivak challenges this "knowability": "In the meantime I remain a consensus breaker among metropolitan activists, who feel they can know everything in a non-vague way if only they have enough information" (Spivak 2003, 204–205). Lack of knowledge, rather than for example power relations, is presented as Grace's only barrier to more sustained exchange. This can first legitimate nonengagement when knowing is presented as an ever-receding horizon, as in the case with Sonia and Grace (cf. Schondelmayer 2010). Or, second, in case understanding a culture is seen as within easy reach, as in Vita's and Eva's case, it can legitimize "quick fix" solution to what they perceive as problematic. To understand the first move, nonengagement justified by lack of knowledge, it is useful to turn to black feminist Audre Lorde, who states that when "different" people are made "Others," this legitimizes unwillingness to reach out across difference, as the "radically other" can never be understood anyway (Lorde 1984). Also, Spivak's notion of an "interested use of cultural relativism" is relevant (Spivak 1999, 297). This addresses Grace's juxtaposition between either confronting the husbands and possibly offending them out of ignorance about "their culture" or leaving the women in their "imposed role." Grace's choice for noninterference exceeds this explanation and instead raises the question whether she is held back from engaging in a dialogue, as it could upset the clear Self-Other distinction she draws on, or whether it could disrupt the image of England she holds onto. The second move, represented by Vita and Eva, where knowledge of culture is seen as easily obtainable, can be situated in liberal democracy's "recognition of cultural *diversity* within the conventional totalizing, knowing frame of Western rationality. It is not an appreciation of serious cultural *difference*" (Bhabha quoted and summarized in McLennan 2003, 76). The latter cannot offer easy closure, as Bhabha argues that it is a matter of living with the "insurmountable ambivalence which accompanies the question of 'knowing' other cultures within the framework of still-dominant host culture" (Bhabha quoted and summarized in McLennan 2003, 76).

Grace's narrative also includes the fear of being perceived as racist. As Philomena Essed stated in the 1990s: "Today many Whites condemn more blatant forms of racism and are often motivated to maintain non-discriminating self-concepts" (1991, 5–6). Two understandings of racism circulate most prominently: one where racism is understood as the expression of extreme right-wing ideology and, to a lesser extent, one where racism is seen as an inevitable, inherent response of all (white) people (Lasch-Quinn 2001). Both accounts of racism are highly psychologized and individualized, prompting responses of denial and preventing engagement with the institutional and structural character of racism. After the Second World War, with decolonization (Duffield 2006), the current discourse on multiculturalism (Malik 1996; Byrne 2006), and national discourses of the "tolerant nation" (Essed 1991), it has not only become more common but also more "appropriate" and accepted to refer to culture instead of "race" when discussing perceived differences. The replacement of "race" by "culture" or "ethnicity" linked to the taboo on explicit expressions of "racial" assumptions has been diagnosed as a shift from a "biological to a sociocultural idiom" (Duffield 2006, 70) or the "culturalization of difference" (Razack 2001, 17). This shift has led to new expressions of racism, "culturalized racism" (Razack 2001, 60), "sociocultural racism" (Duffield 2006, 71), "ethnicism" (Essed 1991, 6), or "post-racism" (Hobson 2007, 105), directed at migrants from and people in the global South. Essed, for instance, defines "ethnicism" as an "ideology that explicitly proclaims the existence of 'multiethnic' equality but implicitly presupposes an ethnic or cultural hierarchical order" (1991, 6).

It is important to note, as Crewe and Harrison point out, and as I have illustrated with the narratives above, that when "race" is replaced by "culture," there is a particular understanding of culture at stake. Rather than understanding every practice to be embedded in "culture" and treating culture as changing and heterogeneous, practices are ascribed to "a culture." White notes that though "international etiquette" no longer allows expressing the view that Western countries are there to save the uncivilized, traditional, passive, and backward developing world, this view "nevertheless lurks within the "discursive *bricolage*" of development" (2002, 418). Her observation implies two things: one, because assumptions about people from the "developing world" can no longer be expressed in explicitly racial terms, the enduring underlying assumptions are articulated differently. Second, the term "bricolage" points to the fact that this postcolonial racialized discourse is not unified and consistent, but an assemblage of different ideas. Crewe and Harrison summarize this ambivalence: "Culture is often reified as a collection of rituals and customs exhibited principally by the less evolved, at times to be celebrated and at other times to be overcome" (1998, 25).

This is apparent in Sonia's reflections about a group of women in an African country that she seeks to support in her international work on peace and security. As discussed earlier, Sonia already talked about cultural difference as both rewarding and challenging. She continues with this last theme:

> So sometimes it is difficult, sometimes, I think that you have to help them a lot, you have to really guide them; you have to be there for very silly things . . . . But many times . . . I think that you really need to be there and reminding them of the things and being very, very pushy and then you get the results, but you have to be behind them.
> Interviewer: And why do you think that is?
> Sonia: I don't know, I don't know. I think it maybe it's the way they are used to doing things.

According to the official vision of Sonia's organization, facilitation of self-representation is central and the women they support are seen as independent and autonomous. While in this light, Sonia's language of supervision and dependence might seem incoherent, it is in line with Eriksson Baaz's observation that NGOs, which work toward empowering people in the global South through partnership, display a "contradiction between the message of partnership and donor images that oppose a superior, active, innovative Self to an inferior, passive, unreliable 'partner'" (Eriksson Baaz 2005, 147). Sonia describes the women as dependent, immature, possibly even childlike in their failure to do even the most "silly things"; this presents continuities with racist colonial representations of the colonized as immature children (Noxolo 2006; Power 2009). During the interview, Sonia offers a more concrete example about a group of African women who were invited by her organization to their strategic political location in the global North to represent themselves politically. Her story is worth quoting in some detail:

> I think they were supposed to travel on a Saturday, and Friday is a holiday there, so they don't work on Friday and Saturday. So on Thursday someone called me and said, "Oh, but my visa is not ready." And I am like, "What do you mean your visa is not ready?" "I went there and they did not have it." And I am like, "I have your ticket for Saturday." So I started calling all of them. None of them have a visa! I called the embassy and they [said], "They did not fill out their papers properly, plus they show up late." And I was like, "People, come on, I am trying to help you. Please help me too!" So I was with the embassy on the phone. They did not get it. I had to change all the tickets, so I felt like, "Okay, I am trying to help you, I am trying to get everything ready, I tell you in advance, I plan everything in advance to make my life easier. You don't do your part; now I have to change everything, because I have to change all the tickets, all the hotels, move everything two days.... And so in that sense sometimes it is frustrating. It is like I am trying to help you, and I am only asking you some silly thing to go to the embassy and get your visa and you don't do it.

The channeling of Sonia's frustration to the women she is supposed to support can be explained with the shift from "race" to culture which came with the assumption that people could now be "blamed" for being different as they chose to "stick to their culture." In contrast, when "race" was assumed to be a natural trait, people could not help being different (Kothari 2006b). Indeed, as Sonia tells me later, she "punished" the women by letting them work even harder when they eventually came. This analysis does not seek to belittle the problems that arose because of the delay with the visas; the organization lost a substantial amount of money, as the flights and hotels had to be rearranged. It is more interesting however to look at Sonia's assumptions and at what is left unquestioned with cultural lenses or blinkers. None of the women Sonia worked with had her visa ready for the journey. Yet Sonia locates the problem with their culturalized lack of responsibility (Verma 2011), rather than considering whether the women had other responsibilities or caring duties that they could not leave behind. Or, perhaps were not keen to travel to the meeting in the first place, as they doubted its political effect, or any other reasons why arranging a visa was not the main priority in their lives at that point. This despite the fact that the women's location in a conflict-ridden area could have prompted such questions. Moreover, the closure that operates in this narrative through reference to an immutable cultural disposition (Schondelmayer 2010) blocks consideration of what researchers have variably called women's "selective engagement" or "active subversion" in development (Jackson 1997, 163), or the *Eigensinn* of people reluctant to be turned into beneficiaries of humanitarianism (Krause 2014, 64). Instead, in Eriksson Baaz's terms, "'resistance'—or advice not taken—is interpreted in terms of passivity" (2005, 76). The situation could also have encouraged Sonia to ask more fundamental questions about the way the relation between her and the women is embedded in (post)colonial structures. Sonia neither questions her own role in the visa problems nor considers that the embassy might be more responsive to her, calling from an organization in the global North, than to the women she invited. However, the dominant understanding of culture understands it as "exist[ing] in a timeless and unchangeable vacuum outside of patriarchy, racism, imperialism and colonialism" (Razack 2001, 58). Presenting culture as *the* reason for the situation that occurred has the effect of forestalling thinking about the effects of imperialism, patriarchy, and racism, in their discursive, institutional, and structural forms. In the next section I will present and discuss some other narratives to make sense of the Other that exceed the cultural lenses and/or blinkers frame.

OTHER RELATING

At this point it is important to stress that some women I interviewed presented more differentiated accounts of culture and Otherness than those discussed in the previous section. If I picture all the women I interviewed in one room, exchanging experiences with each other, I expect that some of the narratives presented above would be met with others' resistance and dismay. At the same time, I warn against a simplistic juxtaposition between those who employed cultural lenses/blinkers, drawing on colonial and racist stereotypes, and those "good" or at least "better" women who related to the "Other" differently. That binary is undermined by variations on the interview narrations presented above that have been widely documented by other studies on development workers (Goudge 2003; Eriksson Baaz 2005; Cook 2007; Heron 2007). That reductionist perspective is also disturbed by the fact that some women had more practice than others in learning to speak the "correct" language about "race." However, taking a position of righteousness on that basis is disrupted by hooks's important warning that awareness and acknowledgment of complicity in racism is only meaningful when it results in different practice: "A woman ... who learns to acknowledge that she is racist is no less a threat than one who does not" (1986, 133). Without reifying the distinction between thought and practice, or perception and reality, this highlights the limits of this analysis, which is based on the women's reflections and self-reported experiences and approaches, rather than on their practice. Equally relevant is Heron's (2007) argument that some development workers she interviewed used a "containment strategy" in which they differentiated themselves from others who expressed themselves in unacceptably racist ways, to maintain a moral sense of self (2007, 84). I will briefly present an example that underlines this logic of containment. At the same time, politically—and, to an extent, analytically—it is important to make normative distinctions and to think about how things can be different and "better." In this vein, this section will continue with discussing the variety of ways in which the women related to Otherness beyond a narrow cultural frame.

Nina, a white North American woman who works in a senior position in Geneva for a women's organization on women's empowerment, speaks about her experiences when she first came to her organization as an intern, and was joined by an intern from an African country. Her positioning of herself as the interested and surprised observer functions to distance herself from the exoticizing racism of others:

> Very often we did things together, and I was really struck by, I don't know what you would label it as, maybe it is a little bit of racism, maybe there is a little bit of interest in the "exotic," which you know is a bit racist. But we would go somewhere ... and somebody was interested in my African friend, because she was really different.... And it was not the only time that that happened. But I was really struck by it and found it very interesting.

And when I ask her whether she experienced a similar curiosity, as she is equally socialized to see "Africanness" as "Otherness," she says: "Well, I don't know, because we had to share a flat together, so I guess you have a natural desire and curiosity to want to get to know someone as a person and a colleague, and I had not been to [her country]." She then continues by mentioning a second example of colleagues inviting NGO representatives from the global South who work in Geneva, to tap into "their difference." This shifts attention away from her own experiences and negotiations with "Otherness," which is described in terms of being friends, housemates, colleagues, that is, as interpersonal. This provides Nina with a privileged proximity that is presented as unmarked by exoticism.

Another moment in Nina's account demonstrates the similarities with the nonengagement discussed in the previous section, despite the very different terms in which Nina expresses herself than, for example, Grace. Nina first describes how Geneva rewards certain privileges based on having English as one's mother tongue and a good education, by which she implicitly seems to refer to whiteness as well. She then presents a story about a meeting to plan a large forum for exchange in an African country, to provide an example of what she calls the "flip side."

> So, you know, people are saying, "You must come, you must do this." And I am like, "Well, I am a white [North American] girl, you know. It does not make sense for me to be there. This is a space for African women. It is not my space and I respect that." . . . When you work at the global level, . . . you can't necessarily wear all the hats or have all the hats that you need. That is when you need to step back and have the wisdom to know that this is not your space, and that you need to enable other women to be in that space instead.

I suggest that this extract reveals a lot about how symbolic acts of demonstrating awareness about racism and power structures can go hand in hand with a depoliticization, which simultaneously belies that consciousness. This depoliticization makes it possible for Nina to present the forum in Africa and her "out-of-placeness" there as the "flip side" of her privileged access to Geneva, with its overrepresentation of English-speaking, white, middle-class, privileged people. It also allows equating the identity markers that are structurally embedded in power inequalities with wearing different or "all the hats," and to have "stepping back" stand alongside her duty to "enable other women," in a way in which African women will never be asked to empower Nina to occupy Geneva as a space. By using "girl" to describe herself and "women" to describe the African women attending the forum, Nina's downplays her privilege alongside her gesture to highlight it. I propose that Nina's "wisdom to know that this is not your space" provides a closure similar to the closure provided by knowledge about "other" cultures (or inaccessibility of that knowledge), as presented in the previous section. In the next examples that I discuss, (relationality to) the Other is less absolutely known. I will analyze how this leaves room for reflection and challenges.

Kate, a white, middle-class woman who works in Brussels for an international aid and development network, for example, resists the cultural blinders of foregrounding culture as an explanatory tool and of women as "victims of culture." She stresses the agency of South Asian women who work in sweatshops: "There is a clear position from most of the women working in this way in India, in Bangladesh in export-processing zones, that they want to work there. They want that bit of cash which gives them more economic independence." While cultural norms and racialized and gendered images combine in the garment industry, with Asian women being seen as docile, disciplined workers, with "nimble fingers" (Harcourt 2009, 734), Kate explores multiple perspectives to understand and intervene in the situation,

> perhaps in opening up that situation, not trying to find one response, but support wherever you can for them to be empowered, be stronger, legal, political, economic, trade unions, employment conditions. Or from the other side you can start from here on conditions for investment, obligations for investors in-country to respect any kind of standard. You can work on the legal system with human rights.

The structural approaches considered by Kate and her attention to economic independence prevent her from framing the situation of female sweatshop workers in the global South in terms of a contrast with the position of women in the global North. At another point in the interview Kate again challenges the "us versus them" divide, which was so prominent in some of the other women's narratives that I have presented in the previous section, deconstructing the North and the South as homogenous categories:

> More people will lose out in globalization, increasingly in our prosperous societies.... And in the South you might have more rich people as well. So this clear divide is [changing], and I think from the gender [perspective], it could be an advantage, because you understand it is not them and us, [but] that [it] keeps changing.

Another example of how Self-versus-Other dynamics can be undermined and framed in more complex patterns of simultaneous identification and differentiation is when Fay, a woman in her early thirties who shares her racialized migrant background with the women she supports, talks about her professional encounters. Fay works for a local organization with migrant women:

> [A migrant woman] is relating her story to me and I understand because there are a lot of structural and other barriers. First there was the communist system; you could not leave your country. And then you have European migratory restrictions; you cannot enter the country. Yes, it is women my age who want to travel, they want to have jobs, they want to do something, and there are just ... no opportunities. And this generates anger also [in me] and even more so if then

they tell me of experiences that they have had of discrimination here, because it is a discriminating and racist society. And you are aware that you are living in the same society and some experiences you have also had and you share, and others not because you are privileged in some way. Then there is the question, how do you look at them and at yourself? At the beginning it was difficult for me, because I also felt guilty for having certain privileges, because I thought the starting point was the same for us, and why is it possible for me to be here and for her to be there?

This narrative underlines once more that an analysis should pay attention to the structural barriers shaping people's lives, and that categories such as nationality and gender should not be read as "universally" determining the experiences of people. In Sotelo's words, "Political and economic transformations may set the stage for migration, but they do not write the script" (quoted in McCall 2005, 1782 n. 15). Fay identifies both commonalities and differences in relation to the women whom she supports. Nancy Fraser uses the notion of "cross-pulls of . . . various affiliations" to point to the conflicting ways in which people can be positioned in relation to others (Fraser 2003, 26). Fay's narrative illustrates the relational aspect of her positionality as a woman NGO worker with a migration background. As Brah and Phoenix argue, the concept of intersectionality has not only opened spaces to think differently about the complexity and variety of power relations but also about "emotional investments" 2004, 82). While on the one hand Fay is more privileged than the women she supports, her emotional (political) investment in challenging a discriminating and racist society stems also from her identification with these women through similar experiences.

I conclude this section with a discussion of three examples of young white women in international work, one based in Geneva, one in Brussels, and one in a Northern European capital, who talk about how they negotiate their position in relations with Others. Spivak has described facilitating her privileged students at Columbia University to "unlearn [their] privilege as a loss" as one of her largest challenges (Spivak 1990, 9). As she understands it, privileges form an obstacle for understanding other people's perspectives (cf. Minh-ha 1991). Both Sylvia and Sarah respond to their realization that their positionality constitutes a barrier for engaging with other people, by making conscious efforts to point out the very present identity markers and stereotypes that they see as obstructing the relation between them and others.

Sylvia explains:

When I am in the South I usually find ways of identifying the things that make me different from wherever I am and then pointing it out in a funny way first. So it is like, "I know what you are thinking. I am assuming this is what is going through you mind, so let me just address it and let you know that I am aware of it too." And then we move on from that. . . . I think more often it is the differences that become the defining things in your identity in relation to the people you are around. And so to try and go through things without acknowledging that difference ends up creating this false sense of who you are in relation to them. Because then that is where any kind of stereotypes are going to come in. . . . That is going to be in the differences. So to be able to just throw that out at the very beginning and acknowledge that it is there, it kind of makes it a bit easier, then, to look past them.

Sylvia's emphasis on acknowledging "differences," especially those "differences" that have been made significant, for example through colonial discourses, racism, and sexism, is a starting point for constructing alternative relations. In the final sentence, however, where she expresses the idea that one can "throw that out at the very beginning" to "mak[e] it a bit easier to look past them," there is an assumption that these differences are both transparent (easy to define and pinpoint) and immediately possible to transcend. Also, the notion of "difference" fails to name the power structures underlying the construction of "difference" and the inequalities that might be at stake in the relationship. Looking at the next interview extract, I suggest that Sarah expresses a more explicit acknowledgment of the challenges that emerge in discussing the assumptions that are made. At the same time, her reflection communicates that only "culture" can be a barrier for an open discussion, and that this can be mitigated by diplomatic strategies, instead of speaking about the power differentials that obstruct open communication (Heron 2007). As can be seen in the extract below, Sarah uses the phrase "[to] have a strong work relationship *beyond* that," which again implies that differences can (always) be transcended. She talks about "get[ting] rid of those assumptions," in an almost literal echo of Sylvia's idea to "throw that out at the very beginning." Sarah:

> There are assumptions made: you have had this kind of background and have had these kind of experiences. And I find that if I notice myself that I am making assumptions, I ask questions. And sometimes this can be very difficult culturally in different situations, because in some cultures, there are some things you ask and some things you don't. And because I am trying to work and do this in a multicultural environment, again it goes back to this diplomacy, to be very delicate in situations and also to really be considerate and attentive to body language, to

also the frequency and level of response.... Because I know if I might be making assumptions, then the other person might be making assumptions about me. So by me asking, I am offering the right to asking back, so to get rid of those assumptions. And again one of the primary things is to develop a core relationship with someone from there, to know a person on a person's sense: "Do you have a family? ... what have you done professionally?" To have a strong work relationship beyond that, those are the relationships that carry.

Ilan Kapoor has pointed out that for "un-learning our privilege as our loss," "it is not enough to try and efface oneself, to benevolently try and step down from one's position of authority" (2008, 55). As can be seen in the earlier narrative of Nina about her decision to decline the invitation to attend an African women's forum, "This gesture is often a reinforcement of privilege, not a disavowal of it" (Kapoor 2008, 56). Instead, "unlearning privilege as a loss" means tracing the origin and route of one's preconceptions and discriminatory practices (Kapoor 2008). I suggest that Sarah and Sylvia both attempt to engage in this act of tracing, by making stereotypes and assumptions that arise explicit. At the same time, they do not critically reflect on their authority to take that initiative, allowing Sarah to take the liberty to ask questions and state that this implies that her counterpart has the right to ask questions back. I argue that in both accounts there is again a remarkable desire for stabilization that comes right after the acknowledgment that differences might bring uncertainties and complicate encounters. This diminishes what first appear to be significant differences between Sarah's and Sylvia's accounts and the narratives presented in the previous section, despite the fact that Sarah and Sylvia employ another kind of language that is not explicitly racialized. Therefore, I suggest that Bhabha's argument that stereotypes have currency because of the illusion of stability they can deliver, and his critique that the recognition of diversity does not amount to accepting difference, remain relevant here (Bhabha 2005).

Sophie's reflections on how her identity affects her work have much in common with what Sarah and Sylvia said, but take an important twist because of the active challenge of her counterparts. Sophie: "Of course it means something. It means I represent money. I can access a lot of people that I would not access if I was born in Zambia. But I come and I have a lot of power coming to Zambia." Immediately, however, she continues:

> But it also means that I am someone that can't understand the situation in Zambia. I mean I have friends in Zambia that I have known for several years, and I always feel that I have so far to [go to] get an equal relationship still. Because even when I think I sort of grasp the situation, they will always say, "But this is

[your own culture]" or "You don't understand Zambian culture." And it is probably true sometimes. Sometimes I don't think it is true. But I think it is very difficult because of class.... But also that I am white, that I come from Europe. It makes it difficult to be honest.

As Sophie realizes, her privilege, expressed in terms of money and access to power, is also a "loss" in the context of her engagement with Zambia and her Zambian friends. For Sophie, her privilege means that "she can't understand the situation in Zambia." This demonstrates (her reflection on) the limits of her own frameworks of interpretation (cf. Schondelmayer 2010). Her Zambian friends deny Sophie the possibility of ever developing a full understanding and thereby reversing a common power imbalance. That the challenge comes from people whom Sophie regards as friends suggests that it is unlikely that Sylvia and Sarah would encounter similar responses from those that stand in a hierarchical relation to them. Though Sophie thinks she sometimes manages to "sort of grasp the situation," her friends perceive her as locked in her own cultural understanding. This is especially relevant in a (post)colonial discourse where those from the global North are generally the ones to act as experts and imbue knowledge (Kothari 2005). It is also significant in the light of the earlier instances where women used the claim to know another culture as a right for intervention. It is relevant to read Sophie's struggle with understanding Zambia with Spivak's revisions to the notion of "un-learning our privilege as our loss." As she writes: "As time passed, and I became aware of the sheer narcissism of the practical politics of unlearning one's privilege, I quietly changed it to 'learning to learn from below,' but nobody paid much attention" (Spivak 2000, 121). Spivak's assertion that we have to *learn to* learn from below speaks to the disruption by Sophie's friends when she thinks that she "sort of grasps it" and forecloses the all-too-easy longing for knowledge as a means to resolve ambivalences. It is also an important corrective to popularized alternative or critical development theories, which call for bottom-up over top-down approaches without engaging with their complexity, such as those discussed in relation to the facilitation of self-representation in chapter 4. Moreover, Spivak's revision is significant in avoiding individualized psychologized understandings of discriminatory structures in the process of reflecting on one's own privilege.

CONCLUDING REMARKS

Since White (2002) observed the silence around "race" and racism in development, much important thinking has been done in relation to development workers' subjectivities, for example in the work of Goudge (2003), Eriksson Baaz (2005), Cook (2007), and Heron (2007). The patterns that I have presented here have much resonance with their work, for example, the gendered and racialized stereotypes of women in the global South, which allow women from the North to present themselves as liberated; the desire for Otherness; or the taboo on speaking about racism. This underlines the similarities between the women that are the focus of this study, namely those who work from the global North on gender and women's issues along a North–South axis and the subjects of these other studies, that is, global-South-based development workers, in particular with regard to their relation to Otherness. In the light of the reality of the recurrence of expressions of colonial logics and racialized cultural explanations, it has been important to present in this chapter what can be regarded as repetitions, or at least parallels. I also align myself with the aforementioned scholars' efforts to contextualize their findings about individual women in a wider postcolonial and racist discourse, going beyond what Goudge has called a "blame culture" (2003, 43), while at the same time refusing abdication of responsibilities. With this chapter I join the efforts by other scholars to make visible such enduring dynamics in the hope that the slight distinctions in emphasis and focus, which I summarize below, contribute to a deeper understanding, which facilitates our struggle against these persistent mechanisms.

Postcolonial theories—and decolonial thought in its distinctive way—have emphasized how colonial configurations have persisted, in our current "post" colonial times, in new but sometimes not so different guises. As I have demonstrated in this chapter, the inconclusive status of the "post" in postcolonialism, which, as postcolonial theorists have emphasized, should not be read as a simple "after" or "beyond," is mirrored in the ambivalent way in which the women talk about colonialism. While some refer directly to colonial times and the continuities they recognize, most often colonialism is presented as firmly situated in the past. I have argued that the fact that colonialism repeatedly appears in the narratives, however, rather (re)affirms its continued relevance.

I have subsequently moved on to discussing understandings of the Other and of Self-Other relations that do not directly name the (post)colonial, but which, as I argue, display strong similarities with colonial discourse, whether in its combined desire and derision of Otherness, in its hierarchical relationality, or in its racialized conceptualization of culture. This chapter has discussed how "civilizing" interventions, which in colonial times were justified on the basis of "race," have been replaced by notions of culture, traditions, and rituals. I have suggested that even though inserting culture into the development discourse as a central component of societies has been an important contribution to development work, merely adding culture does not lead to a nuanced understanding of how "culture" functions and shapes lives in complex and dynamic ways. On the contrary, I have demonstrated with the interview narratives that culture is oftentimes reified and homogenized and that some of the women persistently used a rigid understanding of "culture" to make sense of their work experiences and encounters with the Other. Here cultural lenses became blinkers that blinded the women to alternative structural explanations and downplayed the significance of power differences. In the subsequent section "Other Relating," I presented some alternative understandings of the Other as well as Self-Other relations where cultural frames were less prominent, or got replaced by attention to material and power inequalities. The break between the two sections "Cultural Lenses or Blinkers" and "Other Relating" is inspired by the importance of highlighting the heterogeneous ways in which the women expressed their relation with Otherness. However, I have warned against overstating these differences, by highlighting some continuities in the ways in which power is absent from the accounts and the desire for knowledge about "difference" as a foreclosure of ambivalence. The combined analysis of this chapter has demonstrated that postcolonial articulations of Othering and of centering the Self take place at each of the three levels of this study: in the international headquarters of Geneva and Brussels, in international programs run from privileged capital cities of Europe, and in grounded national projects engaging with migrant women.

CHAPTER 7

Conclusion

Complicit Sisters

This book has presented the reflections of women in the global North whose "doing good" work supports women and addresses gender inequalities. They work either for organizations that operate internationally or through organizations targeting migrant women. Their work broadly situates them at the nexus of two critiques, which respectively address the dimensions of relationality and "helping": first, critical interrogations of the connections between differentially positioned women; second, critical development approaches that problematize aid practices. This study has approached the research participants as "complicit sisters," that is, as women who share certain gendered experiences with the women they seek to support and as women whose subjectivities and positionalities are intertwined with the material inequalities and power structures that have marginalized others. The findings are based on a close analysis of interview material, with a focus on women's understandings, self-presentations, and considerations over practices, and has situated these within wider structures and discourses.

Reading together the narratives of women in the global North who intervene in the global South and those who work in the global North with female migrants from the global South, I have underlined that encounters framed by a "helping imperative" (Heron 2007) do not only take place in the global South and are not only dependent on the transnational mobility of those from the global North. This study has been testimony to the different ways in which mobilities gain meaning depending on the direction and goal of the journey as well as on the actor involved: from field trips to trafficking, from migration to travel, and from fleeing wars to international careers. It has thereby offered an alternative to more common approaches that address development and migration separately and presented a timely intervention in an era of global change and financial, political, and migration "crises" in which "the case for challenging the dichotomies [between domestic and international subfields of the third sector] have become more acute" (Lewis 2014, 1147). I have also extended the more narrow framework of the, in itself promising, notion of the migration-development nexus, which has so far focused primarily on remittances and on the role of diasporas in development. This has also helped to highlight that the issues and concerns that have been identified in the field of development should not be understood as emerging from the international mobility of aid workers and from an imposed presence of Northern workers in the global South, but rather from the structures that make this possible, in other words, from the inequalities that frame global encounters across the world. That means that we need to be cautious about overstating the particularity of international aid careers and about locating solutions in staying (closer to) home.

At different points in the preceding chapters, I have demonstrated that the self-representations, motivations, and dilemmas of women who work internationally follow dynamics similar to those who work locally with migrant women. For example, this has been shown in chapter 3 with reference to what moved women to enter this field of work, in the tensions around representation brought about by internal diversity in the represented group discussed in chapter 4, and in the cultural explanations underpinning Othering in chapter 6. I propose that the points where differences emerged, as in chapter 2, where the younger, international women framed their feminist biographies more strongly in the context of institutionalization of development and women's and gender studies, or in the particular strategies of working across distance in which partner organizations come to stand in for beneficiaries, as discussed in chapter 4, are fruitful starting points for developing further research that systematically compares, rather than analyzes together, the similarities and differences. Such new research direction would shed further light on differences in career trajectories and processes of politicization between those working inside the global North in the area of gendered migration versus those working on gender in the international field. Moreover, such comparative studies could help to further challenge the divide between those understood to work locally and those understood to work globally, and propose more meaningful terms of comparison. For example, between advocacy and service delivery organizations or between organizations, both "local" and "international," that operate in global networks and those that operate as autonomous projects, or between working on gender within organizations that do not consider themselves feminist, versus working for those that explicitly describe themselves as such, as I discussed in chapter 2. The findings of this study, while recognizing some of the classic "fault lines" within feminism, for instance regarding contentious issues like sex work/prostitution, as well as acknowledging differences among the women, such as in the way they spoke about "race" and "culture," demonstrate that these differences do not diminish the women's commonalities based on their structural position as "complicit sisters." The combined analysis of women's work with migrants and women's international work has also served to consolidate the book's theoretical contribution in demonstrating the productive synthesis of feminist and postcolonial critiques with global civil society/citizenship and critical development literature. This joint analysis of international and migration NGOs opens avenues for further studies that apply critical development theories to NGOs in the field of migration, or for research that investigates the continuities between local and global civil society or the parallels between local and global citizenship practices that foreground responsibilities over rights and duties.

In this book, I have drawn on a range of perspectives that allowed me to analyze the connected notions of Self, relationality, and Other from different angles. Synthesizing the insights generated within the different chapters conjures up a rich and interesting picture: at some conjunctures, seeming contradictions are resolved; at others, particular arguments are reinforced, as I will illustrate and demonstrate below. As I have shown, the interviewees' sense of responsibility for global others hinged, on the one hand, on a sense of sameness, a felt connection based on a shared humanity, womanhood, or awareness of global entanglements and, on the other hand, on a position of difference that relegated the one to the giving and the other to the receiving end of aid. The motivating force that emerges from a perception of difference is, as I have argued, often articulated with reference to the privileges and possibilities that the women enjoyed and their wish to provide others with similar access to opportunities. When combining this with the finding that when the women reflected on their own positionality and identity in relation to their work, most of them concentrated on the structures where they were marginalized (often gender, sometimes in combination with other components such as class), an apparent incongruence emerges. Whereas explaining the motivation for the work prompted reflections on privilege, considering identities at work rather produced silences on and mitigations of these same privileges, in order to perform a "race to innocence" (Fellows and Razack 1998). The arguments made in the respective chapters (3 and 5) demonstrate that this seeming contradiction is sustained by two related moves: first, a liberal assumption that opportunities can be improved for others, without taking into account the relationality between dominance and marginalization and, second, a unitary rather than an interlocking understanding of oppressions. As I have discussed, both of these inclinations have been critiqued by feminist and postcolonial scholars. The fact that these moves underpin as well as potentially undermine practices of aid and solidarity between women globally underlines the relevance of these critiques as well as the enduring complexity of the challenges posed.

A second incongruence appears when placing side by side the desire for sisterhood or other forms of women's solidarity, and the way the women made sense of difference through cultural lenses reminiscent of colonial discourse. To put it starkly, a gap appears between, on the one hand, sharing experiences of motherhood and, on the other hand, Othering immobile sari-clad tsunami victims, or between considering women as sisters in the same struggle versus considering them as not able to speak, as discussed in, respectively, chapters 5 and 6. Whereas in the first a relationality is articulated that emphasizes horizontal connections and shared experiences, in the second a hierarchy places the Northern Self in a superior position vis-à-vis the Other. What—in some instances—reconciles both perspectives is a centering of Self, as I have argued. For example, this is the case when sisterhood is based on an ethnocentric notion of shared victimhood, and when self-presentations of a liberated, rational, and responsible woman are dependent on an Other's lack of those qualities. Connecting the analysis of the narratives around sisterhood/solidarity with those on Othering also reinforces my argument from chapter 5, that alternative relationalities beyond global sisterhood require, at least, the following building blocks: resisting divisions; establishing connections through experience; recognizing the instability of one's own position; and understanding solidarity as a process rather than a given. For example, it demonstrates that the resisting of divisions requires not only fighting external forces that separate women, but also being vigilant of our own moves that drive us apart. In a similar vein, recognizing solidarity as a process (and struggle), as one key component of developing alternative alliances beyond sisterhood, is a reminder that the desired easy closure established by reference to knowledge about "culture" or cultural relativism hampers the building of such coalitions.

Other arguments that I have made at separate points in this book are so immediately in line with one another that a synthesis of the insights does not require the resolving of apparent contradictions, as I have done above. Instead, bringing those together further demonstrates their fruitful cross-fertilization. I return here to two claims from different sections in chapter 3, which can be simplistically summed up by stating that the women not only want to "do good," they also want to "do it right." I have made two separate arguments about what is considered "right." Demonstrating that it is productive to employ (feminist) political theory literature on global citizenship and global civil society for the analysis of the women's motivations for their work to improving the situation of other women, I have argued that the women in this study respond to a double-edged discourse. As the result of professionalization of the NGO sector and the women's movement, the women are expected, and expect themselves, to display accountability and formal skills as well as the passion and voluntary ethic associated with original movement goals. As noninstrumental commitment to a vocation is associated with the feminized private sphere and the reliable, accountable, and skillful professional with the (moralities of the) masculinized public sphere, the women have to straddle two spheres, which are conventionally seen as mutually incompatible; for instance, the career NGO feminist is constructed as necessarily uncommitted and the passionate, self-sacrificing, activist feminist as inevitably unprofessional. Drawing on the embodied interview narratives and the work of feminist scholars who have deconstructed the divide between the public and the private, I have argued that this is a false distinction. In a similar vein, I have proposed that another dominant discourse, namely the equation of geographical distance with moral detachment, frames the women's felt obligation to justify their Northern-based location when working to support women in the global South. With both those insights I have demonstrated that the women want to "do it right" and are concerned with, and invested in, (re)presenting the "correct" moral position. Wanting to do the "doing good" right also surfaced in various ways in the other chapters. For example, in chapters 2, 4, and 5 I have discussed how the women were conscious of not repeating the "mistakes" of previous feminist generations and their awareness of critiques of representation. I have documented some of the women's explicit efforts to be reflective about their position and about how their identity played out in their work, as well as their worries about being (seen as) racist (chapters 5 and 6).

That women who work on gender and women's issues across North–South divides are concerned with "doing good" right has a range of implications. It shows the resonance and impact of critiques generated by feminist, postcolonial, and critical development scholars that have left their mark on the feminist movement and the development sector, but also have come to occupy a space in the academy, in the political science, sociology, development, and women's studies degrees that some women had access to. Some of these critiques and the women's corresponding ambitions to "do it right" are essential and well developed, with continued relevance, as I have argued, such as the need for developing antiracist responses. Others, such as the implied moral hierarchy between field and headquarters work and the binary between the "truly committed" and the career feminist, are rather implied and in need of critical unpacking, as I did in chapter 3. Tracing the ways in which the women want to do it right also makes visible potential gaps between informed commitment to improving the practice of "doing good" and investment in being a good, moral person. The latter is at points difficult to disentangle from the first, and has particular salience in a study that bases itself on interviews, with the inevitable dynamics between researcher and research participant.

Doing good and doing it right also speak to women's investment in their work. If I sum up in one interview quote how the women in this study engaged with their work in the field of women's and gender issues across North–South and East–West divides, I would return to Rachel's poignant quote from chapter 3: "I can't imagine doing anything else." This seemingly simple quotation, shared in spirit by many of the women of this study, reflects an amalgam in which work, identity, self-understanding, and world vision are intertwined. While expressing a sense of work as vocation, it also suggests what is at stake for women who at the same time consider their own redundancy as a token of their work's success, as discussed in chapter 4. This raises fundamental questions. If a sense of self is tied to "doing good" and doing it right, what does it mean when doing it right means making "doing good" obsolete? And where does not being able to imagine doing anything else turn into a reluctance to imagining doing anything differently?

The various articulations of wanting to do it right addressed in this study support and complement the work of others who have focused on the subjectivities of aid workers, who have presented reflectivity in testimonies of their own experiences or in the narratives of their research participants. For example, in her research on partnership, Maria Eriksson Baaz observed that among the development workers she interviewed "a spirit of critical self-reflection . . . informed many of the interviews, in some cases accompanied by feelings of alienation and self-doubt" (2005, 91; cf. Fechter 2012, 1393; Roth 2015, 3). The rich quotes that I present in this book are testimony to this, and I am indebted to the women's openness and willingness to share their reflections. This study's explicit focus on women working in the field of women and gender with its history of critical feminist struggles enhances the impetus of critical self-reflection and adds an additional layer of critique. As one woman working in Brussels on gender and development issues suggested tentatively at the very end of our conversation when I asked her if there was anything she wanted to add to what she had told me before:

> I think in the women's movement there is an opportunity—I am not sure if it is picked up—but I think there would be a predisposition to look at those issues more clearly and more frankly through engaging with each other. I am not sure if it is done; I doubt it. It happens here and there, but there is a potential, and I would like to encourage the global women's movement to take that up.

As the preceding chapters have demonstrated, this book shares with many of the research participants as well as with other important studies in this field a normative, political commitment to addressing inequalities and injustices globally and a realization that these inequalities and injustices are not simply external to aid, but are also working through and inside the justice-seeking practices in the field of women and gender. This has compelled authors whose work is a source of inspiration for this book to explicitly position themselves in relation to international development and aid and to either provide suggestions for change or to look for ruptures in the hegemonic tendencies they identified. Paulette Goudge, for example, writes in the conclusion of her study of development workers: "I now turn to the question which I anticipate from readers: what do I think can be done to change the situation?" (2003, 206). Silke Roth positions herself in her book *The Paradoxes of Aid Work: Passionate Professionals* by stating: "Does this mean that aid is bad and should be abolished? By no means. Rather, 'aid' needs to go a step further and needs to be transformed" (2015, 170). Similarly, Barbara Heron (2007, 152) explicitly rejects an interpretation of her book as meaning that "we should all stay home" and underlines the good work done by some development workers. At the end of *The Paternalism of Partnership* Maria Eriksson Baaz (2005) refers to Gayatri Spivak's work to argue that the solution does not lie in rejecting development, but in a persistent critique of it. In this book I have made a similar move by identifying moments and strategies that counter hegemonic acts, and by looking for ambivalences and contradictions in dominant narratives (cf. Cook 2007). In different chapters I have presented disruptions of the hierarchies between the women and their "beneficiaries;" for example, focusing in chapter 5 on attempts to build solidarities between women beyond sisterhood, and in chapter 6 at ways of relating to the Other which would counter Othering. This is motivated by a normative perspective concerned with imagining more responsible practice as well as by the analytical task of making visible the instances where research participants positioned themselves apart from the dominant tendency, reflecting the delicate balance that qualitative empirical studies have to find between identifying general patterns and being attentive to heterogeneity and variation.

At the same time, at the conclusion of this study I want to posit a degree of ambivalence and, perhaps, resistance against this anticipated expectation to take a position in relation to aid and to offer an agenda for change. Given that the women in this study not only want to "do good," but are also keen to "do it right," such recommendations would most probably be welcomed and perhaps produce new generations working in the field of global women and gender issues who are, and can express themselves as being, more aware, self-reflective, and critical. However, the continued relevance of critiques articulated by black, antiracist, postcolonial, and feminist activism and scholarship, demonstrated throughout this book, underlines a durability of structures of inequality that cannot simply be countered by more awareness and reflexivity. Moreover, the parallels that exist between this research and the aforementioned studies in the field, despite their difference in focus, as well as Barbara Heron's observation that "it is noteworthy that so little changes in these narratives [of development workers] over time" (2007, 148), suggest the persistence of particular dynamics and the difficulty of forging change. My reluctance to provide proposals for improved practice at the conclusion of research that has as its focus women's self-understandings and reflections rather than actions is further sustained by the fact that a transparent relation between thought and practice cannot be presupposed; the previously quoted statement by hooks, that "a woman . . . who learns to acknowledge that she is racist is no less a threat than one who does not" (hooks 1986, 133), underlines that. This study has presented the women's intrinsic "in-itness" in the material inequalities and power structures that their work also seeks to work against (Ahmed 2000b, 180). From what I consider to be the analytical value of taking individual reflections as a point of departure to gain insight in these broader mechanisms, I argue that it cannot be deduced that this means that normative, political interventions should also be directed at the level of singular subjects. That is, while this study has taken a microlevel approach, the "problem" in helping relations—and thus the potential "solutions"—cannot be situated at the level of the individual "complicit sister" or at the meso level of organizational structures and development discourses. Instead, it is rooted in and tightly intertwined with those macrolevel structures of global inequality that the women's personal reflections have helped to shed light on, solidifying the ever important critiques of neoliberalism, racism, neocolonialism, and heterosexism.

NOTES

CHAPTER 1

1. That Barbara Heron in her book *Desire for Development* also draws on this particular quote (2007, 144) as well as Razack's wider work, demonstrates the relevance of Razack's statement in the context of aid as well as the fact that this study shares and is inspired by many of Heron's central preoccupations.
2. Relevant organizations were identified through Internet research, the use of Internet databases of global women organizations, and on the basis of information from mailings from similar organizations. I hereby want to express my gratitude to Denise Osted for voluntarily compiling the "Global List of Women's Organizations" at http://www.distel.ca/womlist/womlist.html, which proved an invaluable source.
3. For the same reason, some research participants have different pseudonyms in different sections.

CHAPTER 2

1. Ani DiFranco is a singer, guitarist, and songwriter who is known for her political songs, which address sexism, racism, and homophobia.

CHAPTER 3

1. Anheier et al. (2001) recognize three trends in the evolution of the concept of civil society. The first one, associated with the thinkers of the Scottish Enlightenment, contrasts civil society to the state of nature and civil with barbaric people. The words "state," "civil society," and "political society" were used interchangeably (Van Rooy 1998). Hegel's and Tocqueville's works are examples of the second trend, in which civil society became juxtaposed with the state, with civil society being envisaged as a check on state power (Anheier et al. 2001). The third trend is represented by Antonio Gramsci's understanding of civil society as encompassing cultural institutions like the church, which places civil society between the state and the market. This provides a useful backdrop for critical observations about the extent to which NGOs are "truly" nongovernmental.

CHAPTER 5

1. To ensure anonymity for this research participant in the specific context of her contribution to the book *Sisterhood Is Global*, I here neither use the pseudonym that appears in the other sections and chapters nor provide further details on the organization.

BIBLIOGRAPHY

Ackerly, Brooke A. 1995. "Testing the Tools of Development: Credit Programmes, Loan Involvement, and Women's Empowerment." *IDS Bulletin* 26(3): 56–68.

Adkins, Lisa. 2002. "Reflexivity and the Politics of Qualitative Research: 'Who Speaks for Whom, Why, How and When?'" In *Qualitative Research in Action*, edited by Tim May. London: Sage, 332–348.

Agustín, Lise R., and Silke Roth. 2011. "Minority Inclusion, Self-Representation and Coalition-Building: The Participation of Minority Women in European Women's Networks." In *Transforming Gendered Well-Being in Europe: The Impact of Social Movements*, edited by Alison Woodward, E. Jean-Michel Bonvin, and Mercè Renom. Farnham: Ashgate, 231–247.

Ahmed, Sara. 1997. "It's a Sun-Tan, Isn't it? Auto-biography as an Identificatory Practice." In *Black British Feminism*, edited by Heidi S. Mirza. London: Routledge, 153–167.

Ahmed, Sara. 2000a. "Boundaries and Connections: Introduction." In *Transformations: Thinking Through Feminism*, edited by Maureen McNeil. New York: Routledge, 111–118.

Ahmed, Sara. 2000b. *Strange Encounters: Embodied Others in Post-coloniality*. London: Routledge.

Alcoff, Linda. 1988. "Cultural Feminism versus Post-structuralism: The Identity Crisis in Feminist Theory." *Signs* 13(3): 405–436.

Alison, Miranda. 2004. "Women as Agents of Political Violence: Gendering Security." *Security Dialogue* 325(4): 447–463.

Alvarez, Sonia E. 1998. "Latin American Feminisms 'Go Global': Trends of the 1990s and Challenges for the New Millennium." In *Cultures of Politics, Politics of Cultures: Re-visioning Latin American Social Movements*, edited by Sonia E. Alvarez, Evelina Daginino, and Arturo Escobar. Oxford: Westview Press, 293–324.

Alvarez, Sonia E. 2009. "Beyond NGO-ization? Reflections from Latin America." *Development* 52(2): 175–184.

Amoore, Louise, and Paul Langley. 2004. "Ambiguities of Global Civil Society." *Review of International Studies* 30(1): 89–110.

Amos, Valerie, and Pratibha Parmar. 1984. "Challenging Imperial Feminism." *Feminist Review* 17: 3–19.

Anderson, Kenneth, and David Rieff. 2004. "Global Civil Society: A Sceptical View." In *Global Civil Society Yearbook 2004/5*, edited by Helmut Anheier, Marlies Glasius, and Mary Kaldor. London: Sage, 26–39.

Andrijasevic, Rutvica. 2007. "Beautiful Dead Bodies: Gender, Migration and Representation in Anti-trafficking Campaigns." *Feminist Review* 86: 24–44.

Anheier, Helmut, Marlies Glasius, and Mary Kaldor. 2001. "Introducing Global Civil Society." In *Global Civil Society Yearbook 2001*, edited by Helmut Anheier, Marlies Glasius, and Mary Kaldor. London: Sage, 3–22.

Anheier, Helmut, Marlies Glasius, and Mary Kaldor, eds. 2004. *Global Civil Society Yearbook 2004–2005*. London: Sage.

Antrobus, Peggy. 2004. "A Caribbean Journey: Defending Feminist Politics." In *Developing Power: How Women Transformed International Development*, edited by Arvonne S. Fraser and Irene Tinker. New York: Feminist Press, 139–148.

Appadurai, Arjun. 1990. "Disjuncture and Difference in the Global Cultural Economy." *Theory, Culture, Society* 7: 295–310.

Aradau, Claudia. 2004. "The Perverse Politics of Four-Letter Words: Risk and Pity in the Securitisation of Human Trafficking." *Millennium* 33(2): 251–277.

Armbruster, Heidi. 2012. "'Realising the Self and Developing the African': German Immigrants in Namibia." In *The New Expatriates: Postcolonial Approaches to Mobile Professionals*, edited by Anne-Meike Fechter and Katie Walsh. London: Routledge, 41–58.

Armstrong, Chris. 2006. "Global Civil Society and the Question of Global Citizenship." *Voluntas* 17: 349–357.

Aronson, Pamela. 2003. "Feminists or 'Postfeminists'? Young Women's Attitudes toward Feminism and Gender Relations." *Gender and Society* 17(6): 903–922.

Asia Pacific Forum on Women, Law and Development. 2005. *Women's Human Rights Concerns in Tsunami Affected Countries*. Retrieved from http://www.apwld.org/tsunami_humanrights.htm.

Association for Women's Rights in Development. AWID. 2004. "Intersectionality: A Tool for Gender and Economic Justice." *Women's Rights and Economic Change*, August 2004, 9.

Augustín, Laura M. 2005. "Helping Women Who Sell Sex: The Construction of Benevolent Identities." *Rhizomes* 10. http://www.rhizomes.net/issue10/agustin.htm.

Baillie Smith, Matt, and Nina Laurie. 2011. "International Volunteering and Development: Global Citizenship and Neoliberal Professionalisation Today." *Transactions of the Institute of British Geographers* 36(4): 545–559.

Baker, Gideon, and David Chandler. 2005. "Introduction: Global Civil Society and the Future of World Politics." In *Global Civil Society: Contested Futures*, edited by Gideon Baker and David Chandler. London: Routledge, 1–12.

Bakic-Hayden, Milica, and Robert M. Hayden. 1992. "Orientalist Variations on the Theme 'Balkans': Symbolic Geography in Recent Yugoslav Cultural Politics." *Slavic Review* 51(1): 1–15.

Benn, Stanley I. 1983. "Private and Public Morality: Clean Living and Dirty Hands." In *Public and Private in Social Life*, edited by Stanley I. Benn and Gerald F. Gauss. London: Croom Helm, 151–181.

Benn, Stanley I., and Gerald F. Gauss. 1983. "The Public and the Private: Concepts and Action." In *Public and Private in Social Life*, edited by Stanley I. Benn and Gerald F. Gauss. London: Croom Helm, 3–27.

Berman, Jacqueline. 2010. "Biopolitical Management, Economic Calculation and 'Trafficked Women.'" *International Migration* 48(4): 84–113.

Bernstein, Elizabeth. 2012. "Carceral Politics as Gender Justice? The 'Traffic in Women' and Neoliberal Circuits of Crime, Sex, and Rights." *Theory and Society* 41(3): 233–259.

Bhabha, Homi K. 1984. "Of Mimicry and Man: The Ambivalence of Colonial Discourse." *Discipleship* 28: 125–133.

Bhabha, Homi K. 2005. *The Location of Culture*. London: Routledge.

Bhambra, Gurminder K. 2014. "Postcolonial and Decolonial Dialogues." *Postcolonial Studies* 17(2): 115–121.

Bhavnani, Kum-Kum, and Meg Coulson. 2003. "Race." In *A Concise Companion to Feminist Theory*, edited by Mary Eagleton. Oxford: Blackwell, 73–82.

Bowden, Brett. 2003. "The Perils of Global Citizenship." *Citizenship Studies* 7(3): 349–362.

Brah, Avtar. 1996. *Cartographies of Diaspora: Contesting Identities*. London: Routledge.

Brah, Avtar, and Ann Phoenix. 2004. "Ain't I a Woman? Revisiting Intersectionality." *Journal of International Women's Studies* 5(3): 75–86.

Brown, Keith. 2011. "Everywhere and Everthrough." In *Inside the Everyday Lives of Development Workers: The Challenges and Futures of Aidland*, edited by Anne-Meike Fechter and Heather Hindman. Sterling: Kumarian Press, 107–129.

Buchowski, Michał. 2006. "The Specter of Orientalism in Europe: From Exotic Other to Stigmatized Brother." *Social Thought and Commentary* 79(3): 463–482.

Bulbeck, Chilla. 1998. *Re-orienting Western Feminism: Women's Diversity in a Postcolonial World*. Cambridge: Cambridge University Press.

Burton, Antoinette. 1994. *Burdens of History: British Feminists, Indian Women and Imperial Culture, 1865–1915*. Chapel Hill: University of North Carolina Press.

Byrne, Bridget. 2006. *The Interplay of "Race," Class and Gender in Everyday Life*. London: Routledge.

Caraway, Nancie. 1992. *Segregated Sisterhood: Racism and the Politics of American Feminism*. Knoxville: University of Tennessee Press.

Carby, Hazel V. 1992. "White Woman Listen! Black Feminism and the Boundaries of Sisterhood." In *The Empire Strikes Back: Race and Racism in 70s Britain*, edited by Centre for Contemporary Cultural Studies. London: Routledge, 211–234.

Carter, April. 2001. *The Political Theory of Global Citizenship*. New York: Routledge.

Celis, Karin, Sarah Childs, Johana Kantola, and Mona L. Krook. 2008. "Rethinking Women's Substantive Representation." *Representations* 44(2), 113–124.

Chambers, Robert. 2006. "Poverty Unperceived: Traps, Biases and Agendas." IDS Working Paper 270. Sussex: Institute of Development Studies.

Chambers, Robert. 2008. *Revolutions in Development Inquiry*. London: Earthscan.

Chandhoke, Neera. 2005. "How Global Is Global Civil Society?" *Journal of World-Systems Research* 11(2): 355–371.

Charlés, Laurie L. 2007. *Intimate Colonialism: Head, Heart and Body in West African Development Work*. Walnut Creek, CA: Left Coast Press.

Chesters, Graeme. 2004. "Global Complexity and Global Civil Society." *Voluntas* 15(4): 323–342.

Confortini, Catia C. 2011. "Doing Feminist Peace." *International Feminist Journal of Politics* 13(3): 349–370.

Confortini, Catia C. 2012. *Intelligent Compassion: Feminist Critical Methodology in the Women's International League for Peace and Freedom*. Oxford: Oxford University Press.

Cook, Nancy. 2005. "What to Wear, What to Wear? Western Women and Imperialism in Gilgit, Pakistan." *Qualitative Sociology* 28(4): 351–369.

Cook, Nancy. 2007. *Gender, Identity and Imperialism: Women Development Workers in Pakistan*. Houndmills: Palgrave Macmillan.

Cook, Nancy. 2008. "Development Workers, Transcultural Interactions and Imperial Relations in Northern Pakistan." In *Renegotiating Community: Interdisciplinary Perspectives, Global Contexts*, edited by Diana Brydon and William D. Coleman. Vancouver: University of British Columbia Press, 216–233.

Cooper, Frederick, and Randall Packard. 1997. "Introduction." In *International Development and the Social Sciences*, edited by Frederick Cooper and Randall Packard. Berkeley: University of California Press, 1–44.

Cornwall, Andrea, and Mamoru Fujita. 2007. "The Politics of Representing 'The Poor.'" In *Power of Labelling: How People Are Categorised and Why It Matters*, edited by Joy Moncrieffe and Rosalind Eyben. London: Earthscan, 48–62.

Cornwall, Andrea, Elizabeth Harrison, and Ann Whitehead. 2007. "Introduction: Feminisms in Development: Contradictions, Contestations and Challenges." In *Feminism in Development: Contradictions, Contestations and Challenges*, edited by Andrea Cornwall, Elizabeth Harrison, and Ann Whitehead. London: Zed Books, 1–20.

Corry, Olaf. 2006. "Global Civil Society and Its Discontents." *Voluntas* 17: 303–324.

Crenshaw, Kimberlé. 2000. "Demarginalising the Intersection of Race and Sex: A Black Feminist Critique of Antidiscrimination Doctrine, Feminist Theory and Antiracist Politics." In *The Black Feminist Reader*, edited by Joy James and Tracy Sharpley-Whiting. Malden, MA: Blackwell, 208–238.

Crewe, Emma, and Elizabeth Harrison. 1998. *Whose Development? An Ethnography of Aid*. London: Zed Books.

Crewe, Emma, and Priyanthi Fernando. 2006. "The Elephant in the Room: Racism in Representations, Relationships and Rituals." *Progress in Development Studies* 6(1): 40–54.

De Alwis, Malathi. 2009. "'Interrogating the 'Political': Feminist Peace Activism in Sri Lanka." *Feminist Review* 91(1): 81–93.

de Jong, Sara. 2009. "Constructive Complicity Enacted? The Reflections of Women NGO and IGO Workers on Their Practices." *Journal for Intercultural Studies* 30(4): 387–402.

de Jong, Sara. 2011. "False Binaries: Altruism and Selfishness in NGO Work." In *Inside the Everyday Lives of Development Workers: The Challenges and Futures of Aidland*, edited by Anne-Meike Fechter and Heather Hindman. Sterling: Kumarian Press, 21–40.

de Jong, Sara. 2013. "Intersectional Global Citizenship: Gendered and Racialized Renderings." *Politics, Groups and Identities* 1(3): 402–416.

de Jong, Sara. 2015. "Female Migrants as 'Mediators between Two Worlds': Spatio-Temporal Articulations of Intersectional Positions." *Journal of Diversity and Gender Studies* 2(1–2): 111–126.

de Jong, Sara. 2016a. "Mainstreaming Has Never Run Clean, Perhaps Never Can: Gender in the Main/Stream of Development." In *The Palgrave Handbook on Gender and Development: Critical Engagements in Feminist Theory and Practice*, edited by Wendy Harcourt. New York: Palgrave Macmillan, 92–105.

de Jong, Sara. 2016b. "Cultural Brokers in Post-colonial Migration Regimes." In *Negotiating Normativity: Postcolonial Appropriations, Contestations, and*

Transformations, edited by Nikita Dhawan, Elisabeth Fink, Johanna Leinius, and Rirhandu Mageza-Barthel. Berlin: Springer, 45–59.
de Jong, Sara, and Jamila M. H. Mascat. 2016. "Relocating Subalternity: Scattered Speculations on the Conundrum of a Concept." *Cultural Studies* 30(5): 717–729.
de Jong, Sara, and Susanne Kimm. 2017. "The Co-Optation Of Feminisms: A Research Agenda." *International Feminist Journal of Politics* 19(2).
Dean, Jonathan. 2008. "Feminist Purism and the Question of Radicality." *Contemporary Political Theory* 7: 280–301.
Desai, Manisha. 2002. "Transnational Solidarity: Women's Agency, Structural Adjustment, and Globalisation." In *Women's Activism and Globalisation: Linking Local Struggles and Transnational Politics*, edited by Nancy A. Naples and Manisha Desai. New York: Routledge, 15–33.
Desforges, Luke. 2004. "The Formation of Global Citizenship: International Non-governmental Organisations in Britain." *Political Geography* 23(5): 549–569.
Dimock, Elizabeth. 2010. "Women, Missions and Modernity: From Anti-slavery to Missionary Zeal, 1780s to 1840s." *Itinerario* 34(3): 53–66.
Doezema, Jo. 1999. "Loose Women or Lost Women? The Re-emergence of the Myth of 'White Slavery' in Contemporary Discourses of 'Trafficking in Women.'" *Gender Issues* 18(1): 23–50.
Doezema, Jo. 2001. "Ouch! Western Feminists' 'Wounded Attachment' to the 'Third World Prostitute.'" *Feminist Review* 67: 16–38.
Dogra, Nandita. 2011. "The Mixed Metaphor of 'Third World Woman': Gendered Representations by International Development NGOs." *Third World Quarterly* 32(2): 333–348.
Dower, Nigel. 2002. "Global Citizenship: Yes or No?" In *Global Citizenship: A Critical Reader*, edited by Nigel Dower and John Williams. New York: Routledge, 30–40.
Duffield, Mark. 2006. "Racism, Migration and Development: The Foundations of Planetary Order." *Progress in Development Studies* 6(1): 68–79.
Duffield, Mark. 2007. *Development, Security and Unending War: Governing the World of Peoples*. Cambridge: Polity Press.
Duffield, Mark. 2010. "Risk-Management and the Fortified Aid Compound: Everyday Life in Post-interventionary Society." *Journal of Intervention and Statebuilding* 4(4): 453–474.
Dwyer, Claire. 1999. "Veiled Meanings: Your British Muslim Women and the Negotiation of Differences." *Gender, Place and Culture* 6(1): 5–26.
Eade, Deborah. 2007. "Capacity Building: Who Builds Whose Capacity?" *Development in Practice* 17(4–5): 630–639.
Elliott, Charles. 1987. "Some Aspects of Relations between the North and South in the NGO Sector." *World Development* 15(1): 57–68.
Elshtain, Jean B. 1981. *Public Man, Private Woman: Women in Social and Political Thought*. Princeton, NJ: Princeton University Press.
Enloe, Cynthia H. 1989. *Bananas, Beaches and Bases: Making Feminist Sense of International Politics*. Berkeley: University of California Press.
Eriksson Baaz, Maria. 2005. *The Paternalism of Partnership: A Postcolonial Reading of Identity in Development Aid*. London: Zed Books.
Escobar, Arturo. 1995. *Encountering Development: The Making and Unmaking of the Third World*. Princeton, NJ: Princeton University Press.
Escobar, Arturo. 2007. "Worlds and Knowledges Otherwise: The Latin American Modernity/Coloniality Research Program." *Cultural Studies* 21(2): 179–210.

Essed, Philomena. 1991. *Understanding Everyday Racism: An Interdisciplinary Theory*. London: Sage.

European Women's Lobby. 2007. *European Women's Lobby Response to the European Commission Consultation on a Possible New Initiative to Prevent and Combat Discrimination outside Employment*, 15 October.

Eyben, Rosalind. 2006. "Introduction." In *Relationships for Aid*, edited by Rosalind Eyben. London: Earthscan, 1–18.

Eyben, Rosalind. 2007a. "Battles over Booklets: Gender Myths in the British Aid Programme." In *Feminism in Development: Contradictions, Contestations and Challenges*, edited by Andrea Cornwall, Elizabeth Harrison, and Ann Whitehead. London: Zed Books, 65–78.

Eyben, Rosalind. 2007b. "Labelling People for Aid." In *Power of Labelling: How People Are Categorised and Why It Matters*, edited by Joy Moncrieffe and Rosalind Eyben. London: Earthscan, 33–47.

Eyben, Rosalind. 2012. "Fellow Travellers in Development." *Third World Quarterly* 33(8): 1405–1421.

Falk, Richard. 1994. "The Making of Global Citizenship." In *The Condition of Citizenship*, edited by Bart van Steenbergen. London: Sage, 127–140.

Farrer, James. 2012. "'New Shanghailanders' or 'New Shanghainese': Western Expatriates' Narratives of Emplacement in Shanghai." In *The New Expatriates: Postcolonial Approaches to Mobile Professionals*, edited by Anne-Meike Fechter and Katie Walsh. London: Routledge, 23–40.

Farris, Sara R., and Sara de Jong. 2014. "Discontinuous Intersections: Second-Generation Immigrant Girls in Transition from School to Work." *Ethnic and Racial Studies* 37(9): 1505–1525.

Fechter, Anne-Meike. 2011. "Anybody at Home? The Inhabitants of 'Aidland.'" In *Inside the Everyday Lives of Development Workers: The Challenges and Futures of Aidland*, edited by Anne-Meike Fechter and Heather Hindman. Sterling: Kumarian Press, 131–149.

Fechter, Anne-Meike. 2012. "The Personal and the Professional: Aid Workers' Relationships and Values in the Development Process." *Third World Quarterly* 33(8): 1387–1404.

Fechter, Anne-Meike, and Heather Hindman, eds. 2011. *Inside the Everyday Lives of Development Workers: The Challenges and Futures of Aidland*. Sterling: Kumarian Press.

Fechter, Anne-Meike, and Katie Walsh. 2012. "Examining 'Expatriate' Continuities: Postcolonial Approaches to Mobile Professionals." In *The New Expatriates: Postcolonial Approaches to Mobile Professionals*, edited by Anne-Meike Fechter and Katie Walsh. London: Routledge, 9–22.

Fellows, Mary L., and Sherene Razack. 1998. "The Race to Innocence: Confronting Hierarchical Relations among Women." *Journal of Gender, Race and Justice* 1: 335–352.

Ferree, Myra M., and Carol McClurg Mueller. 2004. "Feminism and the Women's Movement: A Global Perspective." In *The Blackwell Companion to Social Movements*, edited by David A. Snow, Sarah A. Soule, and Hanspeter Kriesi. Oxford: Blackwell, 576–607.

Fox, Mary-Jane. 2004. "Girl Soldiers: Human Security and Gendered Insecurity." *Security Dialogue* 4(35): 465–479.

Frankenberg, Ruth. 1993. *White Women, Race Matters: The Social Construction of Whiteness*. Minneapolis: University of Minnesota Press.

Frankenberg, Ruth, and Lata Mani. 1993. "Crosscurrents, Crosstalk: Race, 'Postcoloniality' and the Politics of Location." *Cultural Studies* 7(2): 292–310.

Frantz, Christiane. 2005. *Karriere in NGOs: Politik als Beruf jenseits der Parteien*. Wiesbaden: VS Verlag für Sozialwissenschaften.

Fraser, Arvonne S., and Irene Tinker, eds. 2004. *Developing Power: How Women Transformed International Development*. New York: Feminist Press.

Fraser, Nancy. 2003. "Rethinking Recognition: Overcoming Displacement and Reification in Cultural Politics." In *Recognition Struggles and Social Movements: Contested Identities, Agency and Power*, edited by Barbara Hobson. Cambridge: Cambridge University Press, 21–34.

Fraser, Nancy. 2009. "Feminism, Capitalism and the Cunning of History." *New Left Review* 56 (March–April): 97–117.

Freedman, Jane. 2001. "'L'Affaire des Foulards': Problems of Defining a Feminist Antiracist Strategy in French Schools." In *Feminism and Antiracism: International Struggles for Justice*, edited by France W. Twine and Kathleen M. Blee. New York: New York University Press, 295–312.

Gal, Susan. 2004. "A Semiotics of the Public/Private Distinction." In *Going Public: Feminism and the Shifting Boundaries of the Private Sphere*, edited by Joan W. Scott and Debra Keates. Urbana: University of Illinois Press, 261–277.

Gandhi, Leela. 1998. *Postcolonial Theory: A Critical Introduction*. New York: Columbia University Press.

Ghodsee, Kristen. 2004. "Feminism-by-Design: Emerging Capitalisms, Cultural Feminism, and Women's Nongovernmental Organizations in Postsocialist Eastern Europe." *Signs* 29(3): 727–753.

Ghodsee, Kristen. 2014. "Research Note: The Historiographical Challenges of Exploring Second World–Third World Alliances in the International Women's Movement." *Global Social Policy* 14(2): 244–264.

Gillis, Stacy, and Rebecca Munford. 2004. "Genealogies and Generations: The Politics and Praxis of Third Wave Feminism." *Women's History Review* 13(2): 165–182.

Goetz, Anne M., ed. 1997. *Getting Institutions Right for Women in Development*. London: Zed Books.

Goetz, Anne M. 1998. "Mainstreaming Gender Equity to National Development Planning." In *Missionaries and Mandarins: Feminist Engagement with Development Institutions*, edited by Carol Miller and Shahra Razavi. London: Intermediate Technology Publications, 42–86.

Goetz, Anne M. 2001. *Women Development Workers: Implementing Rural Credit Programmes in Bangladesh*. New Delhi: Sage.

Goudge, Pauline. 2003. *The Power of Whiteness: Racism in Third World Development and Aid*. London: Lawrence and Wishart.

Grewal, Inderpal. 2005. *Transnational America: Feminisms, Diasporas, Neoliberalism*. Durham, NC: Duke University Press.

Grewal, Inderpal, and Caren Kaplan. 1994. "Introduction: Transnational Feminist Practices and Questions of Postmodernity." In *Scattered Hegemonies: Postmodernity and Transnational Feminist Practices*. Minneapolis: University of Minneapolis Press, 1–36.

Hacker, Hanna. 2012. *Queer Entwickeln: Feministische und Postkoloniale Analysen*. Vienna: Mandelbaum.

Hadj-Abdou, Leila. 2011. "Women's Mobilization in Conflicts over Female Muslim Covering: An Opportunity for the Well-Being of Women?" In *Transforming Gendered Well-Being in Europe: The Impact of Social Movements*, edited by Alison

Woodward, E. Jean-Michel Bonvin, and Mercè Renom. Farnham: Ashgate, 213–230.

Hahn, Kristina, and Anna Holzscheiter. 2005. The Ambivalence of Advocacy: International NGOs and Their Discursive Power of Attributing Identities. Paper presented at the conference "Bringing International Studies Together," Bilgi University, Istanbul, August 24–27.

Hampson, Tom. 2006. "Twelve Months On." In *2025: What Next for the Make Poverty History Generation?*, edited by Tom Hampson. London: Fabian Society, 5–12.

Harcourt, Wendy. 2009. *Body Politics in Development: Critical Debates in Gender and Development*. London: Zed Books.

Harcourt, Wendy, ed. 2016. *The Palgrave Handbook for Gender and Development: Critical Engagements in Feminist Theory and Practice*. Houndmills: Palgrave.

Harding, Sandra. 1991. *Whose Science? Whose Knowledge? Thinking from Women's Lives*. Ithaca, NY: Cornell University Press.

Harper, Ian. 2011. "World Health and Nepal: Producing Internationals, Healthy Citizens and the Cosmopolitan." In *Adventures in Aidland: The Anthropology of Professionals*, edited by David Mosse. New York: Berghahn Books, 123–138.

Hašková, Hana. 2005. "Czech Women's Civic Organising under the State Socialist Regime, Socio-economic Transformation and EU Accession Period." *Czech Sociological Review* 41(6): 1077–1110.

Helms, Elissa. 2003. "Women as Agents of Ethnic Reconciliation? Women's NGOs and International Intervention in Postwar Bosnia-Herzegovina." *Women's Studies International Forum* 26(1): 15–33.

Hemming, Clare. 2008. "The Life and Times of Academic Feminism: Checking the Vital Signs of Women's and Gender Studies." In *Travelling Heritages: New Perspectives on Collecting, Preserving and Sharing Women's History*, edited by S. E. Wieringa. Amsterdam: Aksant, 263–284.

Heron, Barbara. 2005. "Self-Reflection in Critical Social Work Practice: Subjectivity and the Possibilities of Resistance." *Journal of Reflective Practice* 6(3): 341–351.

Heron, Barbara. 2007. *Desire for Development: Whiteness, Gender and the Helping Imperative*. Waterloo, ON: Wilfred Laurier Press.

Higgs, Eleanor Tiplady. 2016. "Becoming Multi-racial: The Young Women's Christian Association in Kenya, 1955–1965." In *Gender and Diversity Issues in Religious-Based Institutions and Organizations*, edited by Blanche Jackson Glimps and Theron N. Ford. Hershey, PA: IGI Global, 24–50.

Hilhorst, Dorothea. 2003. *The Real World of NGOs: Discourses, Diversity and Development*. London: Zed Books.

Hill, Felicity, Mikele Aboitiz, and Sara Poehlman-Doumbouya. 2003. "Nongovernmental Organizations' Role in the Buildup and Implementation of Security Council Resolution 1325." *Signs* 28(4): 1255–1269.

Hill Collins, Patricia. 1986. "Learning from the Outsider Within: The Sociological Significance of Black Feminist Thought." *Social Problems* 33(6): 14–32.

Hill Collins, Patricia. 1993. "Toward a New Vision: Race, Class, and Gender as Categories of Analysis and Connection." *Race, Sex and Class* 1(1): 25–45.

Hill Collins, Patricia. 2000. *Black Feminist Thought: Knowledge, Consciousness and the Politics of Empowerment*. New York: Routledge.

Hill Collins, Patricia. 2012. "Looking Back, Moving Ahead: Scholarship in Service to Social Justice." *Gender and Society* 26(1): 14–22.

Hindman, Heather, and Anne-Meike Fechter. 2011. "Introduction." In *Inside the Everyday Lives of Development Workers: The Challenges and Futures of Aidland*, edited by Anne-Meike Fechter and Heather Hindman. Sterling, VA: Kumarian Press, 1–19.

Hobson, John M. 2007. "Is Critical Theory Always for the White West and for Western Imperialism? Beyond Westphilian towards a Post-racist Critical IR." *Review of International Studies* 33(S1): 91–116.

Hödl, Gerald. 2010. "'Es tut mir nicht leid, dass ich's gemacht hab': Eine 'Oral History' der österreichischen Entwicklungshilfe." *Journal für Entwicklungspolitik* 26(3): 95–118.

hooks, bell. 1981. *Ain't I a Woman: Black Women and Feminism*. Boston: South End.

hooks, bell. 1986. "Sisterhood: Political Solidarity between Women." *Feminist Review* 23: 125–138.

hooks, bell. 2000. *Feminist Theory: From Margin to Center*. London: Pluto Press.

Hopgood, Stephen. 2006. *Keepers of the Flame: Understanding Amnesty International*. Ithaca, NY: Cornell University Press.

Hudock, Ann C. 1999. *NGOs and Civil Society: Democracy by Proxy?* Cambridge: Polity Press.

Hull, Gloria T., Patricia Bell Scott, and Barbara Smith. 1982. *All the Women Are White, All the Blacks Are Men, but Some of Us Are Brave*. New York: Feminist Press.

Hutchings, Kimberly. 2002. "Feminism and Global Citizenship." In *Global Citizenship: A Critical Reader*, edited by Nigel Dower and John Williams. New York: Routledge, 53–62.

Hutchings, Kimberly. 2005. "Subjects, Citizens or Pilgrims? Citizenship and Civil Society in a Global Context." In *The Idea of Global Civil Society: Politics and Ethics in a Globalizing Era*, edited by Randall D. Germain and Michael Kenny. London: Routledge, 84–99.

Jackson, Cecile. 1997. "Actor Orientation and Gender Relations at a Participatory Project Interface." In *Getting Institutions Right for Women in Development*, edited by Anne M. Goetz. London: Zed Books, 161–175.

Jaggar, Alison M. 2005. "Global Responsibility and Western Feminism." In *Feminist Interventions in Ethics and Politics: Feminist Ethics and Social Theory*, edited by Barbara S. Andrew, Jean C. Keller, and Lisa H. Schwartzman. Oxford: Rowman and Littlefield.

Jain, Devaki. 2004. "A View from the South: A Story of Intersections." In *Developing Power: How Women Transformed International Development*, edited by Arvonne S. Fraser and Irene Tinker. New York: Feminist Press, 128–137.

Kane, Molly. 2013. "International NGOs and the Aid Industry: Constraints on International Solidarity." *Third World Quarterly* 34(8): 1505–1515.

Kapoor, Ian. 2008. *The Postcolonial Politics of Development*. London: Routledge.

Kapur, Ratna. 2005. *Erotic Justice: Law and the New Politics of Postcolonialism*. London: Glass House Press.

Kardam, Nuket. 1997. "Making Development Organizations Accountable: The Organizational, Political and Cognitive Contexts." In *Getting Institutions Right for Women in Development*, edited by Anne M. Goetz. New York: St. Martin's Press, 44–60.

Kennedy, David. 2004. *The Dark Sides of Virtue: Reassessing International Humanitarianism*. Princeton, NJ: Princeton University Press.

Kevlihan, Rob. 2001. "Becoming a 'Player': Ireland and Aid Conditionality with Reference to Sudan." *European Journal of Development Research* 13(1): 70–86.

Kleinman, Sherryl. 2002. "Emotions, Fieldwork and Professional Lives." In *Qualitative Research in Action*, edited by Tim May. London: Sage, 375–394.

Korf, Benedikt. 2007. "Antinomies of Generosity: Moral Geographies and Post-tsunami Aid in Southeast Asia." *Geoforum* 38(2): 366–378.

Kothari, Uma. 2005. "Authority and Expertise: The Professionalisation of International Development and the Ordering of Dissent." *Antipode* 37(3): 425–446.

Kothari, Uma. 2006a. "Spatial Imaginaries and Practices: Experiences of Colonial Officers and Development Professionals." *Singapore Journal of Tropical Geography* 27(3): 235–253.

Kothari, Uma. 2006b. "An Agenda for Thinking about 'Race' in Development." *Progress in Development Studies* 6(1): 9–23.

Krause, Monika. 2014. *The Good Project: Humanitarian Relief NGOs and the Fragmentation of Reason*. Chicago: University of Chicago Press.

Kreutzer, Florian, and Silke Roth, eds. 2006. *Transnationale Karrieren: Biografien, Lebensführung und Mobilität*. Wiesbaden: VS Verlag.

Krizsan, Andrea, Hege Skjeie, and Judith Squires. 2012. "European Equality Regimes: Institutional Change and Political Intersectionality." In *Institutionalizing Intersectionality: The Changing Nature of European Equality Regimes*, edited by Andrea Krizsan, Hege Skjeie, and Judith Squires. New York: Palgrave Macmillan, 209–239.

Lang, Sabine. 1997. "The NGOization of Feminism: Institutionalization and Institution Building within the German Women's Movements." In *Transitions, Environments, Translations; Feminism in International Politics*, edited by Joan W. Scott, Cora Kaplan, and Debra Keates. London: Routledge, 101–120.

Lang, Sabine. 2014. *NGOs, Civil Society, and the Public Sphere*. Cambridge: Cambridge University Press.

Lasch-Quinn, Elisabeth. 2001. *Race Experts: How Racial Etiquette, Sensitivity Training and New Age Therapy Hijacked the Civil Rights Revolution*. Oxford: Rowman and Littlefield.

Lazreg, Marnia. 2000. "The Triumphant Discourse of Global Feminism: Should Other Women Be Known?" In *Going Global: The Transnational Reception of Third World Women Writers*, edited by Amal Amireh and Lisa S. Majaj. New York: Garland, 29–38.

Lee, Theresa M. L. 2007. "Rethinking the Personal and the Political: Feminist Activism and Civic Engagement." *Hypatia* 22(4): 163–179.

Leonard, Pauline. 2012. "Work, Identity and Change? Post/Colonial Encounters in Hong Kong." In *The New Expatriates: Postcolonial Approaches to Mobile Professionals*, edited by Anne-Meike Fechter and Katie Walsh. London: Routledge, 59–75.

Letherby, Gayle. 2003. *Feminist Research in Theory and Practice*. Buckingham: Open University Press.

Lewis, David. 2011. "Tidy Concepts, Messy Lives: Defining Tensions in the Domestic and Overseas Careers of U.K. Non-governmental Professionals." In *Adventures in Aidland: The Anthropology of Professionals*, edited by David Mosse. New York: Berghahn Books, 177–189.

Lewis, David. 2014. "Heading South: Time to Abandon the 'Parallel Worlds' of International Non-governmental Organization (NGO) and Domestic Third Sector Scholarship?" *Voluntas* 25(5): 1132–1150.

Loftsdóttir, Kristín. 2012. "Whiteness Is from Another World: Gender, Icelandic International Development and Multiculturalism." *European Journal of Women's Studies* 19(1): 41–54.

Lorde, Audre. 1984. *Sister Outsider: Essays and Speeches*. New York: Crossing Press.

Lugones, María. 2010. "Toward a Decolonial Feminism." *Hypatia* 25(4): 742–759.

MacKenzie, Megan H. 2012. *Sierra Leone: Sex, Security, and Post-conflict Development*. New York: New York University Press.

Maese-Cohen, Marcelle. 2010. "Introduction: Toward Planetary Decolonial Feminisms." *Qui Parle: Critical Humanities and Social Sciences* 18(2): 3–27.

Mahood, Linda. 2008. "Eglantyne Jebb: Remembering, Representing and Writing a Rebel Daughter." *Women's History Review* 17(1): 1–20.

Malik, Kenan. 1996. *The Meaning of Race: Race, History and Culture in Western Society*. London: Macmillan.

Massey, Doreen. 2004. "Geographies of Responsibility." *Geografiska Annaler* 86B(1): 5–18.

Maxey, Ian. 1999. "Beyond Boundaries? Activism, Academia, Reflexivity and Research." *Area* 31(3): 199–208.

Mayoux, Linda. 1998. "Gender Accountability and NGOs: Avoiding the Black Hole." In *Missionaries and Mandarins: Feminist Engagement with Development Institutions*, edited by Carol Miller and Shahra Razavi. London: Intermediate Technology, 172–193.

McCall, Leslie. 2005. "The Complexity of Intersectionality." *Signs* 30(3): 1771–1800.

McClintock, Anne. 1995. *Imperial Leather: Race, Gender and Sexuality in the Colonial Contest*. London: Routledge.

McEwan, Cheryl. 2001. "Postcolonialism, Feminism and Development: Intersections and Dilemmas." *Progress in Development Studies* 1(2): 93–111.

McEwan, Cheryl. 2009. *Postcolonialism and Development*. London: Routledge.

McEwan, Cheryl, and Michael K. Goodman. 2010. "Place Geography and the Ethics of Care: Introductory Remarks on the Geographies of Ethics, Responsibility and Care." *Ethics, Place and Environment* 13(2): 103–112.

McLennan, Gregor. 2003. "Sociology, Eurocentrism, and Postcolonial Theory." *European Journal of Social Theory* 6(1): 69–86.

McLeod, John. 2000. *Beginning Postcolonialism*. Manchester: Manchester University Press.

McRobbie, Angela. 2004. "Postfeminism and Popular Culture: Bridget Jones and the New Gender Regime." In *Interrogating Post-feminism: Gender and the Politics of Popular Culture*, edited by Yvonne Tasker and Diane Negra. Durham, NC: Duke University Press, 27–39.

Menon, Nivedita. 2004. *Recovering Subversion: Feminist Politics beyond the Law*. Urbana: Permanent Black/University of Illinois Press.

Merill, Heather. 2001. "Making Space for Anti-racist Feminism in Northern Italy." In *Feminism and Antiracism: International Struggles for Justice*, edited by France W. Twine and Kathleen M. Blee. New York: New York University Press, 17–36.

Miller, Carol, and Shahra Razavi, eds. 1998. *Missionaries and Mandarins: Feminist Engagement with Development Institutions*. London: Intermediate Technology.

Mindry, Deborah. 2001. "Nongovernmental Organizations, 'Grassroots,' and the Politics of Virtue." *Signs* 26(4): 1187–1211.

Minh-ha, Trinh T. 1991. *When the Moon Waxes Red*. New York: Routledge.

Moghadam, Valentine M. 2001. "Transnational Feminist Networks: Collective Action in an Era of Globalization." *International Sociology* 15(1): 57–85.

Moghadam, Valentine M. 2005. *Globalizing Women: Transnational Feminist Networks*. Baltimore: John Hopkins University Press.

Mohanty, Chandra T. 1984. "Under Western Eyes: Feminist Scholarship and Colonial Discourses." *boundary 2* 12(3): 333–359.

Mohanty, Chandra T. 1992. "Feminist Encounters: Locating the Politics of Difference." In *Destabilizing Theory: Contemporary Feminist Debates*, edited by Michèle Barrett and Anne Phillips. Cambridge: Polity Press, 74–92.

Mohanty, Chandra T. 2003. *Feminism without Borders: Decolonizing Theory, Practicing Solidarity*. Durham, NC: Duke University Press.

Morgan, Robin. 1996. *Sisterhood Is Global: The International Women's Movement Anthology*. New York: Feminist Press.

Morgan, Robin. 2008. *Goodbye to All That (#2)*. February 2. http://www.womensmediacenter.com/feature/entry/goodbye-to-all-that-2.

Mosse, David, ed. 2011. *Adventures in Aidland: The Anthropology of Professionals in International Development*. New York: Berghahn Books.

"Most Tsunami Dead Female—Oxfam." 2005, March 26. *BBC News*. http://news.bbc.co.uk/go/pr/fr/-/1/hi/world/asia-pacific/4383573.stm.

Mügge, Liza M., and Sara de Jong. 2013. "Intersectionalizing European Politics: Bridging Gender and Ethnicity." *Politics, Groups and Identities* 1(3): 380–389.

Munck, Ronaldo. 2002. "Global Civil Society: Myths and Prospects." *Voluntas* 3(4): 349–361.

Naples, Nancy A. 2002a. "Changing the Terms: Community Activism, Globalisation, and the Dilemmas of Transnational Feminist Praxis." In *Women's Activism and Globalisation: Linking Local Struggles and Transnational Politics*, edited by Nancy A. Naples and Manisha Desai. New York: Routledge, 3–14.

Naples, Nancy A. 2002b. "The Challenges and Possibilities of Transnational Feminist Praxis." In *Women's Activism and Globalisation: Linking Local Struggles and Transnational Politics*, edited by Nancy A. Naples and Manisha Desai. New York: Routledge, 267–282.

Narayan, Uma. 1997. *Dislocating Cultures: Identities, Traditions and Third World Feminism*. New York: Routledge.

Nazneen, Sohela, and Maheen Sultan. 2012. "Contemporary Feminist Politics in Bangladesh: Taking the Bull by the Horns." In *New South Asian Feminism: Paradoxes and Possibilities*. London: Zed Books, 87–107.

Nederveen Pieterse, Jan. 2006. *Development Theory: Deconstructions/Reconstructions*. London: Sage.

Neumann, Pamela J. 2013. "The Gendered Burden of Development in Nicaragua." *Gender and Society* 27(6): 799–820.

Nowicka, Magdalena. 2005. *Transnational Professionals and Their Cosmopolitan Universes*. Frankfurt am Main: Campus Verlag.

Nowicka, Magdalena. 2006. "'Feste Beziehung oder One-Night Stand?': Hochmobile und ihre Bindung zu Orten." In *Transnationale Karrieren: Biografien, Lebensführung und Mobilität*, edited by Florian Kreutzer and Silke Roth. Wiesbaden: VS Verlag, 190–208.

Noxolo, Patricia. 2006. "Claims: A Postcolonial Geographical Critique of 'partnership' in Britain's Development Discourse." *Singapore Journal of Tropical Geography* 27(3): 254–269.

Noxolo, Pat, Parvati Raghuram, and Clare Madge. 2012. "Unsettling Responsibility." *Transactions of the Institute of British Geographers* 37(3): 418–429.

Nyhagen Predelli, Line, and Beatrice Halsaa. 2012. *Majority-Minority Relations in Contemporary Women's Movements: Strategic Sisterhood*. New York: Palgrave Macmillan.

Oxfam. 1997. *What Is Global Citizenship*. http://www.oxfam.org.uk/coolplanet/teachers/globciti/whatis.htm.

Oxfam. 2005. *The Tsunami's Impact on Women*. March 25. http://policy-practice.oxfam.org.uk/publications/the-tsunamis-impact-on-women-115038.

Pateman, Carol. 1983. "Feminist Critiques of the Public/Private Dichotomy." In *Public and Private in Social Life*. London: Croom Helm, 281–303.

Petras, James. 1997. "Imperialism and NGOs in Latin America." *Monthly Review* 49(7): 10–27.

Pfeffer, Clemens. 2012. "Koloniale Phantasien Made in Austria: Koloniale Afrikarepräsentationen im österreichischen Nationalrat am Wendepunkt zum Postkolonialismus, 1955–1965." In *Afrika im Visier*, edited by Manuel Menrath. Zurich: Chronos Verlag, 99–122.

Phoenix, Anne. 1994. "Practicing Feminist Research: The Intersection of Gender and 'Race' in the Research Process." In *Researching Women's Lives from a Feminist Perspective*, edited by Mary Maynard and June Purvis. London: Taylor and Francis, 49–71.

Piálek, Nicholas. 2008. "Is This Really the End of the Road for Gender Mainstreaming? Getting to Grips with Gender and Institutional Change." In *Can NGOs Make a Difference? The Challenge of Development Alternatives*, edited by Anthony J. Bebbington, Samuel Hickey, and Diana C. Mitlin. London: Zed Books, 279–297.

Pigg, Stacy L. 1997. "'Found in Most Traditional Societies': Traditional Medical Practitioners between Culture and Development." In *International Development and the Social Sciences*, edited by Frederick Cooper and Randall Packard. Berkeley: University of California Press, 259–290.

Plummer, Kenneth. 2003. *Intimate Citizenship: Private Decisions and Public Dialogues*. Montreal: McGill-Queen's University Press.

Power, Marcus. 2009. "The Commonwealth, 'Development' and Post-colonial Responsibility." *Geoforum* 40(1): 14–24.

Prins, Baukje. 2006. "Narrative Accounts of Origins: A Blind Spot in the Intersectional Approach?" *European Journal of Women's Studies* 13(3): 277–290.

Prokhovnik, Raia. 1998. "Public and Private Citizenship: From Gender Invisibility to Feminist Inclusiveness." *Feminist Review* 60: 84–104.

Pupavac, Vanessa. 2010. "Weaving Postwar Reconstruction in Bosnia? The Attractions and Limitations of NGO Gender Development Approaches." *Journal of Intervention and Statebuilding* 4(4): 475–493.

Puwar, Nirmal. 1997. "Reflections on Interviewing Women MPs." *Sociological Research Online* 2(1). http://www.socresonline.org.uk/2/1/4.

Quijano, Aníbal. 2000. "Coloniality of Power, Eurocentrism, and Latin America." *Nepantla: Views from South* 1(3): 533–580.

Raghuram, Parvati, Clare Madge, and Pat Noxolo. 2009. "Rethinking Responsibility and Care for a Postcolonial World." *Geoforum* 40(1): 5–13.

Rajak, Dinah, and Jock Stirrat. 2011. "Parochial Cosmopolitanism and the Power of Nostalgia." In *Adventures in Aidland: The Anthropology of Professionals*, edited by David Mosse. New York: Berghahn Books, 161–176.

Rao, Aruna, and David Kelleher. 2000. "Leadership for Social Transformation: Some Ideas and Questions on Institutions and Feminist Leadership." *Gender and Development* 8(3): 74–79.

Razack, Sherene H. 2001. *Looking White People in the Eye: Gender, Race, and Culture in Courtrooms and Classrooms*. Toronto: University of Toronto Press.

Razack, Sherene H. 2004. *Dark Threats and White Knights: The Somalia Affair, Peacekeeping, and the New Imperialism*. Toronto: University of Toronto Press.

Razavi, Shahra. 1998. "Becoming Multilingual: The Challenges of Feminist Policy Advocacy." In *Missionaries and Mandarins: Feminist Engagement with Development Institutions*, edited by Carol Miller and Shahra Razavi. London: Intermediate Technology, 20–41.

Rees, Teresa. 2002. "Mainstreaming: Misappropriated and Misunderstood?' Paper presented to the Department of Sociology, University of Sweden, February 21.

Reeves, Audrey. 2012. "Feminist Knowledge and Emerging Governmentality in UN Peacekeeping." *International Feminist Journal of Politics* 14(3): 348–369.

Roggeband, Conny. 2010. "Agent Dilemma: How Migrant Women's Organizations in the Netherlands Deal with a Contradictory Policy Frame." *Signs* 35(4): 943–967.

Rose, Gillian. 1997. "Situating Knowledges: Positionality, Reflexivities and Other Tactics." *Progress in Human Geography* 21(3): 305–320.

Roth, Benita. 2004. *Separate Roads to Feminism: Black, Chicana, and White Feminist Movements in America's Second Wave*. Cambridge: Cambridge University Press.

Roth, Silke. 2003. *Building Movement Bridges: The Coalition of Labor Union Women*. Greenwood, CT: Praeger.

Roth, Silke. 2006. "Humanitäre Hilfe: Zugänge und Verläufe." In *Transnationale Karrieren: Biografien, Lebensführung und Mobilität*, edited by Florian Kreutzer and Silke Roth. Wiesbaden: VS Verlag, 100–121.

Roth, Silke. 2007. "Sisterhood and Solidarity? Women's Organizations in the Expanded European Union." *Social Politics* 14(4): 460–487.

Roth, Silke. 2012. "Professionalisation Trends and Inequality: Experiences and Practices in Aid Relationships." *Third World Quarterly* 3(8): 1459–1474.

Roth, Silke. 2015. *The Paradoxes of Aid Work: Passionate Professionals*. New York: Routledge.

Roy, Arundhati. 2004. "Help That Hinders." *Le Monde Diplomatique*, November. http://mondediplo.com/2004/11/16roy.

Roy, Srila. 2011. "Politics, Passion and Professionalization in Contemporary Indian Feminism." *Sociology* 45(4): 587–602.

Sawer, Marian. 1998. "Femocrats and Ecorats: Women's Policy Machinery in Australia, Canada and New Zealand." In *Missionaries and Mandarins: Feminist Engagement with Development Institutions*, edited by Carol Miller and Shahra Razavi. London: Intermediate Technology, 112–137.

Scharff, Christina. 2011. "Disarticulating Feminism: Individualization, Neoliberalism and the Othering of 'Muslim Women.'" *European Journal of Women's Studies* 18(2): 119–134.

Schondelmayer, Anne-Christin. 2006. "Begegnung mit dem Fremden: eine qualitative Untersuchung zu Handlungspraktiken und Handlungskompetenzen von Entwicklungshelfer(inne)n." In *Transnationale Karrieren: Biografien, Lebensführung und Mobilität*, edited by Florian Kreutzer and Silke Roth. Wiesbaden: VS Verlag, 174–189.

Schondelmayer, Anne-Christin. 2010. *Interkulturelle Handlungskompetenz: Entwicklungshelfer und Auslandskorrespondenten in Afrika. Eine narrative Studie*. Bielefeld: Transkript.

Schwenken, Helen. 2008. "Beautiful Victims and Sacrificing Heroines: Exploring the Role of Gender Knowledge in Migration Policies." *Signs* 33(4): 770–776.

Scott, Joan W., ed. 2008. *Women's Studies on the Edge*. Durham, NC: Duke University Press.

Sennett, Richard. 2003. *Respect: The Formation of Character in a World of Inequality*. London: Penguin.

Sharpe, Jenny. 1993. *Allegories of Empire: The Figure of Woman in the Colonial Text*. Minneapolis: University of Minnesota Press.

Shiva, Vandana. 1989. *Staying Alive: Women, Ecology and Development*. London: Zed Books.

Silliman, Jael. 1999. "Expanding Civil Society: Shrinking Political Spaces—the Case of Women's Nongovernmental Organizations." *Social Politics* 6(1): 23–53.

Simpson, Kate. 2004. "'Doing Development': The Gap Year, Volunteer-Tourists and a Popular Practice of Development." *Journal of International Development* 16(5): 681–692.

Sin, Harng L. 2010. "Who Are We Responsible To? Locals' Tales of Volunteer Tourism." *Geoforum* 41(6): 983–992.

Sizoo, Edith. 1996. "The Challenge of Intercultural Partnership." In *Compassion and Calculation: The Business of Private Foreign Aid*, edited by David Sogge. London: Pluto Press, 191–197.

Sjoberg, Laura, and Carol E. Gentry. 2007. *Mothers, Monsters, Whores: Women's Violence in Global Politics*. London: Zed Books.

Sjoberg, Laura, and Carol E. Gentry. 2008. "Reduced to Bad Sex: Narratives of Violent Women from the Bible to the War on Terror." *International Relations* 22(1): 5–23.

Smillie, Ian. 2000. *The Alms Bazaar: Altruism under Fire. Non-profit Organisations and International Development*. London: Intermediate Technology.

Smirl, Lisa. 2009. "Plain Tales from the Reconstruction Site: Spatial Continuities in Contemporary Humanitarian Practice." In *Empire, Development and Colonialism: The Past in the Present*, edited by Mark Duffield and Vernon Hewitt. Woodbridge: James Curry, 88–101.

Snyder, Margaret. 2004. "Walking My Own Road: How a Sabbatical Year Led to a United Nations Career." In *Developing Power: How Women Transformed International Development*, edited by Arvonne S. Fraser and Irene Tinker. New York: Feminist Press, 38–49.

Sogge, David. 1996. "Settings and Choices." In *Compassion and Calculation: The Business of Private Foreign Aid*, edited by David Sogge. London: Pluto Press, 1–23.

Spelman, Elizabeth V. 1990. *Inessential Woman: Problems of Exclusion in Feminist Thought*. London: Women's Press.

Sperling, Valerie, and Myra M. Ferree, Barbara Risman. 2001. "Constructing Global Feminism: Transnational Advocacy Networks and Russian Women's Activism." *Signs* 26(4): 1155–1186.

Spivak, Gayatri C. 1988. "Can the Subaltern Speak?" In *Marxism and the Interpretation of Culture*, edited by Cary Nelson and Lawrence Grossberg. London: Macmillan, 271–313.

Spivak, Gayatri C. 1990. *The Postcolonial Critic: Interviews, Strategies, Dialogues*, edited by Sarah Harasym. London: Routledge.

Spivak, Gayatri C. 1993. "Interview with Gayatri Chakravorty Spivak." Interview by Sara Danius and Stefan Jonsson. *boundary 2* 20(2): 24–50.

Spivak, Gayatri C. 1999. *A Critique of Postcolonial Reason: Toward a History of the Vanishing Present*. Cambridge, MA: Harvard University Press.

Spivak, Gayatri C. 2000. "Claiming Transformation: Travel Notes with Pictures." In *Transformations: Thinking Through Feminism*, edited by Sara Ahmed, Jane Kilby, Celia Lury, Maureen McNeil, and Beverley Skeggs. London: Routledge, 119–130.

Spivak, Gayatri C. 2003. "Righting Wrongs." In *Human Rights, Human Wrongs: The Oxford Amnesty Lectures 2001*, edited by Nicholas Owen. Oxford: Oxford University Press, 164–227.

Sprague, Joey. 2005. *Feminist Methodologies for Critical Researchers: Bridging Differences*. Walnut Creek, CA: Rowman and Littlefield.

Squires, Judith. 2001. "Representing Groups, Deconstructing Identities." *Feminist Theory* 2(1): 7–27.

Squires, Judith. 2004. *Gender in Political Theory*. Cambridge: Polity Press.

Squires, Judith. 2007. *The New Politics of Gender Equality*. New York: Palgrave Macmillan.

Staudt, Kathleen. 2004. "Straddling Borders: Global to Local." In *Developing Power: How Women Transformed International Development*, edited by Arvonne S. Fraser and Irene Tinker. New York: Feminist Press, 312–323.

Stirrat, Roderick L., and Heiko Henkel. 1997. "The Development Gift: The Problem of Reciprocity in the NGO World." *Annals of the American Academy of Political and Social Science* 554: 66–80.

Stoler, Anne L., and Frederick Cooper. 1997. "Between Metropole and Colony: Rethinking a Research Agenda." In *Tensions of Empire: Colonial Cultures in a Bourgeois World*, edited by Frederick Cooper and Anne L. Stoler. Berkeley: University of California Press, 1–58.

Stroup, Sarah S. 2012. *Borders among Activists: International NGOs in the United States, Britain, and France*. Ithaca, NY: Cornell University Press.

Sunderland, Ruth. 2009. "After the Crash, Icelandic Women Lead the Rescue." *Observer*, February 22. http://www.guardian.co.uk/world/2009/feb/22/iceland-women.

Syed, Jawad, and Faiza Ali. 2011. "The White Woman's Burden: From Colonial Civilisation to Third World Development." *Third World Quarterly* 32(2): 349–365.

TakingITGlobal. N.d. "Ethiopia Millennium Project." http://projects.tigweb.org/EthiopiaMillenniumProj/about.

Taylor, Rupert. 2002. "Interpreting Global Civil Society." *Voluntas* 13(4): 339–347.

Tickner, J. Ann. 2006. "Feminism Meets International Relations: Some Methodological Issues." In *Feminist Methodologies for International Relations*, edited by Brooke A. Ackerly, Maria Stern, and Jacqui True. Cambridge: Cambridge University Press, 19–41.

Timothy, Kristen. 2004. "Walking on Eggshells at the UN." In *Developing Power: How Women Transformed International Development*, edited by Arvonne S. Fraser and Irene Tinker. New York: Feminist Press, 50–61.

Tully, James. 2005. "Two Meanings of Global Citizenship: Modern and Diverse." Presented at the conference "Meanings of Global Citizenship Conference, University of British Columbia, September 9–10.

Urry, John. 1999. "Globalisation and Citizenship." *Journal of World-Systems Research* 5(2): 311–324.

Urry, John. 2003. *Global Complexity*. Cambridge: Polity Press.

Valenti, Jessica. 2007. *Full Frontal Feminism: A Young Woman's Guide to Why Feminism Matters*. Emeryville, CA: Seal Press.

Van Rooy, Alison. 1998. "Civil Society as Idea: An Analytical Hatstand?" In *Civil Society and the Aid Industry*, edited by Alison Van Rooy. London: Earthscan, 6–27.

Vaux, Tony. 2001. *The Selfish Altruist: Dilemmas of Relief Work in Famine and War*. London: Earthscan.

Verloo, Mieke. 2001. "Another Velvet Revolution? Gender Mainstreaming and the Politics of Implementation." IWM Working Paper no. 5/2001, Vienna.

Verloo, Mieke. 2006. "Multiple Inequalities, Intersectionality and the European Union." *European Journal of Women's Studies* 13(3): 211–228.

Verloo, Mieke. 2009. "Intersectionaliteit en Interferentie: Hoe Politiek en Beleid Ongelijkheid Behouden, Bestrijden en Veranderen." *Tijdschrift voor Genderstudies* 12(3): 34–46.

Verma, Ritu. 2011. "Intercultural Encounters, Colonial Continuities and Contemporary Disconnects in Rural Aid: An Ethnography of Development Practitioners in Madagascar." In *Inside the Everyday Lives of Development Workers: The Challenges and Futures of Aidland*, edited by Anne-Meike Fechter and Heather Hindman. Sterling, VA: Kumarian Press, 59–82.

Verschuur, Christine, and Blandine Destremau. 2012. "Decolonial Feminisms, Gender, and Development: History and Narratives of Southern Feminisms and Women's Movements." *Revue Tiers Monde* 1(209): 7–18.

Von der Lippe, Berit, and Tarja Väyrynen. 2011. "Co-opting Feminist Voices for the War on Terror: Laura Bush Meets Nordic Feminism." *European Journal of Women's Studies* 18(1): 19–33.

Wadia, Khursheed. 2015. "Women from Muslim Communities in Britain: Political and Civic Activism in the 9/11 Era." In *Muslims and Political Participation in Britain*, edited by Timothy Peace. New York: Routledge, 85–102.

Walker, Alice. 1984. *In Search of Our Mothers' Gardens: Womanist Prose*. London: Women's Press.

Walker, Anne S. 2000. "The Women's Movement and Its Role in Development." In *Theoretical Perspectives on Gender and Development*, edited by Jane L. Parpart, M. Patricia Connelly, and V. Eudine Barriteau. Ottawa: International Development Research Centre, 191–202.

Waterman, Peter. 1993. "Hidden from Herstory: Women, Feminism and the New Global Solidarity." Women's History and Development Working Paper no. 17. The Hague: ISS.

Weintraub, Jeff. 1997. "The Theory and Politics of the Public/Private Distinction." In *Public and Private in Thought and Practice: Perspectives on a Grand Dichotomy*, edited by Jeff Weintraub and Krishan Kumar. Chicago: University of Chicago Press, 1–42.

White, Sarah C. 2002. "Thinking Race, Thinking Development." *Third World Quarterly* 23(3): 407–419.

White, Sarah C. 2006. "The 'Gender Lens': A Racial Blinder?" *Progress in Development Studies* 6(1):55–67.

Whitworth, Sandra. 2005. "Militarized Masculinities and the Politics of Peacekeeping: The Canadian Case." In *Critical Security Studies and World Politics*, edited by Ken Booth. Boulder, CO: Lynne Rienner, 89–106.

Wiegman, Robyn. 2005. "What Is the Subject of Women's Studies? The Possibility of Women's Studies." In *Women's Studies for the Future: Foundation, Interrogations, Politics*, edited by Elizabeth Lapovsky Kennedy and Agatha Beins. New Brunswick, NJ: Rutgers University Press, 40–60.

Wieringa, Saskia E. 2009. "From Solidarity to Affinity and Feminist Communal Identities." In *The European Feminist Forum: A Herstory (2004–2008)*, edited by Gisela Dütting, Wendy Harcourt, Kinga Lohmann, Lin McDevitt-Pugh, Joanna Semeniuk, and Saskia Wieringa. Amsterdam: Aletta Institute for Women's History, 29–38.

Willetts, Peter. 2002. "Non-governmental Organizations." *UNESCO Encyclopaedia of Life Support Systems*. Section 1, Institutional and Infrastructure Resource Issues, Article 1.44.3.7.

Wilson, Kalpana. 2011. "'Race,' Gender and Neoliberalism: Changing Visual Representations in Development." *Third World Quarterly* 32(2): 315–331.

York, Jodi. 1998. "The Truth about Women and Peace." In *The Women and War Reader*, edited by Lois A. Lorentzen and Jennifer Turpin. New York: New York University Press, 19–25.

Young, Iris M. 2006. "Responsibility and Global Justice: A Social Connection Model." *Social Philosophy and Policy* 23(1): 102–130.

Young, Robert. 1990. *White Mythologies: Writing History and the West*. London: Routledge.

Yuval-Davis, Nira. 2006. "Intersectionality and Feminist Politics." *European Journal of Women's Studies* 13(3): 193–209.

INDEX

abolitionist feminism, 24–25
advocacy
  stories for, 98;
  by WIDE, 17
affiliation cross-pulls, 185
Ahmed, Sara, 88–89, 154
aid:
  in the colonial era, 161, 166;
  and global citizenship, 47;
  industry of, 4, 9, 11, 15, 18, 65, 121, 160, 192;
  international, participatory approaches in, 122;
  local and global, 24;
  and NGOs, 66, 79, 100;
  and partnerships, 100, 102, 104;
  professionalization trends in, 77;
  unworthy recipients of, 27;
  women unresponsive to, 27
All the Women Are White, All the Blacks Are Men, but Some of Us Are Brave (Hull, Bell-Scott, and Smith), 133
altruism, 54–56, 59, 62, 86
Amoore, Louise, 114–15
Anderson, Kenneth, 115–16
Anheier, Helmut, 47, 199n1
Appadurai, Arjun, 11
asylum seekers, 3–4, 9, 69, 176. *See also* migrants; refugees

Bell-Scott, Patricia, 133
beneficiaries, 99–100, 102;
  distance influence on, 88–91, 96, 129;
  Fechter on, 101–2;
  partner organizations as, 100–1, 192, 197

Bhabha, Homi:
  on culture 178;
  on Other, 109, 169–70
biography, 15, 28, 151
black feminism, 5, 43. *See also* black feminists; black women's movement
black feminists, 6, 131–32, 154. *See also* black feminism; black women's movement
black women's movement, 2–3
Brah, Avtar, 6
British imperialism, 162, 167–68
Brussels, 9–10, 78–81
buddy program, 58–59, 71–72
bureaucratic work, 79, 84
Burton, Antoinette, 131
Byrne, Bridget, 7

"Can the Subaltern Speak?" (Spivak), 118, 128
capitalism, 146
Caraway, Nancie, 132, 135, 142
Carby, Hazel, 132
career feminist, 31;
  feminist activist *versus*, 87, 195;
  Roy on, 55
careerism:
  against altruism, 56, 85;
  in NGO, 65;
  privilege of, 120
Carter, April, 47
CATW. *See* Coalition Against Trafficking in Women
CEDAW. *See* Convention on the Elimination of All Forms of Discrimination against Women

Chambers, Robert:
    on international career system, 98;
    PRA by, 124;
    on "project bias," 92
Chandhoke, Neera, 114–16
class, 5, 6, 8, 16, 27, 29–30, 133, 134, 145, 153;
    global citizens, 3;
    middle-class women, 2, 7, 30, 42, 52, 132, 136, 137–38, 143, 145, 152, 183;
    and women's movements, 1–2, 23–24, 121, 140
Coalition Against Trafficking in Women (CATW), 24–25
collective injustice, 17
collective standpoint, 120, 146
college education, 30, 50–51
colonialism, 164 166;
    closure and, 163;
    decolonization of, 163;
    development as, 160–61, 191–92;
    identity and, 166–67;
    NGO in, 161–62
commitment, 41, 53, 59, 73–78, 81, 83, 85, 94, 195–96;
    and exclusionary mechanism, 22;
    to feminism, and politics, 155;
    to gender equality, 41;
    of NGO workers, 55, 95, 156;
    of public/private divide, 12, 62–63, 71, 86–87
communication:
    A Critique of Post-colonial Reason on, 128;
    through grass-roots work, 108;
    of public/private divide, 67, 85
compassion, 58
conscious-raising groups, 143
constructive complicity, 84
constructivist approach, 84
Convention on the Elimination of All Forms of Discrimination against Women (CEDAW), 21–22
Cook, Nancy, 53
Crenshaw, Kimberlé, 6, 139
A Critique of Post-colonial Reason (Spivak), 128
culture, 175;
    and Other, 161, 169, 181–82, 190, 194;
    as race, 177–80, 190;
    and victimhood, 173

DAWN. *See* Development Alternatives with Women for a New Era
decolonization, 163, 189
"Demarginalizing the Intersection of Race and Sex" (Crenshaw), 6
Developing Power: How Women Transformed International Development (Fraser, A., and Tinker), 23
development:
    as colonialism, 160–61, 191–92;
    gender and, 20–21, 45, 195–96;
    and Other, 175;
    relational positions and, 191;
    "selective engagement" in, 181;
    Southern NGOs for, 105–6;
    women's movement for, 23
Development Alternatives with Women for a New Era (DAWN), 17
development workers:
    community distancing of, 79–80;
    experiences of, 4–5;
    Goudge on, 197;
    Heron on, 197, 198;
    racism and, 189
difference, 29, 49–50, 125, 185–87. *See also* Other
DiFranco, Ani, 30, 159, 199n1
discrimination, 139
distance:
    beneficiaries influenced by, 88–91, 96, 129;
    Chandhoke on, 114;
    feminism influenced by, 88–89;
    field visits bridging of, 12–13;
    of global civil society organizations, 129–30;
    of NGO, 89, 195;
    power relations of, 129;
    representation and, 88–89, 114, 149;
    responsibility from, 88–89
"diverse" citizenship, 61
Doezema, Jo, 25–26
dominant groups, 6

[220] *Index*

donor, 19, 92–93
"double bind," 71

education, 30, 126–27, 133. *See also* learning
ego, 54
elite, 48, 108
Elliott, Charles, 112
Elshtain, Jean, 63
empowerment:
    for marginalization, 1–2;
    of partner organizations, 105–6;
    by women's movement, 22–23
Enloe, Cynthia, 66–67, 148
entryism, 19–20
equality, 139–40, 163–64
Eriksson Baaz, Maria:
    on partner organizations, 104, 129, 179–80, 196;
    The Paternalism of Partnership by, 111, 197;
    on postcolonialism, 161
Essed, Philomena, 178
ethnic identity, 28–29
ethnocentrism, 142, 145
"ethnoscape," 11
European Women's Lobby (EWL):
    Czech women NGOs against, 107;
    on discrimination, 139;
    minority women inclusion by, 26–27;
    for sex work, 24–25
EWL. *See* European Women's Lobby
expats, 70

Falk, Richard, 48, 81
Fechter, Anne-Meike, 70, 101–2
Fellows, Mary Louise, 134–35, 156
feminine virtue discourse, 15–16
feminism. *See also* abolitionist feminism; first-wave feminism; second-wave feminism; transnational feminism; Western feminism
    conscious-raising groups for, 143;
    distance and, 88–89;
    Elshtain on, 63;
    ethnic identity and, 28–29;
    gender and, 3–8, 28, 38–39;
    generational interactions influence on, 45;
    NGOization of, 77;
    in organizations, 38–45;
    of Oxfam, 41;
    participation for, 22–23;
    on politics, 63, 153;
    postcolonialism and, 160;
    professionalism influenced by, 42, 46, 76–77;
    representation in, 117;
    sex work and, 24–25;
    sisterhood of, 146;
    stereotypes of, 33;
    young women's view on, 32–33
"feminism-by-design," 121
feminist, 32, 36–37, 42;
    biography of, 15, 28;
    on equality, 139;
    GAD by, 20–21;
    institutional engagement by, 20;
    perspective of, 1–2;
    public/private divide of, 61, 63, 195;
    support for Clinton, 139;
    trajectories of, 12;
    veiling and, 171–72;
    WID by, 20–21
feminist activist, 87, 195
feminist theory, 42, 61, 64, 88, 117
femocrat, 19–20
field visits, 81–82, 95;
    bridging distance by, 12–13;
    bureaucratic work *versus*, 79, 84;
    connection through, 129;
    experience from, 94, 98;
    HQ person *versus*, 81, 196;
    information by, 91;
    of international organizations, 90–91;
    of NGO, 82;
    of partner organizations, 93;
    "project bias" of, 92;
    "reality" of, 91
first-wave feminism, 16, 131
foreign language, 150–51. *See also* language barrier
Fourth World Conference on Women, 17–18
fractal distinction, 67–68
Frankenberg, Ruth, 133, 156
Fraser, Arvonne S., 23
Fraser, Nancy, 185
funding, 100, 104–5
fundraising, 96

Gal, Susan, 67
Gandhi, Leela, 160
gender, 30–32, 37–38, 40–41;
    development and, 20–21, 45, 195–96;
    establishing connections through experience, 149
    feminism and, 3–8, 28, 38–39;
    in global South, 152;
    hierarchies of, 152;
    marginalization by, 135–36, 159;
    oppression by, 138;
    organizations for, 5;
    positional instability of, 153;
    professionalism influenced by, 122;
    race and, 6, 135, 195;
    as "race to innocence," 134;
    Southern NGOs and, 114;
    values and, 77;
    by Western feminism, 121
gender inequality, 28–29, 41, 133, 137–38, 140, 148
gender studies, 34. *See also* women's studies
generations:
    dialogue of, 36;
    feminism influenced by, 45;
    interactions, 35;
    postfeminism and, 33
Geneva, 9–10, 78–80
"geographical promiscuity," 9–10
Ghodsee, Kristen, 23–24, 121
gift, 103–4, 113
global citizenship. *See also* "diverse citizenship"; intimate citizenship
    global civil society for, 46–47, 195;
    Hutchings on, 49, 51–52;
    Oxfam on, 48;
    postcolonialism and, 52;
    privilege of, 48, 52, 57–59;
    public/private divide of, 60, 85;
    responsibility and, 12, 46, 85
global civil society:
    Amoore on, 114–15;
    Anheier on, 47, 199n1;
    critique of, 89;
    by Fourth World Conference on Women, 17–18;
    for global citizenship, 46–47, 195;
    Gramsci on, 47, 199n1;
    Kaldor on, 114;
    Langley on, 114–15;
    public/private divide of, 60–61, 85;
    responsibility in, 85
global civil society organizations:
    Anderson on, 115–16;
    distance of, 129–30;
    Rieff on, 115–16
global justice, 51–52
"Global List of Women's Organizations," 8, 199n2
global North:
    aid of, 11;
    "helping imperative" of, 191–92;
    issues from, 10;
    knowledge from, 188;
    migrants in, 9, 108
global South:
    DAWN and, 17;
    experience in, 98–99;
    gender in, 152;
    homogenization of, 107–8, 182;
    stereotypes of women in, 189;
    transnational women's movement participation by, 24;
    women autonomy of, 126–28
Goudge, Paulette, 197
Gramsci, Antonio, 47, 199n1
grass-roots work, 79, 83;
    communication through, 108;
    against international organization, 80–81

Hampson, Tom, 167
Harding, Sandra, 157
headscarf, 170, 172. *See also* veiling
hegemonic geography, 94–95
"helping imperative," 191–92
Henkel, Heiko, 103–4
Heron, Barbara:
    on containment, 181–82;
    on development workers, 197–98;
    on power relations, 93;
    Razack and, 2, 199n1
hierarchies:
    of compassion, 58;
    difference through, 49–50;
    of gender, 152
Hilhorst, Dorothea, 121
Hill Collins, Patricia:
    on collective standpoint, 120;

"matrix of domination" by, 149;
  on motherhood, 145;
  on oppression, 127–28, 151–52;
  on racism, 139–40;
  on "voyeurism," 3–4
HIV/AIDS, 117
homogenization:
  of global South, 107–8, 184;
  Mohanty on, 142;
  opportunities and, 49–50;
  by Western feminism, 131–32;
  of women, 119
hooks, bell, 42, 181–82, 198
Hull, Gloria T., 133
Hutchings, Kimberly, 49, 51–52

ideal worker, 76
identity, 85, 135–36, 153, 157, 185–86;
  colonialism and, 166–67;
  and postcolonialism, 168–69, 195–96;
  and religion, 171;
  responsibility of, 56–57;
  of women, 125–26;
  work influenced by, 7–8
ideology, 115–16, 119
inequality, 2, 3, 5, 20, 44, 48, 58, 103, 132, 135, 137–38, 140, 144, 198
international career system, 98
international development, 3, 10–11, 20, 23–24, 28, 99–100, 114–15
international organizations:
  in Brussels, 9–10, 78;
  field visits of, 90–91;
  in Geneva, 9–10, 78;
  grass-roots work against, 80–81;
  resources of, 84
International Women's Year, 16–17
intersectionality, 29;
  constructivist approach of, 84;
  Crenshaw on, 6, 139;
  of "race to innocence," 136;
  Razack on, 136–37
interviews, 5, 7–9
intimate citizenship, 60–61
Islamophobia, 172

Jain, Devaki, 23–24

Kaldor, Mary, 114
Kapoor, Ilan:
  on gift, 113;
  on politics, 84;
  on PRA, 124;
  on privilege, 187;
knowledge, 177–78, 188
Kothari, Uma, 108

Lang, Sabine, 54–55
Langley, Paul, 114–15
language barrier, 176. *See also* foreign language
leadership, 16
learning, 109–10. *See also* education
legitimacy, 121
liberalism:
  oppression and, 194;
  patriarchy in, 61;
  of politics, 60
local organizations, 118
locations:
  Brussels justification of, 80–81;
  Geneva justification of, 80–81;
  organizations and, 3–4, 8–11
Lorde, Audre:
  on oppression, 156;
  on Other, 177;
  on sisterhood, 131–32

marginalization, 137, 156, 164;
  competition of, 139–40;
  from education, 132, 133;
  empowerment for, 1–2;
  Frankenberg on, 156;
  by gender, 135, 159;
  privilege and, 120, 193–94
Massey, Doreen, 94–95
"matrix of domination," 149
McRobbie, Angela, 31
migrants, 184. *See also* asylum seekers; refugees
  in global North, 9, 108–9;
  organizations for, 123–24
Miller, Carol, 19–20
Mindry, Deborah, 15–16
minority women, 26–27
mobility, 90, 175–76
"modern" citizenship, 61
modernity, 163
Mohanty, Chandra, 142, 171
morality, 73, 76, 79

Morgan, Robin, 40, 139, 142–44
motherhood, 38;
  Hill Collins on, 145;
  sisterhood of, 144–45, 194
motivation for career, 45, 46, 52, 56–57, 85, 99, 113, 144, 193–94, 195
"myths," 96

Nairobi conference, 17
nationality, 133–34
neoimperialism, 3
NGO. *See* non-governmental organization
NGOization, 19, 31, 55, 77, 85–86
non-governmental organization (NGO), 172–73;
  British imperialism of, 162;
  careerism in, 65;
  for CEDAW, 21–22;
  in colonialism, 161;
  defining dimensions of, 18–19;
  distance of, 89, 195;
  donor accountability by, 19;
  employee benefits of, 53–54;
  against EWL, 107;
  experience of, 4–5;
  field visits of, 82;
  against gender inequality, 41;
  for immigrants, 10, 167
  morality of, 79;
  partner organizations of, 100;
  power relations of, 100;
  professionalism of, 54–55, 85, 195;
  for refugees, 3–4;
  for self-representation, 179, 192;
  target group involvement of, 124;
  of VFDW, 21–22;
  women in, 15–16, 18, 23;
  women's movement influenced by, 54–55
North–South, 1, 3–4, 8–9, 11, 15, 24–25, 58, 160, 195–96

opportunities, 52–53;
  homogenization and, 49–50;
  responsibility of, 50, 57–58
oppression:
  by gender, 138–39;
  Hill Collins on, 127–28, 154;
  liberalism and, 194;
  Lorde on, 156–57;
  of "race to innocence," 134, 156–57, 159, 194;
  of veiling, 171–72
organizations. *See also* global civil society organizations; international organizations; local organizations; non-governmental organization (NGO)
  feminism in, 38–45;
  locations and, 3–4, 8–11;
  for migrants, 121–22;
  milestones of, 15;
  politics of, 41;
  range of, 8–9;
  stories for, 97
Other:
  Bhabha on, 109, 169–70;
  conceptions of, 12, 192, 193;
  culture and, 161, 169, 181–82, 190, 194;
  desire for, 189;
  development for, 175;
  and headscarf, 172–73;
  Lorde on, 177;
  postcolonialism influence on, 169;
  relational positions of, 13–14, 185;
  Self *versus*, 168–70, 173, 176–78, 184–85, 189–90, 193–94
Oxfam:
  feminism of, 41;
  on global citizenship, 48;
  on Indian women tsunami death, 174–75

The Paradoxes of Aid Work: Passionate Professionals (Roth, S.), 197
Participatory Rural Appraisal (PRA) approach, 124
partner organizations, 105, 109;
  as beneficiaries, 100–1, 192, 197;
  empowerment of, 105–6;
  for equality, 163–64;
  Eriksson Baaz on, 104, 129, 179–80, 196;
  field visits of, 93;
  funding of, 100;
  learning about, 109–10;
  legitimacy by, 113;
  as main contact, 101;

mutual dependency of, 129;
of NGO, 100, 101;
power relations of, 111;
responsibility for, 103;
selection of, 124
partnerships. *See* partner organizations
passion, 65, 73–74, 81
The Paternalism of Partnership (Eriksson Baaz), 111, 197
peace, 39–40, 167
personal politics, 63–64, 148
policymaking, 119
political symbolism, 172–73
The Political Theory of Global Citizenship (Carter), 47
politics:
    feminism on, 63, 155;
    Kapoor on, 84;
    liberalism of, 60;
    of organizations, 41;
    private life influenced by, 62;
    professionalism and, 59–60;
    of representation, 129–30;
    republican view of, 60
positional instability, 147, 151–54
postcolonialism:
    decolonization and, 163, 189–90;
    Eriksson Baaz on, 160–61;
    feminism and, 160;
    geography of, 89;
    of global citizenship, 52;
    identity from, 168–69, 198;
    Other influenced by, 168–69;
postfeminism, 31, 33–34
power relations:
    of distance, 129;
    Heron on, 93;
    of NGO, 100;
    of partner organizations, 111–12;
    reflections on, 5;
    responsibility of, 47;
    of UN, 83–84
PRA. *See* Participatory Rural Appraisal approach
prejudices, 165
private life, 73–74;
    politics influence on, 63;
    Squires on, 68–69
privilege, 50–51;
    of careerism, 120;
    of funding, 104–5;
    of global citizenship, 48, 52, 57–59;
    Kapoor on, 187;
    marginalization and, 120, 193–94;
    and professionalism, 59–60;
    by proximity, 94–95;
    in public/private divide, 67;
    responsibility and, 47, 85, 120, 132, 193;
    sisterhood and, 144;
    Spivak on, 188;
    of victimhood, 141
professionalism, 44;
    feminism influence on, 42, 46, 76–77;
    gender influence on, 122;
    good characteristics of, 74–75;
    of ideal worker, 76;
    Kothari on, 108;
    Lang on, 54–55;
    of NGO, 54–55, 85, 195;
    politics and, 59–60;
    privilege and, 59–60;
    responsibility in, 59–60;
    Wieringa on, 55
professional/personal divide, 75–76;
    commitment and, 76;
    Enloe on, 66–67;
    Fechter on, 69;
    necessity of, 65
"project bias," 92
Prokhovnik, Raia, 75
proximity, 90, 94–95
public/private divide, 77–78;
    "agency" dimension of, 71;
    boundaries of, 69–70;
    communication of, 67, 85;
    "double bind" of, 71;
    and feminism, 61, 63, 195;
    Gal on, 67;
    of global citizenship, 60, 85;
    of global civil society, 60–61, 85;
    privilege in, 67;
    Prokhovnik on, 75;
    responsibility in, 67;
    Western feminism and, 62
public space:
    and friendship, 72;
    for morality, 73, 77;
    state as, 61–62, 63

race:
    Ahmed on, 153;
    culture as, 177–80, 190;
    gender and, 6, 136, 193–94
"race to innocence":
    by Fellows, 134;
    gender as, 133–34;
    intersectionality of, 136;
    oppression of, 134, 156–57, 158–59, 193–94;
    by Razack, 134;
    reasons for, 137
racism:
    and depoliticization, 183;
    development workers and, 189;
    Essed on, 178;
    expats and, 70;
    Hill Collins on, 140;
    hooks on, 181, 198
rational man, 76–77
Razack, Sherene:
    Heron and, 2, 199n1;
    on intersectionality, 136–37;
    and "race to innocence" conept, 134–35;
    on relational positions, 2–4, 131, 199n1;
    on social justice, 156
Razavi, Shahra, 19–20
reflexivity, 157–58, 198
refugees, 3–4. *See also* asylum seekers; migrants
relational positions, 185;
    development and, 191;
    discourse of, 15–16;
    of Other, 13–14, 185;
    Razack on, 2–4, 131, 199n1;
    of "segregated sisterhood," 135;
    of sisterhood, 13, 140;
    for solidarities, 158–59;
    support through, 12, 158
representation, 119–20;
    Chandhoke on, 116;
    construction of, 118;
    and distance, 88–89, 114, 149;
    facilitation of, 125;
    in feminism, 117;
    for HIV/AIDS, 117;
    of ideology, 116, 119;
    by local organizations, 118;
    of migrants, 123;
    politics of, 130;
    of sex workers, 118;
    Spivak on, 128–30
resisting divisions, 147–49, 159
responsibility, 141;
    from distance, 88–89;
    global citizenship and, 12, 46, 85;
    in global civil society, 85;
    for global justice, 51–52;
    and identity, 56–57;
    and opportunities, 50, 57–58;
    for partner organization, 103;
    of power relations, 47;
    privilege and, 47, 85, 120, 132–33, 193;
    in professionalism, 59–60;
    by proximity, 94–95;
    in public/private divide, 67
Rieff, David, 115–16
Rose, Gillian, 158
Roth, Benita, 26
Roth, Silke, 196–97
Roy, Srila, 55

safe space, 124
sati (widow sacrifice), 128
second-wave feminism, 16–17, 26, 132
"segregated sisterhood," 132, 135
"selective engagement," 181
Self:
    Other *versus*, 168–70, 173, 176–78, 184–85, 189–90, 193–94;
    redundancy and, 196
self-development, 95
selfishness, 55–56, 59, 62, 85
self-representation, 117–18;
    awareness of, 123, 195;
    NGO for, 179–80, 192;
    platform for, 125;
    of sex worker, 120;
    simplification of, 126
self-understanding, 12, 14
seniority, 7–8
Sennett, Richard, 58
sexism, 137
sex worker:
    EWL on, 24–25;
    feminism and, 24–25;
    movement for, 120;

representation for, 118;
self-representation of, 120;
state engagement with, 26
Sin, Harng Luh, 49
sisterhood, 156;
   of feminism, 146;
   Lorde on, 131;
   of motherhood, 144–45, 194;
   privilege and, 144;
   relational positions of, 13, 140–41;
   reviving of, 142–43;
   victimhood and, 132–33, 141, 147, 158–59, 194
Sisterhood Is Global (Morgan), 40, 139, 142–43, 144, 199n1
Smith, Barbara, 133
social connection model, 59
"socialist feminism," 37
social justice, 156, 197
solidarities, 155;
   establishment of connection through experience, 147, 158–59;
   positional instability for, 147, 151;
   as process, 154–58;
   relational positions for, 158–59;
   resisting divisions for, 147–49, 158–59
Southern NGOs:
   for development, 106;
   diminishing capacities of, 108;
   gender and, 114
Spelman, Elizabeth, 43, 142, 155
Spivak, Gayatri:
   "Can the Subaltern Speak?" by, 118, 128;
   on constructive complicity, 84;
   A Critique of Post-colonial Reason by, 128;
   on knowledge, 177;
   on privilege, 188;
   on representation, 128–30;
   on sati, 128;
   on "strategic essentialism," 98;
Squires, Judith, 68–69
standpoint theory, 157
state:
   cooperation with, 26;
   as public space, 61–62, 63;
   victimhood and, 27
stereotypes:
   of feminism, 33;
   of global South, 189;
   as a process of subjectification, 170
Stirrat, Roderick L., 103–4
stories, 95;
   advocacy through, 98;
   connection through, 129;
   for legitimizing organizations, 97;
   "myths" and, 96
"strategic essentialism," 98
strategic framing, 41
subaltern, 84, 121, 124, 126, 128, 130
subjectification, 170

Timothy, Kirsten, 84
Tinker, Irene, 23
traditions, 175
trafficking, 40
transgender employees, 43
transnational feminism:
   Ahmed on, 88–89;
   history of, 2–3;
   and second-wave feminism, 16–17, 132
transnational women's movement, 24, 45
Tully, James, 61

UK domestic third sector, 10–11
"Under Western Eyes" (Mohanty), 171
United Nations (UN), 16–17, 83–84

veiling, 171–72. *See also* headscarf
VFDW. *See* Voluntary Fund for the UN Decade for Women
victimhood:
   culture and, 173;
   privilege of, 141–42;
   and sisterhood, 131–32, 141–42, 147, 158, 194;
   by state, 27
"victim narrative," 40
violence, 44
Voluntary Fund for the UN Decade for Women (VFDW), 21–22
Voluntary Service Oversees (VSO), 53
volunteering, 99, 100;
   autonomy of, 71;
   boundaries of, 69–70, 71–72;
   Sin on, 49

"voyeurism," 3–4, 95
VSO. *See* Voluntary Service Oversees

WAD. *See* Women and Development
Walker, Alice, 43
"Walking on Eggshells at the UN" (Timothy), 84
WAND. *See* Women and Development
WAVE. *See* Women Against Violence Europe
Western feminism:
  Gandhi on, 160;
  gender in, 121–22;
  homogenization by, 131;
  and public/private divide, 62
"white ally," 7–8
white feminist movement, 2–3
White Lives: The Interplay of "Race," Class and Gender in Everyday Life (Byrne), 7
whiteness, 3, 52, 123, 133–35, 137, 139, 146, 153, 156, 166, 183. *See also* race; racism
"White Woman, Listen!" (Carby), 132
White Women, Race Matters (Frankenberg), 133
WID. *See* Women in Development
WIDE (Women in Development Europe), 17
widow sacrifice. *See* sati

Wieringa, Saskia, 55
WILPF. *See* Women's International League for Peace and Freedom
"womanism," 43
Women Against Violence Europe (WAVE), 26–27
Women and Development (WAD; WAND), 20–21
Women in Development (WID), 20–21
Women's International League for Peace and Freedom (WILPF), 16
women's movement:
  for development, 23;
  empowerment by, 22–23;
  Ghodsee on, 23–24;
  institutional change by, 1–2;
  international orientation of, 16;
  NGO influence on, 54–55
women's studies, 30. *See also* gender studies
work ethic, 74
work experience, 94, 95, 98–99

Young, Iris Marion, 59
Young Women's Christian Association (YWCA), 16
YWCA. *See* Young Women's Christian Association

CPSIA information can be obtained
at www.ICGtesting.com
Printed in the USA
BVHW032057150919
558515BV00002B/99/P